EXPERIMENTATION
IN
PSYCHOLOGY

EXPERIMENTATION
IN
PSYCHOLOGY

by

BENTON J. UNDERWOOD

Northwestern University

and

JOHN J. SHAUGHNESSY

Northwestern University

John Wiley & Sons, Inc.

New York • London • Sydney • Toronto

Library of Congress Cataloging in Publication Data:

Underwood, Benton J   1915–
Experimentation in psychology, by— and —.   236p.
                                              c1975
Includes index.
1. Psychology, Experimental. 1. Shaughnessy, John
H, 1947–   , joint author. 1. Title. [DNLM: 1. Psy-
chology, Experimental. BF181 U56ea]

BF181.U53   150.7'24   74-31157
ISBN 0-471-89636-5

Printed in the United States of America

10-9 8 7 6 5 4 3 2 1

5/31/77 - $10.95

PREFACE

At a number of colleges and universities the undergraduate sequence in experimental psychology has consisted of a basic course followed by one or more courses in specialized content areas (animal learning, human learning, perception, information processing, social, personality). The basic course is intended to provide a common background in the fundamentals of experimental design, while the courses in particular areas are oriented toward content and toward specialized research techniques. The present book, written for the basic course, evolved as a result of the above described sequence being introduced into the curriculum at Northwestern University a few years ago.

As textbooks go, the present one is short. We believe, however, that the student will not find it light reading throughout. To transmit a comprehension of the problems of experimental design and of the problems of interpreting experimental findings as they in fact exist requires dealing with abstract notions and with methods of thinking that the usual undergraduate does not commonly meet in other pursuits. We have not attempted to avoid the difficult issues, although we have tried to work into them gradually across chapters. The understanding may be facilitated by a course in elementary statistics.

It will be apparent to the reader that a majority of our illustrations have come from studies of memory functioning. This results from the simple fact that the area of human memory is the one in which we feel most competent. Nevertheless, we believe that almost all of the problems of experimental design which are covered have their counterparts in other areas, and that the instructor whose specialty lies outside the area of memory will have no problem in finding the counterparts.

We wish to thank Mrs. Phyllis Van Hooser for the careful preparation of the manuscript.

Benton J. Underwood
John J. Shaughnessy

November 1974

CONTENTS

EXPERIMENTATION
IN
PSYCHOLOGY

THE EXPERIMENT

In 1973 the following study was reported by Schwartz and Humphreys.[1] Two groups of college students served as the subjects in the experiment. One group was designated a control group, the other an experimental or treatment group. The subjects in both groups were given a learning task known as a free-recall list. Each subject was presented a list of words, one word at a time, for a few seconds each. After all of the words had been presented, he was asked to recall as many of the words as possible, writing them in any order he wished. On each successive study trial the order of presenting the words differed but still the subject wrote the words on each recall trial in any order he chose.

The control group (C Group) in the experiment was given two trials on one list of 18 words (List A) followed by ten trials on quite a different list of 18 words (List B). We may schematize this sequence, along with the procedures applied to the experimental group (E Group), in the following manner:

C Group: 2 Trials on List A, followed by 10 Trials on List B
E Group: 2 Trials on List B, followed by 10 Trials on List B

It can be seen that the subjects in the E Group had two trials on List B followed by ten additional trials on the same list—List B. One further bit of information is necessary to complete the description. The subjects in the C Group, following the initial trials on List A, were told: "Now, we will learn another list." These subjects then were given List B. The critical part of the experiment was introduced when the subjects in the E Group were given exactly the same instructions following the initial two trials on List B—just before they were presented the *same* list for an additional ten trials.

Just why an investigator would perpetrate this innocuous hoax on a group of subjects is a matter for later comment. We should first look to see whether behavior was influenced and we can do this by examining the performance of the two groups on the ten trials on List B after the critical instructions were given. The mean number of correct responses given on each trial for the two groups is shown in Figure 1.1. Successive trials are equally spaced along the baseline (horizontal or X axis), with the behavioral measure—the dependent variable—along the ordinate (vertical, or Y axis).

It can be seen that the performance of the two groups differed. Although the subjects in the E Group showed initially higher performance than did those in the C Group, their increase in performance over trials was very slow and they actually produced fewer correct responses on later trials than did the subjects in the C Group. This was true in spite of the fact that the members of the E Group had two more trials on the list than did those in the C Group. Clearly, a subtle behavioral difference was produced by the treatment differentiating the two groups in this experiment. Or, as is frequently said, the results were positive, positive in the sense that treatment differences were followed by differences in performance for the two groups.

In 1972 Jones[2] published a report dealing with two questions. First, he asked about the precision with which the kinesthetic sense modality develops in blind children as compared with sighted children. Second, he asked if the precision differed as a function of age for both the blind and sighted children. Kinesthetic precision was defined by the accuracy with which a horizontal

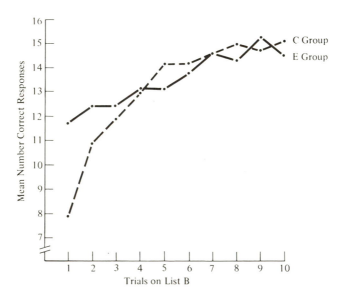

Fig.1.1 Mean number of correct responses on ten free-recall trials. The text describes the treatment differences for the E and C Groups. (Schwartz, R. M., & Humphreys, M. S., List differentiation in Part/whole free recall. *American Journal of Psychology*, 1973, **86**, 79–88.) Data courtesy of Dr. Humphreys.

movement of the arm could be reproduced. The subject inserted the index finger in a thimble mounted on a track. He then moved the thimble along the track until he hit a stop which had been inserted there by the experimenter. Immediately the thimble was returned to the starting position, the stop removed, and the subject tried to reproduce the extent of the original movement as accurately as possible. The subjects with normal vision were, of course, blindfolded.

Blind and sighted subjects were included at eight different age levels, age 5 to age 12 inclusive. The measure of accuracy was the mean error (in inches) in positioning the thimble. The outcome is shown in Figure 1.2. The two questions were given quite definitive answers. The blind children were able to position the thimble with a smaller error than were the sighted children, and the precision increased markedly with increasing age for both groups.

One of the many different visual illusions to which we are susceptible is known as the autokinetic illusion. To demonstrate this illusion, the subject is

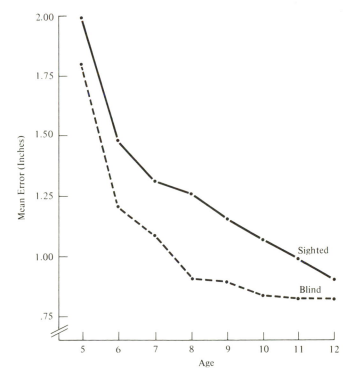

Fig. 1.2. Mean errors made in a positioning task as a function of age for blind and sighted children. (Data from Jones, B., Development of cutaneous and kinesthetic localization by blind and sighted children, *Developmental Psychology*, 1972, **6**, 349–352.)

placed in a dark room. The only visible stimulus is a pin-point of light. If the subject fixates this light it will usually appear to move after a few moments in spite of the fact that it is stationary. The amount of movement can be measured by any of several techniques which need not be of concern here.

A study was published in 1972 by Sharma and Moskowitz[3] in which they examined the extent of the autokinetic movement immediately after the subject had smoked two cigarettes. The treatment differences consisted of the combined amount of marihuana in the two cigarettes. There were four different doze sizes, or in more general terms, four different levels of the independent variable. These dose sizes may be identified as 0, 50, 100, and 200, where the increasing numbers reflect increasing amounts of marihuana in the two cigarettes. A subject smoked the two cigarettes (he was allowed 20 minutes to do so) and then was immediately given a series of trials to determine the extent of the autokinetic illusion. There were 12 subjects and each subject served under all four dose levels, a different dose being given on each of four different days. All of the subjects had had experience with marihuana before serving in the experiment. The findings of this study are shown in Figure 1.3. As is quite apparent from this figure, the extent of apparent movement for the autokinetic illusion was directly related to the dose size of the marihuana.

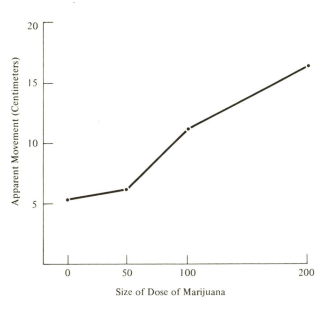

Fig. 1.3. Magnitude of the autokinetic illusion as related to dose size of marihuana. (Data from Sharma, S., & Moskowitz, H., Effect of marihuana on the visual autokinetic illusion, *Perceptual and Motor Skills*, 1972, **35**, 891–894.)

In a 1972 study by Guzy and Axelrod[4], the task of the subject was simply to count and report the number of clicks delivered through earphones. Perhaps it was not a simple task, however. The investigators varied the rate at which the clicks were presented, the rates being 2, 4, 6, or 8 per second. They also varied the number of clicks before the subject made his announcement of the number of clicks heard. These numbers, as delivered to the ear or ears, were 2, 3, 4, 5, 6, 8, 10, and 20. Finally, the subject either heard all clicks in one ear (monotic) or the clicks alternated between two ears (dichotic). This experiment is obviously somewhat more complex than the three already described. The complexity arises from the fact that there were three independent variables: number of clicks presented (8 levels); rate of click presentation (4 levels); and monotic vs. dichotic presentation. All levels of each variable were combined with all levels of every other variable. This results in 64 unique conditions of presentations (8 x 4 x 2). Furthermore, each subject made 10 judgments (there were 10 trials) for each unique condition so that 640 trials were given to each subject. Although 15 different subjects were employed, the conditions were so arranged that the results for each subject alone would be perfectly valid.

When the rate of presentation of the clicks was slow (2 per second), the counting, when summed across subjects, was essentially perfect for both monotic and dichotic presentation. However, as the rate increased, and as the number of clicks in a string also increased, the reported number of clicks became less than the number actually presented. The discrepancy between true and reported frequency was less for monotic than for dichotic listening. The results for the 8 per second rate are shown in Figure 1.4.

BASIC COMPONENTS OF THE EXPERIMENT

The descriptions of the four experiments just presented are mere skeletons of the procedures and results as provided by these investigators in their reports. The areas of research represented by these four studies are so diverse that it might seem as if they were chosen randomly from among the many articles in available journals. On the contrary, each was chosen for particular reasons, reasons which will emerge as the discussion develops in this and later chapters. Initially, references to the four experiments will be used to outline the scope of the book and its organization. Essentially we need to identify the basic components of the experiments because the study of these components constitutes the purpose of the book.

Background Thinking

As we have described the four experiments thus far, the most glaring omission is the lack of any rationale for doing the studies. The investigators did, of course, have reasons for undertaking the work. What were these reasons? What led Schwartz and Humphreys to give these odd instructions to the sub-

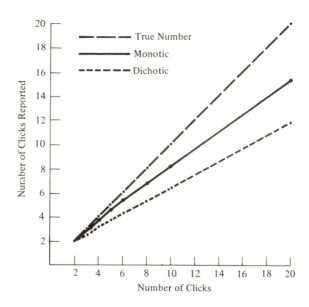

Fig. 1.4. Reported number of clicks as a function of total number of clicks delivered (at the rate of eight per second), and as related to the stimulation of one (monotic) or both (dichotic) ears. (Data from Guzy, L. T., & Axelrod, S., Interaural attention shifting as response, *Journal of Experimental Psychology*, 1972, **95**, 290–294.)

jects in the E Group? Guzy and Axelrod had their subjects count clicks, a task which on the surface seems a little preposterous in spite of the beauty of the results as exemplified in Figure 1.4. As we will see, click counting was not their major concern. It becomes clear that the first component of a piece of research which requires study is the nature of the background thinking which leads to a particular experiment.

No serious experimenter ever performs an experiment just for the sake of doing it. An experiment asks a question of nature and questions are seldom generated in an intellectual vacuum. But having said this, it is necessary to add quickly that there are many, many different routes by which the inquiring, skeptical, or analytical mind may articulate questions which can be posed to nature by means of experiments. The questions range from those generated by everyday observations to those generated by a highly formal theory. Sometimes one experiment is done to secure information needed to undertake another. Sometimes experiments are done to determine the generality of the influence of an independent variable. It may be known that the independent variable X influences behavior on Tasks A, B, and C. What about its effect on a somewhat different task, D? Will a relationship between an independent variable and performance on a given sample of college students hold for fifth-grade children? For the aged? For the white rat? All of this is to say that investigators who use the experiment as a means of trying to understand behavior differ widely in the techniques they use to arrive at a particular question. A research report will always afford some minimum background thinking which led to the experiment. So, bearing in mind that there are many ways by which experimental questions may come to be formulated, let us look briefly at the background thinking of the investigators who produced the four studies described earlier.

The Schwartz-Humphreys experiment arose from certain experimental findings and from theories that attempted to explain these findings. The basic phenomenon behind the work is known as the part-whole effect in free-recall learning. This effect would be found if procedures like the following were administered. A C Group learns a 10-word list, then a 20-word list composed of entirely new words. An E Group learns a 10-word list, but this is followed by a 20-word list consisting of the 10 words which constituted the first list plus 10 new words, all intermingled. The results of such an experiment would be remarkably similar to those found by Schwartz and Humphreys. One interpretation which has been offered for the part-whole effect emphasizes a disruption of organization. During the learning of the first list (the theory goes), subjects are said to acquire a particular organization of the words, a fact which has been inferred from the increase in the consistency of the order in which each subject recalls the words from trial to trial. Then, when the E Group receives a second list consisting of old words (which presumably have been organized) and new words mixed with them, a disruption of the old organization is said to occur and in trying to acquire a new organization, learning is retarded (as compared with the C Group).

There were bits of evidence which did not support the disruption-of-organization theory, and some of these bits suggested an alternative explanation. This alternative emphasized that a subject may have difficulty in discriminating how many of the words from the first list were included in the second. Schwartz and Humphreys reasoned that if the *same* words were used in both lists, there could be no issue concerning the disruption of organization. On the other hand, if the subject could be led to believe ("we will now learn another list") that at least some of the words in the second list were new, he would have a problem in determining just which words from the first list were carried over to the second list. If, therefore, the results resembled those for the usual part-whole experiment, it would be argued that the disruption of organization is not an appropriate explanatory notion. At the same time, such results could be used to support the discrimination hypothesis. In view of the findings, Schwartz and Humphreys leaned toward the discrimination hypothesis, and away from the disruption-of-organization hypothesis.

Jones studied the accuracy of reproducing a kinesthetic movement by blind and sighted subjects. Thoughtful people have long wondered if a deficit in the functioning of one sense modality might be accompanied by an enhanced sensitivity in another. This "compensatory effect" might be expected on the grounds that a person with a deficit (particularly a congenital deficit) in one modality might have to depend more on information from other modalities. Thus, persons with the deficit would have more practice with the intact modalities than would normal subjects. That the blind have super-sharp hearing certainly seems to be a common belief held by fiction writers. Jones studied the previous work on the problem and reached the conclusion that it was difficult to draw a conclusion. Some of the outcomes of previous studies were contradictory, some had involved too few subjects to expect stable findings, and some had not used subjects in whom a sensory deficit had been present at birth. Essentially, then, Jones wanted to see if consistent effects could be produced.

Sharma and Moskowitz (and others) were engaged in a research program aimed at ascertaining the effect of marihuana on attention and perception, with particular emphasis on how such effects (if present) might influence driving skills. In an earlier study in this program, visual stimulation was being used in a fairly dark room. Some of the subjects voluntarily reported that a signal light appeared to move, when in fact it was fixed. The investigators immediately recognized that these reports suggested an autokinetic illusion and they therefore proceeded to study the role of marihuana on the magnitude of the illusion. As we have seen in Figure 1.3, the effects were marked.

What prompted Guzy and Axelrod to ask subjects to count clicks presented successively to the same ear or alternately to the two ears? There is an extensive literature on monotic versus dichotic stimulation. From one perspective, this literature can be viewed as dealing with the general problem of attention. Consider the dichotic situation in which a signal is presented only to the right ear and then is shifted to the left ear only, and thus continues in alternating fashion. If we are to extract any information from these successive signals, it seems appropriate to say that we must constantly shift our attention from one ear to the other. We normally do not recognize the shifting of attention because most signals enter both ears. Dichotic stimulation simply forces the shifts.

How is attention to be characterized? Guzy and Axelrod believe that a shift in attention can be likened to a motor response, and that successive occurrences of a motor response produce fatigue. If this is a reasonable analogy, the greater the number of shifts the greater the fatigue. In their experiment Guzy and Axelrod used two variables to manipulate the number of shifts prior to the time the subject was asked to report the number of clicks. That is, they varied the length of the chain or string of clicks, and the number of clicks per unit of time. If the analogy with a motor response is appropriate, fatigue should increase as both of these variables increase and counting performance should be influenced correspondingly. Guzy and Axelrod interpreted their findings as consonant with their position.

These sketches of the background thinking leading to experiments emphasize a diversity of approaches. Background thinking puts flesh on the report and adds a perspective which the reader obviously deserves. The discussion has emphasized that such thinking leads to a question which is given to an experiment for an answer. The question asked may not always be obvious in the introduction to an experimental report. We often obscure it by stating hypotheses about the outcome of the experiment, or by stating predictions concerning the precise relationship between the independent variable and behavior. But the question is always implicit if not explicit. Hypotheses about the influence of certain complex independent variables often determine the specific questions asked. For example, we might ask about the influence a given children's television program has on the viewer's behavior. What behavior? Would we try to measure the influence on *all* forms or types of behavior? It is quite unlikely. Rather, by observations, background study, or even intuition, the investigator identifies certain forms of behavior which he believes are likely to be influenced by the program. He then may state these as hypotheses, e.g., aggressive behavior will be decreased, or reading skills will be accelerated. He could state these as questions, but in fact he chooses these behaviors to study because he has reached the tentative belief that they would be influenced.

Let us assume that we have an explicit question, and we have decided that it will be worthwhile to devote the time and energy to an experiment. In effect, we have done the background work and thinking necessary to supply a meaningful introduction to the report of the experiment. We are now ready, we say, to design the experiment.

Basic Experimental Designs

As will be elaborated later, an experiment is defined here as a procedure in which at least two different treatments are applied to subjects and the differential influence (if any) on behavior is measured. In choosing a basic experimental design to carry out the experiment, our alternatives are rather sharply limited. We must understand the rationale of the designs, we must recognize their pitfalls, their strong and weak points, and other lesser matters which may enter into the choice. Such information will be handled in later chapters. At this point the types of designs will be identified with a minimum of discussion.

Independent groups.   In this design, one group of subjects is given one of the treatments, a different group the other treatment. Of course, when we have more than two treatments, there will be as many groups as there are treatments. The most frequently used design within this type is called the *random-groups design*. Subjects are assigned randomly to the different groups to receive the different treatments. The assumption is that the random assignment of subjects to the different groups results in "equivalent groups" in the sense that if the groups were now measured on the same task, under the same conditions, their performance would be shown to be statistically equivalent. Or more generally, it is assumed that the groups do not differ (within statistical limits) on any characteristic relevant to the experimental task. Therefore if differences between the groups emerge these differences are attributed to the effect of the treatments—to the independent variable. The Schwartz-Humphreys experiment used this design. Acceptance of their results simultaneously rejects any idea that the differences in the two free-recall learning curves could have been produced by differences in the characteristics of the two groups of subjects when they came to the laboratory. Rather it is presumed that the independent variable (the instructions) was responsible for the differences.

A second type of independent-groups design is called the *matched-groups design*. Contemporary research does not make frequent use of this design. Nevertheless we should have it in our repertoire for potential use. None of the four experiments described above used this design. The idea is to "make" the groups equal, *then* give the treatments. If differences in behavior are found, it is said that they must be due to treatment differences since the different groups were known to be equal. The logic seems undeniable but, as we shall see, there are problems in working this through.

Within-subjects designs.   These types of designs are differentiated from the independent-groups designs by the fact that each subject is given all treatments. There is a single group of subjects and all subjects in the group are given all of the different treatments. If the subjects behave differently under the different treatments it is concluded that these differences *must* be due to the treatments. The attractiveness of this type of design lies in the fact that it does not involve an assumption about equality of the different groups, as the random-groups design does. But again, the value of this characteristic must be weighed against other implications.

One type of within-subjects design is said to be a *complete* design. Each subject is given all treatments in such a manner that the data are not contaminated by processes which change as the subject is given successive treatments. For example, if the subject gets more and more fatigued with each successive treatment, the procedures are arranged so that the effect of the fatigue falls equally on all treatments. Thus the data for each subject can be considered as those from a complete experiment.

The second type of within-subjects design is called the *incomplete* design. Here again, each subject receives all treatments, but the conditions are not arranged so that the results for a given subject are valid estimates of the effect of the treatments. Conclusions about the treatment effects are valid only when the data are combined across subjects.

The Sharma-Moskowitz study on the effects of marihuana on the auto-kinetic illusion was an incomplete within-subjects design. Each subject had all four dose sizes but the arrangements for ordering these conditions were not such as to balance out biasing effects for any single subject. The data were meaningful only when combined across subjects. The Guzy-Axelrod study, on the other hand, was a complete within-subjects design. If these investigators had chosen to do so, they could have presented the results for a single subject with knowledge that the results for that subject were a fair estimate of the different treatments.

The natural-groups design.   Jones compared positioning accuracy of blind and sighted children of different ages. Of necessity, such an experiment requires the use of independent groups. When the influence of a particular characteristic of the subject is being investigated, it is obvious that the subjects cannot be assigned randomly to the different groups. It is equally obvious that we should not match the subjects across the different groups since we do not want the groups to be equivalent. The independent variables in the Jones experiment result from the fact that the groups were not equivalent on age and on vision. The subjects were selected so that the groups would be different on certain specifiable characteristics which had developed in nature's course of events. The question which the experiment asks is whether the groups will differ on the behavior measured in the experiment. It might be argued that such procedures do not really constitute an experiment since the experimenter does not *administer* different treatments. Nonetheless, the thinking that is brought to such procedures and to their outcomes is the thinking which surrounds experiments. In fact, as we will see, the natural-groups design provides some very stark illustrations of the problems which may be present in a far more subtle way in the other designs.

Mixed designs.   If more than one independent variable is manipulated in an experiment (as in the Guzy-Axelrod study) it is quite possible to use a mixed design. That is, the effect of one variable might be determined by using the random-groups design, while the effect of another variable might be determined by a within-subjects procedure. For example, in the Guzy-Axelrod experiment, one group of subjects might have been used to obtain data on dichotic stimulation and a different group used to obtain data on monotic stimulation. The effects of the other two variables could have been assessed in each group through the use of a within-subjects design.

Independent and Dependent Variables

Having chosen a basic design for the experiment, we must insert within this design the independent variable which the background thinking has led us to believe should be evaluated. Of course different levels of the independent variable represent the different treatments. They also represent the only systematic variation allowed in the stimulus complex called the experimental situation. The subjects process the stimuli we present them, and if we find that their behavior changes in some consistent fashion as the independent variable changes, we say that it is a relevant independent variable. It is relevant in the sense that it causes the measured changes in behavior.

At any given stage in the development of an area of research we may speak of three general classes of independent variables. There are those which have been manipulated in an experiment and have been shown to influence behavior. We call these *relevant* independent variables. *Irrelevant* independent variables are those that have been shown not to influence behavior systematically. The third class, almost without limit in number, is called *potential* independent variables because their influence has not been investigated. As background thinking demands, some of these will be brought under experimental scrutiny in the future and thus enter either the relevant or irrelevant classes. Sometimes an independent variable will be relevant for performance on one task and irrelevant for performance on another task that seems very much like the first one. The analytical or theoretical problem, then, is to try to pinpoint the difference in processes which underlies the performance on the two tasks.

We say that we measure the behavior, and that these measurements constitute the dependent variable. What behavior do we measure? And what do we mean by measure? Questions and issues regarding the manipulation of the independent variable and the measurement of behavior require somewhat extended discussion. Chapter 2 will be devoted to these matters.

Data Reduction and Analysis

In the Guzy-Axelrod study there were 640 trials for each of 15 subjects for a total of 9600 observations. Each observation consisted of the number of clicks reported by the subject. It is a little difficult to examine these 9600 values directly and reach a conclusion concerning the relationships between the independent and dependent variables. These data must be compressed, summarized, or reduced so that the investigator can comprehend what he has discovered. The Guzy-Axelrod study was, to be sure, quite complex or extensive in the sense that there were three independent variables. Yet, the "rules" we follow in reducing the data are much the same as for any less extensive experiment. The essential first step is to get a single value for each unique condition, of which there were 64 in the Guzy-Axelrod study. Each subject had 10 trials under each of the 64 conditions, so we would first get a mean for each subject for each condition, thus reducing the number of scores to 960 (a score for each of the 15 subjects for each of the 64 conditions). We may then get a mean for the 15 subjects for each condition and our number of scores is reduced to 64, one for each of the 64 conditions (one for each combination of the levels of the three independent variables).

A fair comprehension of the results of the experiment can be obtained from a graph which exhibits all 64 data points. In Figure 1.4 we had plotted only one-fourth of these points. We could have had four panels, each like Figure 1.4, but each representing a different rate used in presenting the clicks. But suppose we wished to reduce the data further, so that we have fewer than 64 different values yet retain all of the measurements in the reduced number of points? The only sensible way to make such a reduction is to ask about the effect of each independent variable separately. In doing so, we use all of the data so that we say we collapse or sum across the other independent variables. This procedure may be illustrated. To simplify the illustration, we will assume that there were only three levels of the number-of-clicks variable (2, 10, 20), and only two rates (2 and 8 per second). The entries in the table below represent the appropriate means (as taken from the table of 64 means provided by Guzy and Axelrod) for number of clicks reported.

| | Monotic | | | | Dichotic | | |
| | Number of clicks | | | | Number of clicks | | |
Rate	2	10	20		2	10	20
2	2.0	10.0	20.0		2.0	10.0	20.0
8	2.0	8.2	15.3		2.0	6.5	11.9

Thus, for monotic listening, when the number of clicks was 10, presented at a rate of 8 per second, the mean number of clicks reported was 8.2, appreciably under the number of clicks which actually occurred, but still more than reported for the same condition under dichotic presentation (6.5).

Now, we may ask about the influence of each of the three variables, summed across the other two variables. There are six values representing the number of clicks reported for monotic listening and six representing the number reported for dichotic listening. The means of these six means are 9.5 for monotic and 8.7 for dichotic. Also, there are six values for the 2-second rate and six values for the 8-second rate when we collapse across the other two independent variables (monotic versus dichotic, and number of clicks). Thus, we sum across each of the rows and obtain the means of the six values in each row; these means show that at the 2-second rate a mean of 10.7 clicks was reported, and at the 8-second rate a mean of 7.7 clicks was reported. Finally, we may ask about the reporting as a function of the number of clicks presented (2, 10, 20). There are four values for each of these three levels when we collapse across the other two variables and the means are 2.0, 8.7, and 16.8, for 2, 10, and 20 clicks presented, respectively.

Two independent variables may interact in their influence on behavior. By this is meant that the influence of one independent variable differs in magnitude as a function of the level at which another independent variable is set. The data abstracted from the Guzy-Axelrod study seen above show an interaction. For either monotic or dichotic listening, rate had no effect when the number of clicks was two in number. But, as the number of clicks increased to 10 and then to 20, the reported number of clicks was less at the 8-second rate than at the 2-second rate. The quick identification of an interaction and the ability to state it verbally requires practice. Therefore, we will be particularly persistent in referring to interactions throughout the book.

Data reduction usually includes a statistical analysis. Data from the Guzy-Axelrod study as shown in Figure 1.4 might be an illustration of an exception; a statistical analysis could only tell us what is apparent from the graph. Statistics are normally used to evaluate the differences between or among means as given in tables or graphs to determine if we are willing to conclude that a repetition of the experiment will produce the same outcome. Statistical tools are of great benefit in helping us arrive at sound conclusions concerning whether or not our independent variable produced a reliable effect on behavior. This book is not a book on statistics; yet it assumes some knowledge of statistics, particularly in the area of testing the statistical reliability of differences between means. In various problems in the design of experiments, and in the interpretation of their results, we will find that conceptual statistical thinking is very useful, if not necessary, to understand the issues fully.

Many experiments yield information over and above that for which they were explicitly designed. For example, each subject in the Guzy-Axelrod experiment had ten trials on each of the 64 conditions. Did performance change over these ten trials? One could, for example, examine performance on the first 5 trials versus the second 5 trials to get an answer to this question. Sharma and Moskowitz could ask whether the magnitude of the autokinetic illusion changed across sessions, independent of the size of the dose of marihuana. Such questions, it can be seen, really ask about the effect of an additional independent variable, frequently identified as "stage of practice" or "stage of testing." This is not the only variable that might have representation within the body of data and which was not explicitly "put in" the original design. Other illustrations of such analyses, frequently called subanalyses, will arise. Such subanalyses have two values. First, they add to our knowledge without our having to perform an additional experiment. Second, these subanalyses are sometimes useful for a theoretical interpretation of the results of the experiment.

Interpretation

Reports of experiments usually include a separate section following the presentation of the results, commonly called the "discussion" section. The purpose of this section is to try to give some perspective to the findings of the experiment. In a real sense, it is the responsibility of the investigator *not* to leave the reader shrouded, or dripping in specific data. Who is better situated than the experimenter to provide the broader perspective?

The nature of the discussion section can vary widely because it will be tied closely to the background thinking as given in the introduction and, as we have seen, the background thinking will vary from experiment to experiment. Yet there are some guidelines. First, the investigator should summarize what he believes to be the critical findings. Second, he should fit these into previous findings. If the results are in contradiction to previous findings some resolution may be attempted. Initially, then, the discussion section becomes an extension of the background thinking.

Beyond tying together the empirical results, discussion sections may diverge markedly from study to study. If the purpose of the experiment was to make a test of a theory, the investigator is obliged to evaluate his findings in light of the theory. He may find a need to suggest a modification of the theory. He may conclude that his findings were not consistent with a theory, or, if he prefers his conclusion to be somewhat more sharply etched, he may say his findings refute a theory. He may propose a tentative new theory and suggest new manipulations to test it. Sometimes, after completing the first two steps noted above, the investigator has nothing further of substance to say. Regrettably, we sometimes proceed to say more anyhow, as if a short discussion section is intellectually demeaning.

STRENGTHS AND LIMITATIONS OF THE EXPERIMENT

The critical strength of the experiment lies in the fact that when it is properly executed we learn about the cause-effect relationships existing in nature. It is as near a foolproof technique for making these discoveries as has yet been devised. Those who have sought other approaches for determining cause-effect relationships in behavior have usually become discouraged.

The experiment is often believed to be tied to a laboratory, a laboratory in which there is complex equipment, white coats, and cages of animals. In principle the experiment is not wedded to a laboratory in a physical sense. Experiments can be executed in the classroom, on the highways, and in the bureaucracies of governments. It may be mechanically difficult to carry out such field experiments cleanly, but it should be clear that different treatments can be administered in environments other than the laboratory.

There are many pointed issues about cause-effect relationships in behavior which, because of the nature of our society, cannot easily, if at all, be arbitrated by the experiment. How would one carry out an experiment on the effect of noise pollution on various kinds of behavior? Suppose an investigator had a very reasonable theory about the cause of schizophrenia. How could he carry out his experiments with human subjects, experiments in which he would try to induce schizophrenia? What is the brightest light a person can see without retinal damage occurring? What is the effect of religious training during childhood on honesty in adulthood? The answers to such questions, and many, many others must come from sources other than the experiment with human subjects.

An experiment, to varying degrees, represents an abstraction of nature in the sense that certain variables are not allowed to influence the behavior being investigated. Furthermore, we may use tasks which have no apparent counterpart in real life. It is rather doubtful if many people have either as a vocation or as an avocation the counting of clicks delivered to one ear. The analytical requirements of experimental research often necessitate this new or abstracted environment in order to allow some of the normal forces of nature to be blunted. But the separation of the laboratory from real life need not be, and often is not, as great as some would believe. Schwartz and Humphreys did their experiment in the laboratory but they could have done it with groups of subjects in a school classroom. Had they done so, the results would probably have been much the same as they found in the laboratory. Nevertheless, there is an issue here which should be given some thought.

In an experiment with one independent variable we say that we hold all variables constant except the one we are manipulating. Such a situation is a far cry from nature where behavior occurs under conditions where many potential independent variables are changing in their magnitude from moment to moment. How then, it may be asked, can the results from a laboratory have any applicability to behavior as we observe it every day?

1. When we say that we hold all variables constant except one, we must understand that literally we do not hold all variables constant. We may hold some constant (in the sense of a fixed or static value), but not others. It is more appropriate to say that we may hold some potential independent variables constant but that in general the strategy of an experiment is not to hold these variables constant. Rather, we devise our procedures in such a way that any effects of these uncontrolled variables will influence the behavior equally under the different levels of the independent variable. Or, to say this another way, we do not allow these potential independent variables to act differentially on our conditions of interest. Only in this sense are they held constant— we presume their effects (if any) are equivalent under all levels of the independent variable of central interest. This rather delicate matter will be given more extended discussion later. For the moment we should recognize that in many experiments the separation between laboratory and real life is not very great, and therefore the problem of applying laboratory findings to real life is not as formidable as it might seem.

2. Consider a simple and well-known relationship between an independent variable and memory for verbal materials. The subject is given a long list of pairs of words to be learned. Within this long list pairs occur with varying frequencies. Some may occur twice, some five times, some eight times. As any third-grade student would know, the likelihood of recalling a pair is directly

related to the number of times it was presented for study within the list. Now, suppose the teacher in a classroom carries out much the same procedure. She is helping her students learn the English equivalent of French words by presenting pairs consisting of French-English words. Within the long list the pairs are presented with varying frequencies. She tests her students and finds that unlike the laboratory findings the effect of frequency of presentation is very small. A pair presented eight times is recalled only slightly more frequently than is a pair presented once. What are we to make of this outcome?

The first obvious conclusion we would draw is that the magnitude of the laboratory finding did not maintain itself in the classroom. That is saying nothing other than repeating the facts of the case. Why did the same effect not manifest itself? We would be likely to say that some potential variable (or variables), controlled in the laboratory, was not controlled in the classroom. Whatever variable was involved, it markedly decreased the effect of frequency. Or, to put this in the language we will be using, some independent variable interacts with frequency of the pairs (the manipulated independent variable) to depress the frequency effect. It is a part of the experimental enterprise within an area to discover independent variables which do interact, i.e., to discover variables which jointly influence behavior. The major reason for manipulating two or more independent variables in an experiment is to make such discoveries. These discoveries cannot be made directly by any other means.

In the classroom illustration, suppose that the students were excited about a field trip they were going to take during the next period and that, in effect, they could not care less about learning the pairs of words. Their motivation for learning was low and they paid little or no attention to the pairs as they were presented. Thus, we might infer that in the classroom the motivation was low, in the laboratory it was high. If this independent variable (motivation) is responsible for the discrepancy between the laboratory and the schoolroom results it means we have identified two variables which interact. To repeat our earlier definition, an interaction between two variables is present when the magnitude of the effect of one independent variable (frequency of pair presentation) differs depending upon the level of another independent variable (motivation).

We see, therefore, that an experimental finding may not hold in real life because the level of other relevant independent variables may differ between the two situations. Such a discrepancy does not mean that the laboratory finding is not applicable to real life, but it does mean that it is applicable only when certain other conditions prevail.

3. It is a fact that experimental psychologists frequently find themselves dealing with effects or phenomena of small, even miniscule, magnitude. It is quite possible, indeed likely, that an independent variable which has only a

small effect under the controlled conditions of the laboratory would have no effect in real life where other variables may mask it entirely. Why, then, might we bother to investigate such effects in the laboratory?

In the first place, independent variables which produce large effects, really large effects, often do not need laboratory study. These effects are observable to anyone who is at all alert, and an experiment is not needed. If you spend ten minutes in concentrated study you are not going to learn as much (or as well) as if you spend three hours in concentrated study on the same material. Why do an experiment? The experimentalist might be interested in the precise law which relates time spent in study and amount learned, and he might be interested in the way study time interacts with other independent variables, but the basic effect of the independent variable per se (study time) does not require a laboratory demonstration. It is natural, therefore, that experiments would be directed toward the influence of other variables of less potency, or to variables whose influences are not directly observable by the senses. The laboratory is an adjunct and corrective device for uncontrolled observations, not a substitute.

"Small phenomena" are sometimes investigated vigorously to see if they could represent an "iceberg" effect. That is, only the tip may be being measured, and given the right set of other variables the magnitude of it may be increased. If under a wide variety of conditions the effect is consistently small, however, it may remain as an interesting laboratory phenomenon judged to be of small consequence in the overall behavior. This conclusion is possible only after the phenomenon of interest has been studied, and studied carefully.

4.   As has been apparent, when we ask about the applicability of laboratory phenomena to real life we are asking about their generality. *Within* the laboratory the question of generality of principles is always a persistent and important issue. Will a relationship between an independent variable and behavior discovered with college students as subjects hold for fifth-grade students? For chimpanzees? If we find a relationship between two levels of an independent variable and behavior, can we generalize between and beyond these levels? Will the relationship hold for all settings of other independent variables? We will return to such questions as we discuss the design of experiments and their interpretation. For the time being, we need to understand that the question of whether we can generalize between the laboratory and real life is an extension of the issue of the generalizability of results within the laboratory. Under any circumstances, the question of the generalizability of results is not one to be taken lightly or to be answered off the cuff. For the most definitive answer we must bring field research, laboratory findings, and theoretical thinking together.

OTHER RESEARCH APPROACHES

Even a slight acquaintance with psychological research shows that systematic attempts to understand behavior are by no means limited to the experiment. It was noted above that many answers to questions about behavior simply cannot be resolved by an experiment. Either we ignore these questions or we get less powerful but relevant evidence by other means.

Naturalistic Observations

The essence of the method of naturalistic observation is to observe and record specified behavioral events as they naturally occur. Most of the extensive descriptions of animal behavior have been obtained using this technique. Points of interest associated with increasing age of a baby (e.g., age of expected first step) have been identified by averaging the actual age at which many, many babies were first observed to behave in a given way. Naturalistic observation provides many substantial facts about behavior and many hypotheses about the cause of certain behaviors, and hence it may help us to identify potential independent variables.

In carrying out a study by the method of naturalistic observation, the investigator has one cardinal rule he must follow. He must not allow himself to intrude in any way upon the situation in which the behavior is to be observed. He must allow the conditions of the environment to produce their effects without in any way being modified by his presence. Naturalistic observation is quite the opposite of an experiment on this score. In an experiment the investigator tries to control the conditions or variables; in a naturalistic-observation study he must not impose any control. This may be illustrated.

Students in the authors' classes usually perform a study using naturalistic observation. It provides experience in collecting data outside of the laboratory, but more importantly, it brings into sharp focus the problems which prevent the drawing of cause-effect conclusions from naturalistic observation. In carrying out the assignment, one student hypothesized that drivers of high priced automobiles would be less likely to come to a complete halt at a certain street intersection having a stop sign than would drivers of low priced automobiles. To collect his data he stationed himself directly on the corner, in full view of the drivers, with a clipboard plainly in evidence. It was not until he discovered that all cars were coming to a complete stop that he realized he was responsible. When he secreted himself he found that stopping behaviors changed abruptly. The basic rule: the investigator must not in any way be responsible for the behavior he wishes to observe.

A naturalistic-observation study may proceed at either of two levels. At the most elementary level the investigator merely asks about the frequency (or some other quantitative index) with which a given behavior occurs. What is the forage range of a chipmunk? What is the stopping behavior of drivers at a given intersection? How many stop completely, almost stop, maintain the same speed, or actually speed up? Such observations describe what may be called a behavioral segment or phenomenon. At a second level, the investigator "inserts" an independent variable into the situation. This independent variable must also consist of some naturally occurring event which can be clearly identified as having at least two levels (two treatments). The student observed stopping behavior as a function of the cost of the automobile; the cost, he believed, might reflect differences in the characteristics of the drivers. What is the forage range of the chipmunk during a summer month versus a fall month? A naturalistic-observation study might ask about nearly any kind of measurable or countable behavior as related to a factor or factors which changed levels or values in the natural scheme of things. Here are some other illustrations.

The idea was advanced that students driving cars with out-of-state licenses would be less likely to purchase a parking permit required by the university than would students driving within-state cars. The student's reasoning was that the owner of a car with an out-of-state license would be more difficult to "track down" than would the owner of a car carrying a within-state license. Consequently, an owner from out of the state would be less likely to purchase a university permit. The student went to a large university parking lot. He went up and down the rows of automobiles. Whenever he found an out-of-state license he would record whether or not it also carried a university permit. He would then observe the first car to the right which had a within-state license and record whether or not it carried a university permit. Thus, the independent variable was within-state license versus out-of-state license, and the nominal dependent variable was the number in each class holding university permits. Fifty in each class were observed and his findings thoroughly discredited his hypothesis. Only 2 of the 50 out-of-state cars failed to have a university permit while 4 out of the 50 within-state cars failed to show a permit.

Another student had the notion that it was more difficult to put in concentrated study before dinner than after. He observed students in the library between 4:00 and 5:00 P.M. and again between 7:00 and 8:00 P.M. He used several indices of concentration and they all showed that concentration was less before dinner than after. His idea was developed from the premise that hunger makes for general restlessness, hence poor concentration. This student realized, however, that his results did not prove this hypothesis and he proceeded to list a number of other factors having nothing to do with hunger which could produce the same effect. For example, he noted that the students he observed between 4:00 and 5:00 p.m. may have been studying all afternoon and that fatigue may have made them restless. Those he observed between 7:00 and 8:00 P.M. may have been studying for the first time that day. Nature simply does not provide control over alternative causal factors.

The similarities between the natural-groups design and naturalistic observation when different classes of people are observed should be pointed out at this time. Jones might have observed blind and sighted children in their day-to-day behavior and reached a conclusion about kinesthetic accuracy. It was much simpler and more rapid to bring them to the laboratory and measure them on a common task. The student might have brought students into the laboratory and devised a task to measure their attentiveness in studying for varying periods of time to test his hypothesis. Both naturalistic observation and the natural-groups design present problems of interpretation that are best discussed in expanded form in the context of a later chapter.

At this point it must be made manifest that naturalistic observation has great value. In the first place, we at least get data describing certain behavioral phenomena, phenomena which may be judged of sufficient importance to warrant further study by other methods. Second, the observations may suggest independent variables which should be given experimental test. Third, observations may suggest certain kinds of measurements or response indices which would be more appropriate or relevant than would other kinds. For example, naturalistic observation of the effect of frustration on kindergarten children might well suggest certain response measures which would reliably reflect frustration. Finally, naturalistic observation may provide *some* evidence on important issues when it is not possible to gather the evidence by conducting an experiment. If the results of a naturalistic-observation study are treated with great caution concerning their implications, they may be of value in handling these important issues.

Correlation Techniques

Any relationship between two variables represents a correlation existing in nature. The correlation between the click input frequency and reported number of clicks was essentially perfect in the Guzy-Axelrod experiment. Nevertheless, the area of research associated with the use of correlational techniques to determine relationships differs from experimental work in that the interest is fundamentally in the relationships between dependent variables, and not between independent and dependent variables. The speed and quality of wrapping quarter pounds of butter may be correlated with another dependent variable, e.g., the score on a ten-minute test of finger dexterity. For selection of workers to be butter wrappers this is a valuable fact, but we do not know thereby about the role of any independent variables on the development of finger dexterity. Correlational studies are not intended to produce this latter type of information, but this in no way diminishes their usefulness for their intended purpose.

The correlational approach as practiced would essentially have no meaning or use if individual differences did not exist in skills, capacities, aptitudes, and so on. The most elaborate use of this individual difference approach is known as factor analysis. Using the fact that individual differences exist, the purpose of factor analysis is to find out how a variety of perhaps superficially diverse skills or aptitudes or capacities are related. Do verbal skills relate to mathematical proficiency? What are the subskills which might be individually identified and which in sum constitute mathematical skills? How many distinctly different (uncorrelated) factors underlie what is commonly called intellectual or scholastic skills? In a certain sense, factor analytic studies can be viewed as involving independent variables. The investigator constructs a battery of tests which differ in certain ways, these differences reflecting the investigator's notions as to what it is that might constitute different skills or factors. As will be seen, certain experimental work approximates this approach. But the intent differs. The factor analyst asks about the relationships which exist among skills or capacities or aptitudes; in the experiment the question would ask what independent variables were responsible for developing the skills or aptitudes or traits as they now exist.

More and more in recent years the experimentalist has come to view the correlational approach as a useful and powerful support tool for his analysis. More importantly, this tool is a necessity for certain kinds of theoretical approaches. Illustrations of this support will be provided in later chapters.

We have surveyed the critical points in all the phases constituting "doing an experiment," and have contrasted the experiment with other forms of research. Much of this introduction was by way of pointing to matters which will be discussed in detail in later chapters.

In an experiment we "feed" different levels of an independent variable (stimulus variable) into an organism and measure his behavior (dependent or response variable). If the independent variable is a relevant one we find that the behavior changes as the independent variable changes and we say that the independent variable is a causal factor in the behavior. Our first task in the following chapter is to examine certain characteristics of the independent variables which are manipulated in experiments across the various subject-matter areas which constitute the content of psychology.

REFERENCES

1. Schwartz, R. M., and M. S. Humphreys, List differentiation in part/whole free recall. *American Journal of Psychology*, 1973, **86**, 79–88.

2. Jones, B. Development of cutaneous and kinesthetic localization by blind and sighted subjects. *Developmental Psychology*, 1972, **6**, 349–352.

3. Sharma, S., and H. Moskowitz, Effect of marihuana on the visual auto-kinetic phenomenon. *Perceptual and Motor Skills*, 1972, **35**, 891–894.

4. Guzy, L. T. and S. Axelrod, Interaural attention shifting as response. *Journal of Experimental Psychology*, 1972, **95**, 290–294.

INDEPENDENT AND DEPENDENT VARIABLES

It is useful conceptually to think of the independent variable as ranging continuously from very low to very high. At the same time we may visualize the possible results of the experiment for such a widely sampled independent variable. Several possible fictitious, but realistic, outcomes are depicted in Figure 2.1. Panel A shows that the dependent variable (the behavior being measured) increases linearly as the independent variable increases. The slope of the line could vary from shallow to steep and we would still speak of it as a linear relationship. Panel C also shows a linear relationship, but one in which the dependent variable decreases as the independent variable increases—an inverse relationship. Linear relationships are particularly appealing to investigators as outcomes of their research, and the appeal goes somewhat beyond the esthetics of the matter. Such relationships are, of course, easy to express mathematically. In addition, however, there is a prevailing notion that the explanatory or theoretical problem in handling a linear relationship is likely to be somewhat less complicated than that for a nonlinear relationship. Nevertheless, we should understand that a linear relationship is quite dependent upon our scale for the independent variable and upon the units of measurement for the dependent variable. Scales can be transformed to remove linearity, and relationships which are nonlinear may be made linear by transformations.

Panel B shows that the behavior was not influenced by the independent variable. We would say that the independent variable was irrelevant to the behavior being studied. This is not an unusual finding of an experiment. The failure of an independent variable to produce an influence on behavior often produces negative reactions, bordering on dismay, within the investigator. If he overcomes these feelings and submits the results for publication, the editor may have negative reactions because of the negative results. If the editor overcomes his negative reactions and publishes the article, the readers of the journal may have negative reactions. It appears that unless the results of an experiment producing negative results have very pointed theoretical

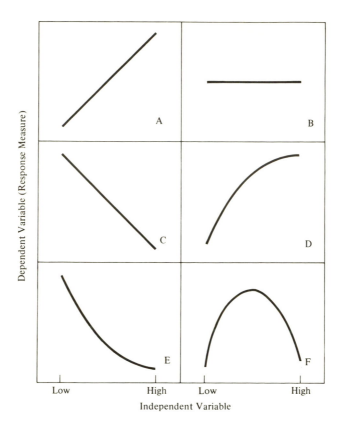

Fig. 2.1. Some possible relationships between dependent and independent variables.

implications, a chain reaction of negative affect, starting with the research assistant, is set off. Yet, in the long run, it is important that we know which independent variables do influence various types of behavior and which do not. Everything cannot influence everything else; there must be selective causality in nature's scheme of things.

While the principle of limited or finite causality must be accepted, it does not mean that all potential independent variables must be put to an experimental test. Suppose that we do a study of concept learning in the laboratory. Our independent variable is separate from the concept task itself, and consists of a number of empty coke bottles standing on a table apart from the subject. Under one condition we have 1 bottle; under another condition, 3; under another, 5; another, 7; another 9. We can visualize a plot of the results with number of empty coke bottles on the baseline and some measure of concept learning on the ordinate. The finding would undoubtedly be like that shown in Panel B. Why would we, as well as an editor, say that this whole thing was absurd? Because there is no reason—intuitive, theoretical, common sense or otherwise—to expect that the number of empty coke bottles has anything to do with concept learning. There is no background thinking which could lead to this expectation. So we can see that we do not draw randomly when we want to choose an independent variable; we impose a great deal of our own beliefs and ideas on the situation in an effort to choose an independent variable that will have an influence, and which we believe others might accept as being "reasonable." By such rational procedures we sharply limit the number of independent variables that need to be given experimental tests. Such procedures may in fact eliminate from consideration certain relevant independent variables, but sooner or later their pertinence will be seen.

Continuing the inspection of Figure 2.1, we see that Panels D, E, and F exhibit nonlinear relationships. The relationships in Panels D and E are like a linear relationship in that they are said to be monotonic. There is a consistent relationship (upward or downward) for both, but each increase in a unit of the independent variable is not accompanied by a constant change in the response measure. The relationship in Panel F would be said to be nonmonotonic or complex, since there is a reversal in the relationship; the dependent variable first increases and then decreases as the independent variable increases. It should be noted (with regard to Panel F) that if an experiment were done in which only two levels of the independent variable, low and high, were used, the response measure would not differ and we would possibly conclude that the independent variable was irrelevant. A minimum of three widely spaced levels of the independent variable is necessary to guard against such inappropriate conclusions.

Types of Independent Variables

Rules for classification seem to have a way of breaking down at certain points. Rules of spelling do not handle all spelling cases. A biologist who discovers an insect that does not fit within the standard classification system might choose to step on the bug and avoid the problem. So it is with types of independent variables. Most can be fitted into one of four types, but there are ambiguous cases.

Task. In most experiments an external task is used if only in the sense that stimuli of some kind must be presented to which the subject must respond. Frequently used tasks are spoken of as standardized tasks, such as a paired-associate list, an operant chamber, letter strings, the Müller-Lyer illusion, and so on. Any characteristic of these tasks which is manipulated as an independent variable is spoken of as a task variable. The characteristics of the words, common or uncommon, might be varied in a paired-associate list. The size of the operant chamber, or the size of the lever or key within it, could be manipulated.

Environmental. Any characteristic of the experimental environment which is varied while keeping the task the same is called an environmental independent variable. The more obvious characteristics which could be changed, such as temperature, humidity, or lighting, would fit this category. One of the most frequently manipulated environmental variables is time. An illustration is the time between the onset of the conditioned stimulus and the onset of the unconditioned stimulus in classical conditioning. Another is the number of clicks per unit of time. The length of the retention interval is still another.

Subject. Jones selected subjects of different ages; age is a subject variable as is any other identifiable characteristic of the subject such as sex, height, race, sociableness, visual acuity, blood type, sense of humor. Subject variables, therefore, are more or less enduring characteristics on which subjects may differ.

Temporary subject variables. Any manipulation which is aimed at changing the characteristics of the subjects within the group as compared to the way these characteristics naturally exist will be spoken of as temporary subject variables. When Sharma and Moskowitz gave subjects different doses of marihuana they were interested in seeing if the subjects' perceptual systems were temporarily changed thereby. A geometric illusion may be presented for viewing monocularly and in doing so we change the way the subject would normally look at the illusion. Guzy and Axelrod presented clicks for monotic processing, a type of processing which does not usually occur. One group of subjects may be instructed to learn a task in a given way, and if this way is not the one the subjects would use customarily, we are temporarily changing the processing characteristics of the subjects. Naturally existing subject differences arise because of genetic or experiential factors; manipulations for producing temporary subject differences may, to some degree, result in changes which simulate the naturally existing permanent subject differences.

When lower animals are used as subjects, the investigator may sometimes produce permanent changes in the characteristics of the subjects. Such would be the case if brain lesions were produced in gerbils to determine if the lesions at different sites influence exploratory behavior. As a way to assess the role played by various sensory modalities on maze learning by rats, different classes of sensory receptors may be systematically destroyed for various groups. The intent of studies of this nature is the same as that for inducing temporary changes in characteristics of human subjects, although the surgical procedures may be viewed as being somewhat more decisive.

CONFOUNDING OF INDEPENDENT VARIABLES

When relationships are obtained between independent and dependent variables our purpose is to conclude that the changes in the behavior were caused by the changes in the independent variable. To say this another way, our aim in doing an experiment is to identify an agent of change explicitly. To do this, we must avoid a confounding of our independent variable by some other independent variable. Two independent variables are confounded when the variation in the magnitude of our intended independent variable is accompanied by a variation in the magnitude of another known or potential independent variable. The relationship between the two may be direct (one increases as the other increases) or inverse (one decreases as the other increases). In both cases we would say there is a confounding. The consequence is that we cannot identify the cause of the behavioral change; it might be due to one or the other independent variable, or to some combination of both. If a balky mule is hit simultaneously on the rear with a paddle and with a switch, there is no way to tell whether the immediate forward movement was caused by the paddle or the switch or whether the combination of the two was responsible.

It might seem that avoiding confounds should be a fairly easy occupation. Any editor of a journal will quietly but firmly inform us that this is not the case. Even those who have been in the business for many years may occasionally goof. It is true, as will be seen later, that the choice of a particular design technique (between or within groups) will automatically avoid certain types of confounding, but the choice of a particular design is not intended as a device to avoid all confoundings. A good and theoretically pointed idea for an experiment is a fine commodity, even somewhat rare, but the idea has to be implemented within a procedure in which there are no confoundings; otherwise, false conclusions may be reached. So far as we have been able to determine, the perception of confoundings, particularly subtle confoundings, results from practice, then more practice.

Illustrations of Confoundings

Let us start with an examination of two studies using naturalistic observation, because these studies (as noted earlier) are particularly vulnerable. They are vulnerable because the so-called independent variable must occur at two or more levels in the natural course of events, and in nature many factors do change simultaneously.

Earlier, a description was given of a study in which the "concentration" of students studying in the library before and after dinner was observed. Those observed after dinner showed better concentration than those observed before dinner. Was the difference to be attributed to difference in hunger? It was pointed out that one matter which prevents such a conclusion is the likelihood that the observations made before dinner were made on students who had been studying all afternoon while those made after dinner may have included students who were studying for the first time that day. Thus, amount of time spent in studying before the observations were made may have been responsible for the difference in concentration, with differences in hunger being quite inconsequential. Another possibility is that the students observed at the two time intervals may have differed in their ability to concentrate. If this is true, the differences in concentration also might have been found if the observations had been recorded during the same time period. There is still another possibility: the topics being studied before and after dinner may not have been the same and concentration could have differed because of this factor. Differences in behavior observed in a single study by naturalistic observation seldom allow an interpretation in terms of a particular independent variable because other independent variables are usually confounded with it.

Assume that an investigator has the hypothesis that a certain animal should feed more frequently at midday than in the evening because of differences in the amount of light available. Assume further that his observations show that this expected difference in feeding does occur. Now we ask ourselves if there is a confounding. One obvious one is that there are likely to be temperature differences between the noon and evening hours. Therefore, amount of light as an independent variable is confounded by temperature.

In trying to discern whether or not a confounding exists in the experiment we are designing, or in research done by others, there are two probabilistic rules which are useful.

1. A confounding is most likely to occur among variables within the same class. When a task variable is being manipulated, it is most likely to be confounded with another task variable if a confound does exist; a subject variable is most likely to be confounded with another subject variable, and so on. This rule, viewed as a probabilistic rule, is a fairly valid one in guiding our attempts to design an experiment without a confounding.

2. After it has been determined that there is no confounding by a variable within the same class as the one being manipulated, the most probable source of confounding is a subject variable when the independent-groups design is used (and when we are studying the effects of an independent variable *other* than a subject variable). In the case of within-subjects designs there is no way by which the results can be influenced by a confounding with a subject variable since all subjects serve in all conditions.

The two probabilistic rules may be illustrated. Assume that we have a notion (for whatever reason) that free-recall learning of words will be more and more difficult the greater the number of syllables in the words. We are going to choose words with one, two, and three syllables, thus having three levels of the independent variable. We go to a word source and obtain a random sample from words having one syllable, another sample from those having two syllables, and a third sample from those having three syllables. There are the same number of words in each sample, and each sample is used to form a different list. Number of syllables is a task variable, so, following our first probabilistic rule, we should ask whether number of syllables (the independent variable we are interested in) is confounded with another task variable—with some other property of the words correlated with number of syllables.

There is certainly at least one other task variable that is correlated with number of syllables, namely, the frequency with which the words are used in the printed language. The correlation is negative; the more frequently used words are shorter words. Other task variables may also be confounded with number of syllables, such as parts of speech, concreteness or abstractness, and perhaps others. If we are truly interested in learning as a function of the number of syllables, we must find some way to hold these other characteristics of the words constant while we manipulate only number of syllables.

Next, we may illustrate the second probabilistic rule. An experiment is done with three levels of an independent variable, say, speed and accuracy of long-division problems as a function of the length of the rest interval between successive problems (one, two, and three minutes). In a given school there are three eighth-grade classes. One of the classes is arbitrarily assigned the one-minute condition, a second the two-minute condition, and the third, the three-minute condition. Differences which may occur could be due to either the length of interval or to differences in the ability level of the students in the classes. The environmental variable (time between problems) may be confounded with a subject variable, in that the students in the different classes may differ on arithmetic ability.

These, then, are illustrations of some relatively obvious confoundings. In subsequent chapters we will have opportunity to illustrate somewhat more subtle cases. We turn next to cases of intentional confoundings.

Complex Independent Variables

There are times when an investigator may intentionally manipulate an independent variable which, considered in total, consists of a number of identifiably different independent variables. There are different situations which could lead an investigator to use this approach. Supposing an advertiser asks whether it would be better to advertise a product using radio commercials or using television commercials. The commercials produced in the two media may differ in a number of identifiable ways. Nevertheless, the study is carried out because the advertiser is not asking an analytical question. He may not at all be interested in the specific factors involved in producing a difference in sales (if such occurs). Rather, he is interested in a very practical problem and needs an answer, an answer which can be supplied to him by the experiment.

Consider another case. In a certain school system it is found that the achievement of the students in the junior high school is far below the national average in mathematics. To see if there is "hope," an experiment is carried out. The students in half the junior high schools in this large city continue to be taught as in the past. The other half of the students are given a markedly changed teaching-study program. New text books are employed, rewards are given for achievement, programmed learning machines are available, and so on. This is sometimes called the sledgehammer approach. Now if these differences in treatments have an influence, it will be quite impossible to identify which one of the several independent variables is responsible. Perhaps only one is responsible, but the experiment was not designed to determine this. So we can say that these nonanalytical experiments, involving a complex independent variable, have a place in the scheme of things. They may be useful for answering applied or commercial questions, and they may be useful in seeing what can be done about certain educational or social problems. We must always evaluate an experiment in terms of the intent of the investigator. If an investigator knows what he is doing, and if he chooses to do a study in which a complex independent variable is used, we cannot deport him so long as his conclusions are not analytical statements about the component variables.

The use of a complex independent variable might be justified as a deliberate research strategy when the long-term goal is highly analytical research, that is, research which attempts to identify the contribution of each identifiable independent variable within the complex stimulus manipulations. For an illustration of this we may return to the investigator interested in the teaching of mathematics. Let us assume that his complex independent variable produced a whopping positive effect on the mathematical skills of the students. Having found that "he had ahold of" some one or more potent independent variables he now starts a series of analytical studies to find out just which ones are largely responsible for the overall effect. He does this by examining the influence of each identifiable independent variable alone. The order of the examinations could be more or less random. The investigator probably would not be this crassly empirical about it, but he might be. It is more likely that he has some notions, perhaps theoretically derived, concerning the critical components in his complex independent variable and it is highly likely that these would be the ones that he would first bring under analytical experimental scrutiny. If he is a very perceptive, or perhaps lucky, theorist he might find his entire effect was produced by the first component variable he brought to the experiment.

We may recognize, then, that under certain circumstances an experimenter may intentionally confound independent variables. Since this is quite easy to do, we need not consider this a matter to be taught here. Our interest will be in the design of analytical experiments, experiments in which there is no confounding of independent variables.

There is one further matter about confounding with which we should come to grips at this point. Suppose we perceive a confounding in our or someone else's experiment, but the confounding variable is one on which there has been no research; that is, it is not known whether the variable does or does not have an influence on the behavior being measured in the experiment. All we know is that its magnitude is correlated with the independent variable of interest. We tend to take a fairly hard line in these situations and conclude that the results are ambiguous as to their cause, and therefore they should not become a part of our literature. However, there are probably cases where we would conclude that the confounding variable could not possibly have produced the effect measured, with this conclusion being based on our past knowledge of what are and are not likely to be relevant independent variables (e.g., variation in number of coke bottles).

Assume that we did a study on the effect of two dose levels of marihuana on the autokinetic illusion, using two groups of middle-aged subjects. Following the data collection, we find that the mean age of the two groups differed by six months. There is a confounding, but we would probably conclude that this age difference could not possibly be involved in our findings. That is, a six-month age difference in the middle forties should be of no consequence even if the age difference was significant statistically. Therefore, we must not always rule against the investigator when the effects of a confounding variable are unknown. Sometimes we can make appropriate tests within the data collected and find out if the confounding variable was involved. For example, within each of the two groups described above we could determine if the magnitude of the illusion was related to age, thus using a correlational approach. If the two are not related, we are in fine shape.

Quantifying the Independent Variable

In thinking about various possible relationships between the independent and dependent variable (such as illustrated in Figure 2.1), it is worthwhile (as suggested earlier) to conceive of the independent variable as changing in small units along a unitary dimension. The conception has direct representation whenever the independent variable can be described through the use of scales reflecting physical properties, such as weight or length. There are similar measures used in describing events which reflect the frequency of recurrent events per unit of time (e.g., clicks per second); and, of course, time per se is often used as an independent variable in psychological experiments. We may also ask about the rate of learning the T-maze as a function of the number of grams of food in the goal box; about the pitch of a tone as a function of the sound wave, or about the persistence of a memory as a function of the time since it was acquired. Thus, scales used to describe events or objects in the physical sciences have some degree of applicability in the description of the independent variables used in studies of behavior.

Many independent variables of interest to psychologists cannot be described in the above fashion. Even if they can, the description may have little behavioral meaning, or may be so complex as to make any understanding quite out of the question. We must use other devices to provide the descriptions of such independent variables, and these other devices consist of using our own discriminal capacities as the quantifying agent.

As we grow from infancy to adulthood we develop capacities to distinguish or discriminate differences among events because they produce differential responses "in" us. We may "read" these reactions, and if appropriate descriptive words can be agreed upon we may report to others how these reactions differ in magnitude along one or more psychological dimensions or continua. A grapefruit and a chocolate pie would probably be universally reported as differing along a sweet-sour dimension of taste. Many reactions are said to differ along a pleasant-unpleasant dimension, and there is frequently high agreement among different people as to the events which produce the differences in pleasantness or unpleasantness. Yet it is not possible to conceive of how many such events could be described meaningfully by measurements along physical scales. Consider two cartoons, one which produces a laugh, the other a ho-hum. It does not seem possible to describe the differences in the two cartoons by using physical scales (length, weight) which would in turn reflect the differences in the two different reactions to the cartoons. It should be clear that physical stimuli are in some way producing the reactions, but the relationship between the critical physical stimuli and their description by physical scales is missing. If we ask a subject to lift two weights, one an ounce and one a pound, he will report the pound weight to be the heavier. Thus there is a direct relationship between his responses to the weights and the physical scale. But there are many, many events or stimuli in the world which produce differences in subjective or phenomenal magnitude which cannot be described meaningfully by the scales used to describe physical properties and the relationships among those physical properties. Let us pursue this still further.

If you are presented two verbal units, TAG and TAC, and are asked to describe your reactions to each, there would be clear differences. The physical properties of the two verbal units are almost identical, but not quite. This tiny difference is associated with reactions which differ considerably. If we reverse the order of the letters, we have GAT and CAT. Now the reactions will differ again although the physical differences have remained much the same. At the present time we have no way to provide a meaningful description of the differences among many stimuli except by referring to the differential responses they produce. We will speak, therefore, of quantifying (in its minimal sense) a psychological stimulus dimension. A psychological stimulus dimension is one which some investigator believes has psychological relevance in understanding behavior but which cannot be described meaningfully by already existing physical scales or derivatives thereof.

To quantify a psychological stimulus dimension requires an experiment. We must understand how such an experiment differs from one in which the independent variable is described by physical scales. In the latter case we ask about the relationship between the independent variable (where units are expressed by a common physical scale) and behavior. In the former case we are asking whether a set of events or stimuli, undifferentiated by apparent physical dimensions, can produce different subjective magnitudes along some specified dimension of responding. If the responses show some consistency across subjects for the events we say we have quantified a psychological stimulus dimension. We have done this by using the responses of the subjects to specify points along the dimension. We have, therefore, established units or quantities by which the events differ.

Having established a psychological stimulus dimension, where are we? So we discover that common words can be reliably scaled along a dimension of pleasantness-unpleasantness, or that there is agreement on the seriousness of various crimes. Having carried out such procedures, what have we gained? There are three gains which may be identified. First, the quantified scale may be useful as a measuring device in further studies. Suppose ten breakfast cereals have been evaluated along a dimension identified as most-liked to least-liked. If we are considering marketing a new cereal, we might be wise to find just where along the scale the new cereal will be placed by potential consumers.

A second use of such a scale is serving as the dependent variable in an experiment. As had been noted, common words can be scaled quite reliably along a dimension running from very unpleasant to very pleasant. Suppose we have a theory which predicts that unpleasant words will become less so as a direct function of frequency of exposure. We conduct an experiment in which the independent variable is the frequency of exposure of unpleasant words. We may use the already established scale as the instrument of measurement to determine if in fact there is a direct relationship between frequency of exposure and reduction in the degree of unpleasantness. If there is, our manipulations are effective.

A third use of an established psychological scale is to employ the stimuli or events which represent various points along the scale as a quantified independent variable for further experiments. To continue the above illustration, we might ask about the relationship between the pleasant-unpleasant dimension of words and the rate of free-recall learning. Thus in thinking how a graph would express the outcome of such an experiment, we might visualize six lists of words differing in their positions along the pleasant-unpleasant scale. These six lists would define six points along the baseline with a measure of learning along the ordinate. On the surface, at least, this seems exactly comparable to manipulating an independent variable described by a physical scale, e.g., learning as a function of the number of grams of food in the goal box of a T-maze.

The three uses to which a psychological scale may be put do not represent the only reasons why the scaling of a psychological dimension would be undertaken. One could ask merely whether or not a reliable scale could be established for a certain class of events. To say this another way, we might undertake to scale a characteristic merely to find out if there is an underlying continuum for which there is agreement among subjects. Certain events may be perceived quite differently by different individuals. Certain esthetic objects or events are sometimes found to be quixotic in that although people may agree that it is perfectly reasonable to be asked to make pleasant to un-pleasant decisions for the events, when the data across people are examined it is found that there is no agreement. If there is zero agreement among subjects concerning their reactions (likes and dislikes) to several works of art, all of the works would end up with the same scale value and we would say that we cannot provide a meaningful measurement of them.

THE DEPENDENT VARIABLE

The dependent variable (the response measure or response variable) is said to index the behavior of interest in the experiment. Schwartz and Humphreys were interested in differences between their E and C Groups in free-recall learning over trials, and they used the number of words correctly recalled on each trial as their index. Jones used the number of inches by which the positioning movement deviated from the true distance as his index of preci-sion in the kinesthetic system. For Guzy and Axelrod the dependent variable was the number of clicks reported by the subject, a measure which they related to attention.

It can be seen that a raw dependent variable is a performance measure; that is, it is something the subject does or says. We could have an experimental psychology which stops with these measures. For example, we could have a psychology of correct responses in free recall, or a psychology of the number of reported clicks. This would be empiricism at its boundless best, or worst. Most investigators are not content with this. They are not interested in the number of reported clicks as such. They are interested in reported clicks because they believe that such reports are telling them something about some process judged to be fundamental in producing not only the behavior mea-sured but also many other behaviors. Changes in the performance measure (as related to changes in the independent variable) are used to make inferences about those more fundamental processes. In certain areas of investigation these inferences are so commonly made that no thought is given to the fact that an inference has occurred. For example, Schwartz and Humphreys in-ferred learning from their response measure and probably few would object to this inference. In other areas there may be disagreement as to just what fundamental processes are to be inferred from the performance measure. The psycho-galvanic response (changes in the electrical resistance of the skin) has been used off and on for decades and yet it is probably fair to say that just what is to be inferred from this measure is in doubt, or at least in some disagreement.

To draw a distinction between what is observed and what is inferred from what is only observed is to point out a distinction that is sometimes difficult to maintain in practice. If a white rat is placed on a table top he is likely to move around on it, poke his head over the edge, and perhaps sniff. It is somehow quite compelling for us to say that the rat is curious, but that is not what we have observed. Tears in the eyes do not always mean sadness; slicing onions may produce tears. So we see that it is difficult to avoid theoretical or conceptual thinking even when we are concerned about the performance we observe in an experiment.

Quantification of the Dependent Variable

Response measures as taken directly in the experimental situation may represent all levels of quantification. At a very simple level it might be whether the subject did or did not respond to a given stimulus condition, and our response measure might be the number of times the response did occur or the number of subjects who did respond. Did you hear that tone? Have you seen this word before? At the other extreme the response measure might be the number of microvolts produced by a muscle contraction or the number of milliseconds required to press a button when a certain stimulus appears.

Sometimes it is necessary to make some rather arbitrary decisions about response measures. An anagram is a set of letters that when rearranged forms a word: *oeepssrn = response*. Anagram problems have been favorite ones for use in studying certain forms of elementary problem solving. Suppose a subject is given four anagrams to solve with the response measure being the total time to solve all four anagrams. This seems clear and clean enough until we run across a subject who solves three anagrams but simply cannot find a solution to the fourth one. What do we do? We might impose an upper time limit, say 30 minutes, and any subject who has not solved all the anagrams within that period will be assigned a score of 30 minutes for his solution time. Another possibility might be to have the 30-minute limit but to measure the average time required to complete the solved anagrams. Thus, a subject who solved only two anagrams within the 30-minute period would get a higher (poorer) score than one who solved three, and of course any subject who solved all anagrams in less than 30 minutes would have a still lower score. If we are measuring the performance of rats in a straight alley the response measure is often the time to run from the start box to the goal box. What do we do if a rat chooses not to go down the alley at all on a given trial? Again, some arbitrary decision will be necessary, but a decision involving extermination is not viewed as being an appropriate one. The basic idea in such arbitrary decisions is to find one that will not bias the outcome of the experiment in the sense that the response measure under one level of the independent variable will not be favored over the measure for another level.

The quantification of the response is not always as simple as the cases discussed up to this point. Suppose a subject is given five minutes to memorize a 500 word passage of prose. At the end of the five minutes we ask him to write the passage verbatim. Few if any subjects could do this. How are we going to score the recall? Suppose in place of the adjective *unclean* the subject writes *dirty*. Is this to be counted correct? It is obvious that some decisions will have to be made in order to obtain a numerical score for each subject.

The raw score values as obtained more or less directly from the subject's performance may be transformed or converted in some manner. This may result as a matter of taste, or from a statistical requirement, or in some cases, it may be a necessity if the effect of the independent variable is to be appropriately assessed. These latter cases are important in that they represent one of the few cases where we may speak of a genuine error in an experiment due to an inappropriate response measure. The following case is an illustration.

The task to be presented to the subject is called a search task. Lines of letters are typed on a sheet of paper with no spaces between the letters. The subject's task is to go through the letters in each line and cancel all of the Ts and Ks. The independent variable is the number of *different* other letters in the lines. In one condition all the remaining 24 letters are used, these letters being positioned randomly around the Ts and Ks. In the other condition only the letters F, H, and N are used. The following two lines will illustrate the two conditions:

QWERTPOIUYKASDKFGHJLMNBTVCPOIKUYREWQASDFTGHJLMNB

FNHNTHFNHNKFHNKFHNHNFNHTHNFHFKHNHNHFNFHNTFHNNH

For both conditions the Ts and Ks in each line are exactly the same in number and position. The only difference is the number of different letters surrounding the Ts and Ks.

We will assume that the subject is allowed three minutes to go through as many lines as possible, crossing out all of the Ts and Ks he can detect, working under instructions which make both speed and accuracy important in the performance. For the response measure we count the number of Ts and Ks which are missed (not detected and crossed out) under each of the two conditions. We find that the two means are statistically equivalent. This would lead us to conclude that the number of different surrounding letters is not a relevant independent variable in this search task. Suppose, however, that under one condition the average subject finished only 10 lines within the three-minute period while under the other condition the average was 15 lines. This means that the number of different letters influenced search speed. Furthermore, it also means that per number of lines inspected in three minutes the error *rate* differed.

There is a general rule which can be used to indicate when we must transform a response measure in the sense just described. If the conditions (independent variable) of an experiment result in a different number of opportunities for the occurrence of the particular event of interest (e.g., errors in the above illustration), the data must be converted to take into account the difference in number of opportunities. This issue is important to the interpretation of many social statistics. To be told that the number of rapes increased or decreased each year over a five-year period in a given locale is not easily interpreted until we have made an adjustment for the number of opportunities. Such an adjustment could be made (roughly) if we knew the number of adults living in the given locale each year. The knowledge that there has been an increase in the number of fatal automobile accidents over successive years does have a sobering effect. However, what it means with regard to driving behavior, traffic control, and so on, cannot become comprehensible unless we at least adjust for the number of automobiles on the roads for each year.

To recapitulate, there are many experiments in which the independent variable causes a difference in the number of opportunities for the occurrence of a given event. If the behavior of interest is the occurrence of such events, adjustment must be made for the differences in opportunities. Of course, the adjustment is usually made by getting a proportion (number of occurrences/ number of opportunities).

Reliability of the Dependent Variable

The reliability of a response measure is normally determined by calculating a correlation between two sets of measurements obtained on the same subjects under the same condition. We say that the response measure is highly reliable if the correlation is high; the rank order of the two sets of scores is much the same for the two distributions.

We normally expect the measures we use as the dependent variable to be reliable and it is a fact that they usually are. Nevertheless, a lack of reliability in the individual scores in no way prevents sound conclusions from an experiment. This may be illustrated with some hypothetical data. Assume we have done an experiment in which there are two conditions, A and B, and in which the same five subjects served in both conditions (a within-subjects design). The scores for the two conditions were as follows:

	Condition A	Condition B
Subject 1	4	15
2	5	23
3	6	12
4	7	14
5	8	18

These two sets of scores are not highly correlated, so we might say that the response measure is not reliable when based on this evidence alone. However, when the scores for each condition are considered as a whole it is quite evident that there is high reliability. The lowest score in Condition B is higher than the highest score in Condition A. We could conclude without the slightest hesitation that the independent variable produced a rather profound effect on performance.

Now assume further that we had two sets of measurements for each subject under each of the two conditions. Given these scores, we could determine the reliability separately under each condition. Suppose that both correlations were very high. Such an outcome would mean that the lack of relationship between the scores under Condition A and Condition B is not due to the unreliability of the individual scores. Rather, it would mean that the independent variable interacts with individual differences. Or, to say this another way, the characteristics of the individual that are responsible for the performance under Condition A are different from the characteristics largely responsible for performance under Condition B, and the two sets of characteristics are not correlated.

What would we conclude if we had two sets of scores on the same individual under each condition and the correlations were near zero in both cases? Would such a state of affairs jeopardize the conclusions from the experiment? Not at all, for we would still retain our high reliability for the difference in the means for the two conditions. We do not require high reliability of individual scores for experimental work, although as noted earlier, such reliability is usually found. Sometimes we wish to relate the scores obtained in an experiment to other scores which are available for the subjects, for example, school grades. If the individual scores obtained from the experiment are unreliable, we could not expect to show any relationship with school grades. It is, therefore, very useful to have high reliability of our response measure for it does give us an opportunity to seek further relationships, but such reliability is not a necessity for research when group means are of primary interest.

Multiple Dependent Variables

Earlier an illustration was given of a task in which the subject was allowed three minutes to cross out as many Ts and Ks as possible. Suppose that instead of imposing the three-minute rule, we required the subjects to go through all lines on the page and we recorded the time each subject took to complete the page. We now have two response measures, namely, time to complete the page and number of errors. These two measures are often spoken of as speed and accuracy measures, but the interest here is in illustrating any type of experiment in which two or more response measures are obtained.

We might ask the following questions first: "Which response measure is the better? Which one will serve as a better reflection of the influence of the independent variable? Or, should we use some composite of the two?" There are no pat answers to these questions, so the best that can be done is to suggest some guidelines.

In the above illustration we might anticipate that the number of errors and time to complete the page would be highly correlated—negatively correlated. A person working through the page very quickly might miss many targets, whereas the person working slowly might miss few targets. If the individual speed and accuracy scores are highly correlated, either may be used and the same conclusion concerning the effect of the independent variable will be reached.

Another consideration would be in terms of the sensitivity of each response measure. Suppose that only a few subjects missed any target letter under either condition? It is not very meaningful to work with a bunch of zero scores, so we would conclude that the independent variable did not influence accuracy and we would turn to the time-to-complete scores to see if the speed was influenced.

The more difficult situation conceptually revolves around a case where two response measures are both highly reliable (and sensitive, therefore) but do not correlate with each other. This situation essentially forces the conclusion that the two response measures are indexing two relatively independent processes. Such a conclusion would be particularly firm if the independent variable did not influence the two response measures in the same way. At this point, theoretical thinking must take over, since the data cannot tell us anything more. The investigator will normally try to suggest what the processes are and how they might be elucidated by further experiments.

It is not unusual in experiments where human subjects are involved to interrogate them after the session is completed. The questions and answers provide a separate set of response measures. If reports from subjects are to have maximal potential for helping us understand the behavior investigated, the questioning should be pertinent and systematic. Pertinence usually results from preliminary ideas of the investigator combined with what is learned from the relatively free reports of pilot subjects. With this information it is possible to construct a questionnaire to be used for all subjects, although some questions may be specific to the condition in which the subject serves. When we develop instructions to be given the subjects prior to the experimental treatment, we frequently have to test them with pilot subjects to make certain a clear understanding will be transmitted. So also, if we are seriously interested in the reports of the subjects after the experiment, we should show the same care in developing the questions to be used in the post-experimental inquiry. Furthermore, such inquiries often lead quite naturally into a "debriefing" of the subject concerning the purpose of the experiment, and just where the condition in which the subject served fits into the overall purpose.

We should by no means expect that reports from the subjects are always going to be useful. Sometimes what a subject reports adds understanding to the more quantitative data, sometimes it does not. Sometimes what a subject tells the investigator may provide an insight which will lead to a new line of research. Sometimes what a subject tells him may lead to a dead end in further research. Sometimes what a subject reports seems to be trivial or of no consequence for interpreting an experiment. Even a careful approach to the gathering of subject reports does not guarantee the usefulness of the reports.

WHERE WE ARE

The background thinking has led us to a particular independent variable. The dependent variable (or variables) to be used to index the behavior of interest has been chosen. We are now ready to decide upon a particular experimental design. The following two chapters should provide information necessary to reach the appropriate decision.

3

INDEPENDENT-GROUPS DESIGNS

We come now to a detailed consideration of the basic designs used for implementing an experiment. The word *design* is used throughout this text to mean the plan by which subjects are assigned to the conditions of the experiment, or the plan by which the order of administering the conditions to a subject is determined. The second case will be discussed in the next chapter. In the present chapter the focus is on plans which may be used for assigning subjects to different conditions when each of the subjects serves in only one condition of the experiment. We have noted earlier that designs which use independent groups are of two types, random groups and matched groups.

RANDOM-GROUPS DESIGN

The random-groups design grows directly out of statistical theory, particularly sampling theory. A short review may be necessary. The theory starts with the idea of a defined population, such as all eighth-grade students in a city, all of the elk on a game preserve, or all of the freshmen students in a given university. Suppose we wanted to know something about the population not as yet known, e.g., the average vocabulary of the eighth-grade students. We could administer a vocabulary test to *all* of the students in the population with the mean of these scores used as the critical information. This would be fine. However, sampling theory allows us to estimate this mean by much more economical procedures, namely, by sampling from the population. We administer the test to a small number of students and use the mean of the sample as an estimate of the population mean. Or, as is frequently said, we generalize to the population from the data obtained from the sample. We can do this, according to the theory, if the sample we use is chosen randomly from the population. Choosing randomly means that each unit (e.g., eighth-grade student) in the population has an equal likelihood of being included in the sample. One may visualize a large drum with 10,000 capsules of identical size and weight in it, each capsule representing a unit in the population. If these capsules are well mixed, and if 100 are drawn blindly, we would expect any measurement we make using the sample to estimate closely the measurement for the entire population.

We are well aware that measurements from random samples will not always provide an accurate estimate of the population values. Or, if we took two random samples from the population we would not expect that the means of the two would be identical, for example on vocabulary score. But we would not expect the difference between the two means to be "statistically significant." However, the theory tells us we will be wrong occasionally if we conclude that the two sample means will never be statistically different.

For the experimental psychologist, there are two matters of critical importance which emerge from statistical sampling theory. First, the whole idea of the random-groups design rests on the assumption that if we draw two or more random groups from the same population, and if we measure these two or more samples under the same conditions, the means will not differ statistically. Therefore, if we give these two or more randomly formed groups different treatments or conditions in an experiment, and if the means *do* differ statistically, we conclude that the differences are due to the differences in the experimental treatments. We know that our conclusion will be wrong occasionally, for we know that randomly formed groups from a given population will differ sometimes even when measured under exactly the same conditions. We must, therefore, accept the unsavory fact that our conclusions concerning the effect of an independent variable will occasionally be in error.

The second fact of importance for our thinking is that when we do experiments we seldom, indeed almost never, draw units randomly from a defined population. We do not do this because we usually cannot define the population in any but a trivial sense, e.g., students taking the elementary psychology course who happened to volunteer for this particular experiment. The purpose of sampling from a defined population is to make statements about the population based on measurements of the sample or samples. If we cannot define the population meaningfully in experimental work, we cannot make statements about the population based upon the measurements in the experiment. To say this another way, we are not in a position to generalize our findings beyond the particular subjects used in the experiment. One might conclude that the whole enterprise is therefore doomed from the start. But it is not, and we need to see why. Furthermore, we have not yet considered how it is possible to speak of a random-groups design when we cannot specify a population from which we could sample randomly.

Generality of Findings

When we define a population we usually do so in broad terms based on obvious classification data such as age, grade, sex, socio-economic level, political party, intelligence, and so on. Expressed in the terms used in the previous chapter, we say that populations are usually specified in terms of particular subject variables. This is not always the case, but other bases for classifications would be used because they presumably reflect differences in subject variables. To identify one population as those people in the United States living west of the Mississippi River, and another as those living east of the river would not be using a very meaningful population characteristic unless it is further assumed that these two populations differ in one or more subject variables associated with the geographical area.

The definition of a population is never exhaustive. If it were, all populations would reduce to one case since an exhaustive classification based on subject variables would result in each person being declared unique. Rather, a population is defined in terms of a few subject variables and all other variables are free to vary. To define a population as all eighth-grade students with IQs of 100 or more still leaves a large number of unspecified differences, for example, reading proficiency, or socio-economic status. If we chose groups of subjects for an experiment by sampling randomly from this population, we must assume that the two or more groups we drew did not differ in subject variables which were relevant to (correlated with) performance on the particular task we were using in the experiment. As previously noted, we will be wrong occasionally in this assumption, but we must proceed upon it. When the experiment is done, we could generalize the findings to eighth-grade students with IQs of 100 or more. Note that we have *not* identified any subject variable that is related to the performance on the task or which interacts with the independent variable of the experiment. To say that the results can be generalized to eighth-grade students with IQs of 100 or more may be of some value, perhaps, but in most cases it would seem to be paying homage to sampling theory in a rather ineffective way if our interest is in understanding behavior.

It must be crystal clear that in one way or another we must be able to state the limits or boundaries within which a given experimental finding may be expected to hold. This is true for all classes of independent variables, not merely for subject variables used to define populations. So, to repeat the earlier question, how do we reach generalized statements about an independent variable when in fact we do not sample from a known population when doing an experiment?

We must first accept the notion that there is *some* underlying continuity in behavior. If we start out with the notion that sophomores and juniors in college represent two distinctly different populations behaviorally, we would be denying the continuity. The assumption of continuity allows us to draw conclusions which we would insist have some generality beyond the particular subjects used in the experiment. The idea that there is some degree of continuity can be supported. Throughout the course of history of experimental work, a given independent variable will have been manipulated in different experiments with subjects who differed so clearly that one would be forced to say that they must represent different populations by any of the usual classification schemes used to define populations. In many, many instances independent variables produce substantially the same effect across these different populations.

Whenever a subject variable enters into an experiment as an independent variable, we are really exploring the effects of a variable which might be used to define different populations. Although we have hinted at the interpretative problems raised by such experiments, these problems are not helped one bit by using the population-sample model. Jones did not sample randomly from precisely defined populations of school children when he did his study on kinesthetic positioning, but the marked and systematic changes he found over grade levels would probably not have been different had he done so.

The point of this discussion is to make it evident that the experimentalist attempts to establish the generality of his findings, not by sampling from a population, but by a process of reasoning, based upon the assumption of continuity in behavior. This assumption is consistently tested by examining experimental findings. In fact, in order to sample knowledgeably from a population we would need to discover first what the critical behavioral characteristics are for defining populations. Having done this, the problem of generality would be solved. Thus, for a given experiment, we use the statistical procedures derived from population-sample theory without really knowing with any precision what population is involved. It must be remembered that these procedures help us reach decisions about the reliability of the findings of a given experiment, but they do not tell us about the generality of the findings. We must now explain what is meant by the random-groups design when a defined population is not involved.

Developing Random Groups

The nub of the matter in developing random groups is to be sure that no bias exists in assigning subjects to the two or more groups to be used in the experiment. Let us first note what this is *not* saying. It is not saying that the particular subjects to be assigned to the various groups need be known before the experiment begins. It says nothing about the number or characteristics of the subjects to be used in the experiment. In short, the statement allows great latitude. The critical word is *bias*. There is bias when some characteristic of the subject, or some factor correlated with a subject variable, determines the group to which a subject is assigned. This must be avoided if we wish to develop random groups.

Let us first see how subjects can be assigned without bias. Then we will look at a number of ways which have bias in the assignment procedure. The basic illustration is hypothetical, but it is a situation which has many of the characteristics with which we are normally confronted in assigning subjects to the groups of an experiment. We will assume that we are going to do an experiment with three conditions, I, II, and III. We are prepared to be satisfied if we have as few as 15 subjects in each condition, or as many as 30 in each condition. In fact, we are going to pay each subject $5 for serving in the experiment and we have $450 which can be used for this purpose. Since the experiment takes only a few minutes of the subject's time, the pay is considered attractive even under inflationary conditions.

An advertisement is inserted in a local paper soliciting residents to serve as subjects, the only restriction being that to qualify the person must be ten years of age or older. The subjects are asked to report at a certain door in a certain building at a certain time, and to form a line in order of arrival. On the specified morning a long line forms and a quick count shows that 90 people are in the line. By any standards, the people in the line are a heterogeneous group. What population they might represent is unknown other than to say that these are the people who showed up on this particular morning in answer to an advertisement in the newspaper. Our problem is to assign them to the three groups without bias, and we must handle this for each subject as he enters the door for his brief session. How do we do this?

The most satisfactory way to do this would be to use a block-randomized schedule of the three conditions of the experiment. Using tables of random sequences of numbers (see Appendix B), we would form successive blocks of three conditions each. In every block each condition would be represented once with the order of the three conditions within a block being random. A random order would be determined independently for each of the 30 blocks. Thus, in Block 1 the order might be III, I, II, in Block 2, I, III, II, in Block 3, II, III, I, and so on. The first subject who enters the door would be administered Condition III, the second Condition I, the third Condition II, the fourth Condition I, and so on. This block-randomized schedule would be prepared ahead of time and would be followed without any exceptions being allowed.

To repeat, the purpose of assigning subjects randomly is to produce three groups which, as groups, do not differ statistically on any subject variable that is relevant to performance on the experimental task. This is to say that we expect the mean ages, IQs, learning abilities, blood types, and so on, to be equivalent. If this assumption is met, any differences we observe among the three groups as a consequence of the different treatments administered will be attributed to the treatment differences.

Now, let us examine some procedures for assigning subjects to groups in this situation, procedures which would produce bias. Suppose we put the first 30 subjects in the line in Condition I, the second 30 in Condition II, and the last 30 in Condition III. This would likely produce groups which did differ on subject variables. We would already know that they differed on one characteristic, namely, how early they arrived at the specified location. This trait might well be correlated with other traits which are relevant to performance on the experimental task.

To make the next point, let us assume that we have only two conditions in the experiment. It might seem that we would really not need to worry about randomizing within blocks. Why not assign the subjects in alternating order to the conditions, I, II, I, II, I, II, etc., rather than randomizing within blocks, II, I, I, II, I, II, II, I, etc.? It would not be unreasonable to assume that many of the subjects came in pairs; two friends might decide to come together. Assuming that there are a number of these pairs of friends, would we expect the order in which the two friends waited in line to be random? Perhaps not; the relationship between the two friends may be such that one is more likely to be first in line than the other. Whatever might produce this dominance in ordering, it can be seen that if we used alternating conditions (I, II, I, II, I, II) we would be introducing a correlation between the position in line for each pair and the particular condition to which assigned. Of course, if pairs of friends were unsystematically separated in the line by people who had come individually, the correlation would be broken.

The question may be raised as to why we do not use complete randomization rather than block randomization. With complete randomization of the three conditions we would simply have a random schedule of the three conditions until all 90 subjects had been completed. This would be satisfactory except that we would probably end with a different number of subjects in each group. Rather than the 30-30-30 assured by block-randomization, we might have 30-34-26. There is nothing wrong with this except that it is inconvenient statistically to work with an uneven number of subjects in the groups. Another alternative would be to arrange a random order of the three conditions subject only to the restriction that each of the three conditions must occur 30 times. In carrying out this plan, the moment one of the conditions had 30 subjects placed in it, it would be dropped, and subjects placed in the remaining two conditions. When one of these reached a total of 30 subjects, all of the remaining subjects would be placed in the final condition. The problem with this procedure is that the last few subjects may be loaded heavily into one or two conditions, and insofar as they may differ from the subjects who were nearer the head of the line, a small bias is introduced.

The fact is that the block-randomized schedule is easy to use, eliminates bias effectively, and is therefore the one to employ in developing random groups.

A Variety of Situations

Except for the fact that all subjects were present at once, the illustration used above is much like the situation normally faced (particularly at universities) in assigning subjects to an experiment. Students volunteer to serve as subjects or are required to serve as a part of their course work. The usual experiment will require several weeks or even months to complete the data collection. Perhaps each day data are obtained from only two or three subjects. A commonly used system is one in which, at a central location, students register for one or more of the several experiments which may be available to them. In effect, therefore, the experimenter does have a long line of subjects who must be assigned to the conditions without bias as they come to the experimental room, and the block-randomized schedule is appropriate.

Group procedures. It is frequently very economical to administer the conditions to several subjects simultaneously by having the subjects participate in the experiment in groups. Special problems arise when these procedures are used. If the experimental treatments require a very short period of time to administer, one might think of using an intact class of students as they have assembled for the usual class period. Several instructors may agree to allow five minutes of the class period for the experiment. It would be very convenient to administer one treatment to one class, a second treatment to another, and so on. In general if there are N conditions, N different classes are used. A little thought will show that this simply will not do. The only possible way by which the criterion of "no bias" could be met would be if the students had been assigned to the classes randomly, all students who had started the course remained, and all were present on the day the experiment was conducted. All three events would be exceedingly rare. The critical point is that the students in the different classes may well differ on subject variables relevant to performance on the task. Even if there were several classes or sections of exactly the same course there would be no reason to believe that the students chose the sections randomly. There is no way by which this situation can be accommodated except by the use of a pretest or matching procedure, a matter for discussion later in the chapter.

Still we may insist that we want to collect our data in groups because of the economy involved. Since the use of intact classes will not work, perhaps having subjects sign up in the central location will. First we will examine the procedure that will not be satisfactory. At the central location subjects discover they can register for one of N sessions, the N sessions corresponding to the number of different treatments of the experiment. Each of the sessions is scheduled at a different time of the day. We see at once that this will be troublesome. The student can only register for a session to be held at a time when he is not in class. The session for which he is available depends upon his class schedule, and differences in schedules for students may reflect differences in subject variables (e.g., Mathematics majors versus English majors). Furthermore, the performance of a subject may differ as a function of the hour of the day. Even if the sessions were scheduled at the same time each day for several successive days there might be reason to believe that a subject who registers for the first session could be different from the one who registers for the fifth session. All such plans simply do not meet the criteria needed to assure "no bias."

There are two solutions to the problem. The first solution will handle the problem for any type of an experiment in which group treatments are feasible. This solution is to schedule a large number of group sessions and assign the treatment conditions to them by a block-randomized schedule. Again, suppose we had three treatments or conditions and wanted to measure 30 subjects in each. We might choose to use groups of five subjects each. Thus, 18 different sessions would be scheduled at the same times on successive days. The three conditions, randomized within six blocks, would be matched with the 18 sessions in order. This would be equivalent mechanically to a block-randomized schedule for individual subjects with 6 subjects assigned to each condition. A general rule for conducting group experiments is to hold many sessions with a few subjects in each session rather than few sessions with many subjects. Of course, if the number of subjects within a session becomes very small, little is to be gained over testing the subjects individually.

The second way of coping with group experiments would apply only to situations in which the different treatments can be given simultaneously to a group of subjects. If this can be done, the different treatments can be assigned randomly to the subjects assembled as a group. Such situations will occur when all subjects are treated the same initially but tested differently. Two illustrations may be given from the authors' work. We undertook an experiment to test the different types of memory for a long list of pairs of words. Thus, all subjects were shown the same list, but they were given different printed instructions for the test. Actually, there were five different printed instructions. These instructions were block randomized and passed out to the subjects row by row.

In another study we wanted to test memory for a list of words immediately after the list was presented and after 24 hours. The same subjects could not be given both tests; thus one group had to be given the immediate test, another group the 24-hour test. When the subjects registered for the experiment they agreed to come for two successive days at the same hour. On the first day, all subjects were given the same list of words to learn. Immediately after presenting the list, half the subjects, randomly identified, were asked to leave and return the following day. The remaining subjects were given the immediate retention test.

Administering treatments to groups of subjects can be highly economical. Furthermore, it can be argued that the conditions are more constant than is true when individual subjects are tested. We simply must be sure that when we use group testing procedures we do not forget that the need of assigning subjects to treatments randomly is just as obligatory as when we deal with the individual subjects.

Multiple experimenters. We may return to our original example in which we advertised for subjects and assigned them randomly to conditions in the order in which they stood in the line. If we did an experiment in this fashion we would undoubtedly use more than one experimenter so that the subjects would have a relatively short time to wait. Assume that we had two experimenters. Any experimenter must be considered as a potential independent variable; two different experimenters may get different estimates of the effect of a given independent variable. Recognizing this, our design must neutralize these possibly different estimates. It would be apparent, for example, that we should not assign all subjects under one condition to one experimenter and all of those under a different condition to another experimenter. For design purposes, we must think of performing two independent experiments, each experimenter testing half of the total subjects in each condition, the other experimenter testing the other half. In our example, each experimenter would have his own block-randomized schedule of 15 blocks, with each condition represented once in each block. We may, if we wish, examine the data to see if there were differences produced by the experimenters. This can be done meaningfully only if it is planned ahead of time. We should block-randomize the line of subjects in twos to determine which experimenter gets each successive subject. Again, it should be obvious that we could not assess appropriately what differential effects, if any, were produced by the two experimenters if one tested the first 45 subjects in line and the other tested the last 45. Given this situation, the differences in the characteristics of the experimenters may be confounded by subject variables.

The extreme case of multiple experimenters would be one in which each experimenter ran a single subject in each condition. This is not an unusual possibility when a class is conducting the experiment. In one of our classes we conducted such an experiment having five different conditions and 25 different experimenters (all of the students in the class). Each experimenter had to search for five students not in the class to serve as subjects. Each experimenter independently determined a random order for the five conditions. Thus, there were 25 blocks of the five conditions. The first subject which any given experimenter wheedled, cajoled, or paid to serve in the experiment was assigned to the first condition in the block, the second to the second, and so on. It was absolutely essential that the experimenter not try to match a given subject with a given condition ("he is my friend so I will give him an easy condition"); the experimenter had to assign conditions to successive subjects in terms of his random order of the conditions. Experiments of this nature, when the results are combined across experimenters, can produce very orderly data.

With multiple experimenters the general rule to follow is that each experimenter must do a complete experiment in the sense that he must run an equal number of subjects in all conditions of the experiment. There is no necessary requirement that all experimenters test the same number of subjects, but it is necessary that each has complete blocks. In one sense, the use of multiple experimenters could be judged to be highly desirable. If the experimenter is thought of as an independent variable, then the results of an experiment using multiple experimenters have greater generality than the results of an experiment having a single experimenter.

Stratified assignment.   A classical technique for assigning subjects to groups in animal research is known as the split-litter technique. White rats from the same litter are likely to be more homogeneous in subject variables than are rats from different litters. Therefore the experimenter might choose to distribute animals from the same litter across his conditions. Of course, it depends upon the number of conditions and the number of animals in the litter as to how evenly this will work out. The idea, however, represents a case of stratified assignment. The split-litter technique is used rarely with human subjects (twins) but the basic notion of stratified assignment is rather frequently implemented in experiments using human subjects. The stratification is based upon a subject variable, usually an obvious one such as age or sex. Let us return to the lineup for an illustration. We decide to stratify on age, so that we will have 30 subjects between the ages of 10–20, 30 in the range 21–40, and 30 with ages of 41 or over. For each age group a block-randomized schedule is used to assign the subjects within an age group to the conditions of the experiment. Age, therefore, becomes another independent variable and the results may be examined for its influence in the experimental results.

It can be seen that even without stratified assignment we could examine the results for the influence of a subject variable such as age (providing we had access to such information). As a consequence of block-randomizing the conditions across all 90 subjects we would expect the different age ranges to be about equally represented in each condition. So we could examine the results to determine the influence, if any, of age. The only advantage of block-randomization within strata is that it assures an equal number of subjects in each condition in each level of the stratified variable.

In the illustration just mentioned, we stratified on only one subject variable. This is not a limit. We could stratify on two variables (age, sex), three variables (age, sex, educational level), or more, providing we had available a sufficient number of potential subjects to fill all of the cells with an equal number of subjects. If we have three age levels, three educational levels, and two sexes, there would be a total of 18 cells representing all combinations of the levels of the three subject variables.

If we push the logic of stratification to its extreme, we essentially have a matched-groups design carried out in a very ponderous manner. As we will see later, in the matched-groups design the ideal would be to have identical twins, assigning one to each of the two treatments in a two-condition experiment. Now consider the consequence of stratification when we gradually increase the number of subject variables on which we stratify. The greater the number of variables used in stratification the greater is the homogeneity of subjects who will "fit" into the same cell. Carried to the extreme, we could have so many different cells that only identical twins would fit into a given cell. Stratification is never carried this far, of course. But it can be seen that the use of stratification in conjunction with random groups moves toward the implementation of the logic of matched groups.

Loss of subjects. In the process of collecting the data of an experiment, it is almost inevitable that there will be a loss of one or more subjects. The meaning of the word "loss" in this context is not its lethal one when human subjects are involved, but it may be when animals are the subjects. We speak of loss of a subject when for one reason or another he does not provide us with appropriate data. There are two types of losses which may occur, one which we will call mechanical loss, the other, selective loss.

A mechanical loss may be produced for a variety of reasons, but the critical commonality is that it is not produced by the behavior of the subject. Rather, it is produced by experimenter failure or equipment failure. If a piece of equipment breaks down while a subject is being tested, we usually have to discard the data for that subject. The experimenter may err, failing to do something that he should have done, so the data are incomplete.

When a mechanical loss occurs we replace the lost subject with another. The convention has been to replace the lost subject with the next subject arriving for the experiment. It is handled as if the lost subject had never entered the picture. There seems to be no way by which the equality of the groups would be threatened by this procedure.

The selective loss of subjects is a serious matter and one that is far more difficult to handle than is the mechanical loss. Selective loss results from some deficiency in the subject. Loss for such a reason becomes critical because the moment a loss is due to the inadequacy of a subject we are now faced with the possibility that the equality of the subject variables across groups, developed by the block-randomization, may be destroyed. If the different conditions of the experiment do not produce differential loss, we are not concerned; but if there is a correlation between number of subjects lost and conditions, we are in trouble. Thus if we have a 20 percent loss in one condition and a 3 percent loss in another, we would have difficulty convincing a reader that the subjects completing the experiment did not differ in subject variables across conditions. Two illustrations of selective loss will be given.

Studies of brain functions are frequently conducted by producing lesions in different loci of the animal brain. Following the operation, the behavior of the animals is observed in a standard test situation. Suppose that different loci of the lesions are associated with different mortality frequencies. If this is due to some inherent difference in the brain systems (as contrasted with differences in the clumsiness in producing the lesions at the different loci), we must be aware that the conditions of the experiment have produced selective loss. Therefore, differences in the behavior of the animals in the test situation may not be due directly to differences in brain functioning at the different lesion sites.

A very powerful variable in human learning is called interitem similarity among verbal units. For example, among nonwords five units such as KRQ, VQR, RKV, QVR, and QRK might be called a high-similarity list in that only four different letters are used. A low-similarity list might consist of the trigrams KRQ, CHV, BPD, SWF, GJL, five units in which no letter is duplicated across units. If we gave these two lists to college students as a free-recall task, some of the students would be unable to learn all of the five high-similarity units within a 50-minute experimental session. If the nature of our experiment calls for complete learning, we are going to have differential loss of subjects for the two lists. Hence we can no longer assume that the successful subjects in the two groups are equivalent on subject variables, particularly the subject variable of learning ability.

There are probably some experiments where nothing can be done when there is selective loss. We would conclude that the data may be quite confounded and there is no ameliorative step which can be taken. In other cases there are ways of dealing with selective loss. Three general ways of handling this problem will be discussed.

1. We could use a pretest to select subjects who would all have a high probability of successfully completing the requirements of the experiment. In the case of the trigram experiment, we might first give subjects a moderately difficult list to learn. Then, those whose learning ability placed them in the 25th percentile or higher would be used in the main experiment, these subjects being assigned randomly to the two lists. Those who fell below the 25th percentile would not be used in the experiment.

2. Another alternative for salvaging some experiments, such as the trigram experiment, follows the same logic as given in the first method but is carried out post hoc. We would proceed on the assumption that a subject who is poor or slow in learning the low-similarity list would also be a subject who would be unable to master the high-similarity list. Therefore whenever we would lose a subject for his inability to learn the high-similarity list we would drop the subject with the poorest score on the low-similarity list. Both are replaced, of course, if we wish to complete the experiment with the number of subjects for which we had originally planned. In the end we will have dropped an equivalent number of subjects from both groups, and those who are dropped are the slowest learners in both groups. It is as if we had given a pretest.

3. Sometimes pretest scores may be used to solve the differential-loss problem. Consider the lesion study. Assume that all of the animals were given a pretest in the standard test situation prior to the operations. We might find that the groups of animals surviving for the posttest did not in fact differ on the pretest. That is, the differential loss of subjects did not produce selection on a subject variable that was related to performance on the standard test. Therefore the scores of the subjects remaining in each group could be used to index directly the effect of the lesions at the different sites. If the groups differ on pretest scores, we might go through a matching procedure (see later). Or we might use change scores as the response measure, a change score indicating the change in performance between the pretest and posttest for each animal. These change scores may differ as a function of lesion site.

One other solution might be mentioned. This would be to refuse to do experiments in which there is likely to be selective loss. Yet there are many problems, judged to be important, which should be attacked experimentally and for which selective loss is a threat. For example, some might judge that it would be important to study long-term retention of students in suburban schools as compared with those in inner-city schools. If the retention interval is, say, six months, it would be highly probable that there would be selective loss of subjects for the two groups. Differences in the mobilities of the families would almost assure this. We would have to be prepared to cope with such selective loss if our data are to be interpreted appropriately.

Holding Conditions Constant

We are now in a position to comprehend fully what is meant when we say that in an experiment we hold all conditions constant except the independent variable. We obviously do not hold all other potential variables constant in the sense that they are maintained at a fixed value, although we may hold some at a fixed or static value. In the first place, it is obvious that it would be essentially impossible to hold subject variables constant. Even many environmental variables cannot be held at fixed values. In forming random groups we do not hold all potential variables at a fixed level; rather, as we have seen, we develop our randomization procedure so that differences in magnitudes of these variables from subject to subject and from moment to moment are not allowed to favor one experimental treatment over another.

Let us assume that we had a measure of the influence of all potential variables which are held constant in an experiment by the randomization of subjects to conditions, and by randomization of conditions and subjects across all environmental conditions. If we knew the influence of each of these variables on performance on the experimental task, presumably we could verify the assumption of randomization that the sum of the effects of all of these variables, whether positive or negative, would be equivalent for all treatment conditions in the experiment. That is what we mean when we say that variables other than the independent variable are held constant.

It seems to be true that the student beginning his study of experimental psychology remains uneasy, or even downright skeptical about the method of random groups as a way of doing research. Some are not willing to put their confidence in an impalpable god of randomness. Although this god, unlike most gods, admits he will be in error occasionally, some students seem to feel that the infrequent occasion will fall on their experiments exclusively. Aren't there other ways to carry out the research which have less of a walking-a-tightrope atmosphere? The answer is affirmative, and we will proceed to consider one of these now. In the next chapter we will discuss design methods which completely eliminate the need for assuming that random assignment will equalize the influence of subject variables.

MATCHED GROUPS

In the discussion of random assignment, we noted that the consequence of such assignment was the neutralizing of the influence of two classes of potential independent variables, subject variables and those in all other classes, with particular emphasis on environmental variables. The matched-groups design, if carried out to perfection, would eliminate completely differences in relevant subject variables across the experimental groups, but would still demand randomization to equalize the influence of variables other than subject variables.

Let us examine the basic thinking behind the matched-groups design. All subjects are given a pretest on which the performance is known to be highly correlated with performance on the experimental task. Then groups are formed on the basis of the pretest scores (as many groups as there are conditions in the experiment) so that all groups have essentially equal means and variances on the pretest scores. The experimental treatments are then administered. Any differences which occur are attributed to the independent variable. These differences could not be due—so the thinking goes—to differences in subject variables among the groups because the groups have been equated on the relevant subject variables, namely, those that are important for performance on the experimental task.

As was suggested earlier, one way to match subjects on subject variables in a precise way is to use identical twins (two conditions), triplets (three conditions), quadruplets (four conditions), and so on. With human subjects only the use of two conditions would be feasible. Pairs of twins are used, one member of each pair being assigned (randomly) to Condition I, the other to Condition II. As a consequence, differences in subject variables between the two groups are essentially eliminated. However if we were to carry out the experiment, we certainly would not test all subjects in Condition I at, say,

8:00 A.M., and all those in Condition II at 5:00 P.M. Instead, we would use a block-randomized schedule to equalize the influence of variables other than subject variables.

If we are to be realistic about the use of matched groups we must concentrate on applying the technique when neither identical nor fraternal twins are available. We might think of using siblings, but the problems are no different from the more typical case, the case in which we have genetically unrelated subjects and we want to match groups.

The Matching Task

The matched-groups technique always requires a pretest of some kind, or at the very least, it requires the availability of certain information about each subject prior to testing the subjects under different conditions. The critical requirement is that performance on the pretest be correlated with performance on the experimental task. Unless pretest scores predict performance on the experimental task, we have added nothing (except our time) beyond the random-groups design. This is to say that before we ever do an experiment it is desirable to show that in fact the pretest and experimental task produce correlated scores. There are certain guidelines to be followed.

Experimental task as the matching task. The likelihood that a pretest would predict performance on the experimental task is maximized if we use the same task for the pretest that we use for the experimental conditions. If we were going to study the influence of certain variables on depth perception, we could give some pretest trials on the apparatus used to measure depth perception. If rats were to be tested on exploratory behavior following certain operative procedures, we could test the exploratory behavior of each rat before the operation. If we were interested in the effect of different teaching techniques on the acquisition of grammatical rules, we could give a pretest that is exactly the same test to be used after the different teaching techniques have been introduced and carried out.

The use of the experimental task as the matching task presumes that we are maximizing the correlation between the pretest and the experimental test. A high correlation is not inevitable in such circumstances but a high correlation is probable as long as the performance scores on both the pretest and experimental test are reliable. Usually if an area of research has been developed, there will be existing evidence on the correlation so that an experiment can be undertaken with the knowledge that the pretest will predict performance on the experimental test. However, there may be occasions in which the experimental task cannot be used as a matching task. If we want to do a study in which particular anagrams are used as the experimental task, we could hardly use the same anagrams for the matching task and for the experimental task. Generally speaking, if performance on the matching task (the pretest) heavily influences performance on the experimental trials or task, we would not use the experimental task as a matching task. Two other alternatives are possible.

Matching task from same class as experimental task. If we wanted to pretest subjects on their anagram-solving abilities, we could use one set of anagrams for the pretest and a quite different set for the experimental test. If we were going to do an experiment on the free recall of words we could use a list of words for a pretest, none of which occurred in the list used for the experiment.

We would anticipate that the performance on a pretest constructed from the same class of materials that is to be used on the experimental task would be correlated with performance on the experimental task. Those subjects who do well on the pretest are likely to do well on the experimental task; those who do poorly on the pretest are likely to do poorly on the experimental task. At the same time, however, we would expect this relationship to be less than if we had used the same task for the pretest and for the experimental test. The magnitude of the correlation becomes an empirical matter; if the correlation is low the matching of subjects is a waste of time.

Beyond establishing the correlation, there is a further matter of concern. As noted above, there exists the possibility that the matching task may influence performance on the experimental task. If this influence is different for the several experimental treatments, we obviously have a confounding and our conclusions concerning the effects of the independent variable will be in error. Unfortunately such possibilities are difficult to detect for the usual experiment, but a fairly blatant illustration may be given. Suppose we are interested in the forgetting of a list of words learned by free recall. The independent variable will be the length of the retention interval; for example, the intervals may be 1 minute, 1 hour, and 24 hours. Three groups are formed by matching based on the learning scores for a list of words different from those words used for the experimental list. Known facts tell us that the words in the pretest may interfere with the memory for the experimental list and the amount of the interference is directly related to the length of the retention interval. Thus the interference would be greater after 24 hours than after 1 minute. As a consequence of using the matching task, we have grossly overestimated the rate of forgetting which would have been obtained had the matching task not been used.

Now, perhaps we are beginning to get some notion that the matched-groups design is not a panacea; it may solve some problems but introduce new ones. We now turn to the third type of matching task.

Different but correlated matching task. In this case, the matching task and the experimental task are, at least superficially, quite different. For matching subjects prior to giving them a free-recall task we might use the scores on an intelligence test, or perhaps school grades. For anagrams, we might use the scores on a vocabulary test as the matching task. The possibilities are without limit; the critical fact to remember is that performance on the pretest must correlate substantially with performance on the experimental task. Ideally, we want a pretest which will predict performance on the experimental task, and yet one which will have little direct effect on the performance itself. To a certain extent these two objectives are incompatible. The greater the pretest differs from the experimental task the less likely it is that the performance on the pretest will be correlated with the performance on the experimental task. The lower this correlation the less the benefit to be derived from the matched-groups design, i.e., the less the likelihood that we are going to avoid those occasional false conclusions which we live with when we use the random-groups design.

The three types of matching tasks have been given in the order reflecting the magnitude of the correlation to be expected between the pretest and the experimental task. Whether or not the pretest might have an undesirable influence on the performance on the experimental task (such as differential interference) must be determined for each proposed experiment. Sometimes the background research will provide an answer. If not, it is the responsibility of the experimenter to convince his reader that the results produced by his independent variable were not in even a small part due to differential effects of the matching task.

How to Match

The above evaluation may seem overly pessimistic, for it is a fact that we can at times use a matched-groups design quite effectively. This is particularly true when we use the first type of matching task (same task as experimental task). Therefore we must be prepared to carry out the actual matching procedure. Assume we have given all of the potential subjects the pretest and we are now ready to carry out the matching. There are two ways this can be done, although the outcome for both is much the same.

Matching subject for subject. Assume we have three conditions in our experiment. In the ideal case, we attempt to find groups of three subjects with identical scores on the pretest. Thus we might find three subjects with scores of 12 on the pretest, three with scores of 13, three with 14, three with 15, and so on. As we move toward the middle of the distribution of pretest scores we would expect to find several groups of three subjects each, all having the same score. When as many subjects as possible have been matched, the three subjects within each group are then assigned randomly to the three conditions, one to each. The outcome of such a procedure is equivalent means and equivalent variabilities for the resulting three distributions. It will be recognized that this method of matching simply carries the stratification of subjects on a given variable (as discussed earlier in the chapter) to the maximum number of strata (different scores) possible.

Matching subject for subject is usually wasteful when carried out as described above. It requires that we always find three subjects (or a multiple thereof) with the same pretest scores. If we had five conditions in the experiment we would always have to have five subjects (or a multiple) who had the same pretest scores. Subjects who are left over after the matching simply would not be used in the experiment. It can be seen that we could decrease the number of discarded subjects by increasing the sizes of the strata. We might, for example, define a stratum as being 14-15 inclusive, 16-17 inclusive, and so on. Thus, we would allow a tolerance of one score point. Or we might increase the strata to a range of three points. Particularly at the extremes of the distribution of pretest scores, our flexibility would be increased and still we would expect equivalent means and variabilities if the subjects were assigned randomly to the experimental conditions from each stratum.

Matching on means and variability. A logical extension of increasing the size of the stratum is to ignore the matching of individual subjects and merely use a scheme which will result in three groups with equivalent means and variabilities. If the distribution of pretest scores does not contain extremely deviant cases, no cases, or at most a few, need be discarded. We could, for example, start at the bottom of the distribution of pretest scores, and assign successive groups of three subjects randomly to the three conditions. If in the unlikely event the means and variabilities do differ somewhat (uncomfortably different even if not statistically different), we might correct by dropping the extremes from each of the three distributions.

Post Hoc Matching

The illustrations used above assumed that pretest scores were available before the data collection under the experimental conditions was initiated. This might be inconvenient or impossible in some situations. Therefore, we would use post hoc matching. This involves giving all subjects the pretest and then immediately giving them the experimental treatments, the particular treatment being determined by block-randomization without regard to pretest scores. After all of the data have been collected, the matching procedures are undertaken without, of course, any reference to the scores under the experimental conditions. The only difference between such post hoc matching and matching prior to testing under the experimental conditions is that the experimental treatments have already been administered to the subjects. Nevertheless, we may proceed just as described earlier. We have three distributions of scores–the scores on the pretests for the three groups of subjects given the three different experimental conditions. We go through our strata matching, subject for subject, discarding subjects who will not fit our scheme.

Suppose we are interested only in matching on means and variabilities. Suppose further that upon examining the pretest scores for the three groups we find that the means and variabilities are equivalent. We would expect this to be the usual finding because by assigning subjects to the conditions by block-randomization we expect any differences in subject variables and environmental variables to be neutralized or balanced across groups. Have we matched? Of course not; what we have shown is that, as expected, randomization did the job. We would really have no use for the pretest scores.

Finally suppose that our block-randomization produced one of those rare occurrences, and we find that the three groups do differ significantly on the pretest scores. Or suppose this happened because we did not think it necessary to assign subjects randomly to experimental conditions since we knew we had the pretest scores and could, on a post hoc basis, make the appropriate adjustments. The fact is that at this point we are in a small heap of trouble. To match three groups on a post hoc basis has some potential for mismatching. The reason for this requires reference to the fact of regression. Genetic regression is illustrated by the fact that the children of very tall parents are likely to be shorter than their parents; children of very short parents are likely to be taller than their parents. So, too, a subject whose score falls at the extreme of a distribution on a pretest is likely to move a little bit toward the mean if he is tested again. Therefore if we attempt to match two (or more) groups from distributions of pretest scores which have appreciably different means, our match will be unreliable since we are matching scores from different points within the distributions and regression effects will differ. The seriousness of this mismatch will be directly related to the magnitude of the difference between the means. This matter will not be pursued further. If we use block-randomization in assigning the subjects to the conditions it would rarely happen that the means will differ in magnitude to the extent that regression differences will be serious.

SUMMARY COMMENTS

A reading of history suggests that when independent-groups designs have been used there has been a decrease in the use of matched groups over the years and an increase in the use of random groups. In the discussion, we have tried to give some of the reasons why this has occurred. Neither the authors nor their students have carried out an experiment with matched groups for many years. Yet it must be admitted that there have been times when we wished we had pretest scores. When the results of a given experiment have seemed quite unreasonable we were prone to conclude that this was an occasion when block-randomization did not result in equivalent groups. Pretest scores would be of great value in such cases in determining whether or not this occurred.

We have seen that with matched groups there may be a problem finding a pretest which does not interact with the experimental task. If we can use the experimental task as the matching task we are almost bound to be successful. However, normally in such cases we do not use a between-subjects design. More frequently we use the within-subjects design (see next chapter) in which a matching task has no meaning.

There is still another reason why the matched-groups design has diminished in use. For simplicity, we have talked about 2 or 3 or perhaps 5 conditions for an experiment. The principles are the same as if we had 50 conditions. Many experiments are done with 8, 12, or 16 different conditions, often with two or more independent variables and with perhaps 200–300 subjects. We could use a matched-groups design for these experiments, but the possibility of matching subjects for 16 different groups, for example, seems never to have been considered seriously.

There is a final matter. We know the random-groups design will occasionally give us a wrong conclusion concerning the effect of an independent variable. The only purpose for using a matched-groups design is to eliminate such occurrences. But we must remember that we can also get statistically significant correlations between pretest and experimental scores by chance. Matched groups will not eliminate chance occurrences; they only reduce the number of false conclusions reached, a number which is relatively small even when matched groups are not used. Yet it would be unwise to legislate against matched groups. There may be experiments that need to be done, particularly field studies, for which it may not be possible to carry through meticulously random assignment. In such cases pretests may allow the experiment to proceed. And, as we noted earlier, whenever there may be losses of subjects for any reason, pretest scores may be valuable whether used for matching or not.

4

WITHIN-SUBJECTS DESIGNS

At the expense of excessive repetition, the basic issue in designing an experiment will be restated. We introduce two or more different treatments and the empirical question we ask concerns the influence (if any) these treatments have on the behavior of interest. We say that all other variables must be neutralized in the sense that their effects must be constant across the treatments; otherwise, we have a confounding. With independent groups the focus is on subject variables as sources of confounding. We accept the fact that with random groups there will be a confounding by subject variables occasionally, although when this event occurs is not likely to be known. The use of matched groups should reduce the likelihood of such events although we have seen that this technique is not without problems of its own. As we move along to within-subjects designs, we find that we completely eliminate any possibility of confounding of the treatments by subject variables. This desirable outcome is produced by the simple procedure of using each subject in all treatment conditions; each subject is given all levels of the independent variable or variables being manipulated in the experiment. Because each subject is measured under each condition, there can be no question raised as to whether or not subject variables were responsible for differences in behavior resulting from the experimental treatments.

There are two kinds of within-subjects designs, both of which were described briefly in Chapter 1. We speak of one as being complete in that the conditions are administered to a subject in such a way that all potential confounding variables are neutralized for that subject. The data, therefore, can be considered as those from a complete experiment in spite of the fact that only a single subject is involved. The click-counting experiment of Guzy and Axelrod was just such a study.

The second kind of within-subjects design is one in which each subject is given each treatment, but the effects of these treatments are confounded by the effects of other variables in each subject's data. The confounding can be removed only by summing the data across subjects for each condition. The

63

study by Sharma and Moskowitz, in which they assessed the effects of the size of the dose of marihuana on the magnitude of the autokinetic illusion, employed this design. The incomplete within-subjects design will be examined in detail in a later part of this chapter.

COMPLETE WITHIN-SUBJECTS DESIGN

An Illustration

As a means of getting at the logic of this design, a simple experiment conducted as a class exercise will be examined. The students in the class were the subjects, the instructor the experimenter. The purpose of the experiment was unknown to the subjects until after the data were collected. The task was that of estimating the duration of temporal intervals, these intervals being 5, 8, 14, and 23 seconds. The duration of the interval, obviously, is one independent variable. A second variable was also treated as an independent variable: the manner in which the subject estimated the duration of the interval. There were two different ways.

For one of the ways, the subjects drew a horizontal line to indicate how long they thought the interval was. A short line implied a short interval, a long line a long interval. The lines were drawn on an ordinary sheet of paper. It was necessary to give the subjects some notion of how long the intervals would be, else they might find themselves wishing to draw a line longer than was possible on the sheet of paper. So preliminary to the data-collection stage, the subjects were given samples of the longest and shortest intervals which would subsequently be used. This allowed each subject to establish for himself what long and short intervals meant with regard to the lines he would draw. The response measure was the lengths of the lines drawn, measured to the nearest sixteenth of an inch.

As a second way of expressing judgments of duration, the subjects drew circles, a circle with a small area representing an interval of short duration, a circle with a large area representing an interval of long duration. The freehand drawing of circles results in figures which may deviate considerably from true circles. As an arbitrary decision, it was decided that the response measure would be the length of the horizontal diameter of the "circles." Because the area of a circle grows disproportionately to the increase in the diameter, we might expect that the slope of the curve relating duration of the interval and the diameter (second method) would be less steep than the slope of the curve relating duration of the interval and the length of the horizontal lines (first method).

Drawing horizontal lines and circles to represent the duration of temporal intervals is an illustration of cross-modality matching or mapping. In the pure form of cross-modality mapping, the subjects express their judgments of the relative magnitudes of stimuli presented to one modality by choosing or producing an event of a given magnitude when this event is appropriate to a modality different from the event being judged. They could express differences in the loudness of a tone by their choice of cylinders from a series of cylinders differing in weight. The gram scale thus becomes a means of reflecting apparent loudness of tones. Although the experience of passage of time has no particular sense modality to which it is tied, the basic logic of cross-modality matching was involved when the subjects expressed their judgments of temporal duration by drawing lines of varying length and circles of varying areas.

There were four intervals and two methods of expressing the judgment; hence there were eight different treatment conditions. How can we administer these eight conditions to a subject so that all other potential confounding variables are neutralized? This is the critical question to be answered in drawing up a complete within-subjects design.

In the experiment, each interval under each type of response mode was given to each subject four times. Suppose we gave four trials using the five-second condition with horizontal-line drawing, then four trials with the eight-second interval still with horizontal-line drawing, and so on. After this is finished we repeat the procedure but use circle drawing as the response mode. You will recognize that a procedure of this type just will not do. When the subject comes to draw the circles he is, in some sense, different from the subject that drew the horizontal lines. Furthermore, giving the intervals in order, with all trials on one completed before moving to the next, has the same problem. If there are changes in performance with successive trials they will not influence the conditions equally. This, then, is the major problem with which we must deal in planning the order in which the trials are administered. When a subject is given successive trials on a task his performance may change over trials—he may become more accurate, less accurate, more variable, or less variable. In a true sense we are changing the subject (at least temporarily) as we test him; we are experimentally inducing a subject change.

Changes which occur as the subject is given more and more experience with a task, or with tasks within a given class of tasks, are sometimes called practice effects. These effects may be positive in that the subject's performance gets better, as if a skill may be developing, or they may be negative in that the performance gets worse, as if boredom or fatigue may be involved. To cover both cases we will speak of progressive changes with practice, or progressive error. The solution to the design problem involves devising a way to neutralize progressive error. As will become clear later, there are several variations of a basic technique which may be used. The particular method chosen for the experiment we have been describing is outlined in Table 4.1.

Each of the eight conditions was administered four times, and since there were eight conditions, 32 trials were required. There is nothing magical about

4 trials; the only requirement is a minimum of 2 trials. If an investigator were interested in individual subjects' data (which we were not), 4 trials might not be a sufficient number of measurements to result in stable data. In any event, the schedule for the 32 trials is shown in Table 4.1. We may now see what the design is presumed to accomplish by the way of neutralizing potential confounding variables.

Table 4.1. Trial orders for a complete within-subjects design in which the task was the judgment of the duration of four intervals (5, 8, 14, and 23 seconds), and in which the judgment was expressed by drawing a horizontal line (L) or by drawing a circle (C).

Trial	Interval	L or C	Trial	Interval	L or C
1	5	L	17	8	L
2	14	L	18	5	L
3	8	L	19	14	L
4	23	L	20	23	L
5	14	C	21	23	C
6	23	C	22	8	C
7	5	C	23	14	C
8	8	C	24	5	C
9	14	C	25	23	C
10	8	C	26	5	C
11	23	C	27	14	C
12	5	C	28	8	C
13	5	L	29	5	L
14	8	L	30	14	L
15	23	L	31	23	L
16	14	L	32	8	L

Purpose and Logic

The order of administering the four intervals across the 32 trials was determined by using a block-randomized schedule. Each successive block of 4 trials includes all four intervals, with the order within each block being random. This plan is assumed to neutralize the effect of progressive error for the four interval durations. The basis for this assumption may be examined graphically in Figure 4.1. For purposes of simplicity and generality, the four intervals in the figure are identified as 1, 2, 3, and 4. The 32 trials, 8 for each of the four intervals, are placed along the baseline. The ordinate is labelled progressive error. Three different relationships are shown, each representing a possible function relating progressive error with successive trials. By having each interval represented at each stage (defined as a block of four), it is assumed that

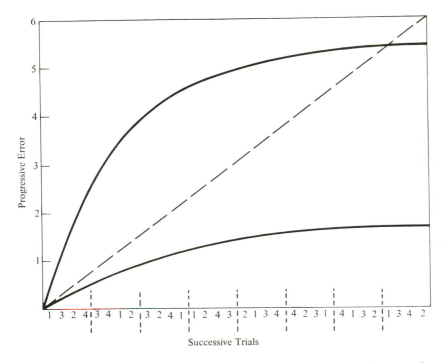

Fig. 4.1. Some possible relationships between trials and progressive error for the experiment outlined in Table 4.1. The numbers along the baseline represent the four intervals, and L and C represent trials on which a horizontal line (L) or a circle (C) was drawn. The numbers are block-randomized, and the L-C variable is counterbalanced.

the progressive error will be about equal for all four interval conditions. The assumption holds (within reason) regardless of the nature of the relationship between stage and progressive error.

You may wish to validate this assumption. If so, proceed as follows. Choose any one of the three relationships shown in Figure 4.1. Then, for each of the eight occurrences of Condition 1, move vertically from the baseline to the curve, then horizontally to the ordinate, and estimate the value representing progressive error. Sum these eight values for Condition 1, and do the same for the other three conditions. The sums of the four conditions should be approximately equal if progressive error is being balanced—if progressive-error effects are falling equally on all four conditions summed across trials. For the upper curve, the authors obtained the following sums for the four conditions in order: 35, 36, 34, 36.

We may now turn to the second variable, mode of response. For the first block of 4 trials, the subject drew horizontal lines; for the next two blocks (trials 5–12), he drew circles; then for a block of 4 more trials he drew horizontal lines, etc. The generalized symbol for this ordering is ABBA counter-balancing. Again, if a series of trials contains several ABBA sequences (in this case LCCL sequences), it is assumed that progressive error will fall about equally on the two conditions symbolized, and that this will be true regard-less of the nature of the relationship between trials and progressive error. This can be tested in Figure 4.1 by using the middle of each block as the point on the baseline from which to move vertically to the curve, then across to the ordinate. The sum of the L blocks and the sum of the C blocks should be about equal. In this case, for the uppermost curve, the sum of the L blocks is 17, the C blocks, 18. The greater the departure of the curve from linearity the less equivalent the sums are likely to be, but even in this case, where the curve rises very sharply at first, the sums are not appreciably different.

To summarize the design: the effect of progressive error was neutralized by block-randomization for one variable (length of interval), and by ABBA counterbalancing for the other variable (line drawing versus circle drawing).

The combined results for the 22 subjects who participated in the experiment are plotted in Figure 4.2, where it can be seen that the data are very orderly. Length of horizontal line drawn to indicate length of a temporal duration in-creases linearly as the interval increases. Length of the diameter of the circles drawn also increases progressively as the interval increases, but at a less rapid rate than is true for the lengths of the horizontal lines. This last somewhat less

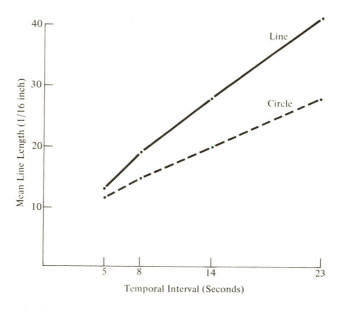

Fig. 4.2. Results of the experiment outlined in Table 4.1.

than world-shaking finding almost had to occur if the area of the circle was the characteristic of the circles which the subjects tried to correlate directly with temporal duration. However this may be, Figure 4.2 provides another illustration of interaction effects between two variables; as the length of the temporal interval increased, the increase in the response measure was less when the subjects drew circles than when they drew the horizontal lines.

Variations, Elaborations, and Cautions

The two techniques described for the above experiment are widely used in complete within-subjects designs to neutralize progressive error. Progressive error is not eliminated from such experiments; rather, its effects are "thrown" equally over all conditions of the experiment so that no bias results. It is always possible to determine the nature of the relationship between stage of practice and progressive error from these experiments. In the design in Table 4.1 we would combine the scores for successive blocks of eight trials, since each of the experimental conditions occurred equally often in each eight-trial block. These four resulting points would describe the relationship between progressive error and successive stages of practice. It can be seen that any complete within-subjects design always includes an independent variable other than those of central interest in the experiment, namely, stage of practice.

It is not unusual for investigators to give a subject a number of trials initially and then to discard the data from these trials. That is, only the data produced on the trials after these initial trials are used to assess the influence of the independent variable. The idea is that the initial trials may show rather sharp changes in progressive error, or these trials may show considerable variability. By eliminating these unstable data a more accurate estimate of the influence of the independent variable may be obtained. Sometimes a subject may serve in the experiment for several successive days and the initial trials on each day are discarded. Again, this discarding is based on the assumption that after the subject becomes adjusted or warmed up, the data will be less variable. This may be illustrated. Assume that we are going to give the subject the same treatment on each of several successive trials. Suppose the scores for a given subject read as follows on the 10 initial trials: 13, 22, 16, 12, 17, 15, 17, 16, 17, 15. The variability among the scores in the second block of 5 trials is much less than that among the first 5 although the means are the same for the two blocks. In this case we would conclude that at least through the first 10 trials there was no progressive error but that there was a change in variability associated with stage of practice. If the first five scores are eliminated, the variability of all scores taken during the session will probably be reduced.

Consider another case, again where we are measuring the subject under exactly the same condition on successive trials—the only varying factor being stage of practice. The successive scores are 5, 7, 8, 10, 12, 14, 13, 14, 14, 15. Changes occur very rapidly initially, after which there is little change. If the scores for the initial five trials are included in the data it again is apparent that the variability in the scores for the session will be increased. Thus an investigator will eliminate the data from the initial trials unless he is interested in the effect of his independent variable when progressive changes with practice are initially sharp, or when the variability is great even if the means do not change. It should be clear that the trials for which the data are retained are still balanced against progressive error no matter how small the progressive-error effects may be.

In the experiment outlined in Table 4.1, the intervals were balanced against progressive error by randomization within blocks of four trials. Another alternative would be to use ABBA. In this case, since there are four conditions, it would be symbolized as ABCDDCBA, translated as 5, 8, 14, 23, 23, 14, 8, 5. With several such blocks we would get a good balance for progressive error. Then why not use ABBA instead of block-randomization? The answer is we must avoid the possibility that the subject will be able to predict the stimulus (particular duration of interval, in this case) to be given and judged on the next trial. Each trial should represent an independent judgment or perception of the stimulus. If the subject believes that a particular stimulus will be given next, his judgment may be influenced by this belief or expectation. To take an extreme case, suppose the subject was given a series of durations as follows: 5, 7, 9, 11, 13, 15, 17, 19, 21. The subject would undoubtedly perceive that the intervals were increasing with each successive trial. Therefore, his judgment on a given trial would be influenced by his expectation that the interval being presented at the moment would be longer than the one presented on the preceding trial. It would be irrational for him to give a judgment reflecting a shorter interval than that given on the previous trial even if he felt it was shorter. The behavior is being seriously influenced by his expectations; he is not making an independent judgment for each stimulus. In most experiments the investigator does not want expectations to influence the response. With ascending and descending series, such as occur in ABBA counterbalancing, such expectations may develop.

In the case of line drawing versus circle drawing, the ABBA sequence is quite satisfactory. In fact, the subjects were necessarily told before each block of four trials which type of response to perform, so it would be of no consequence if they expected a change. The general rule is that if a subject's behavior will be influenced by his anticipation of the stimulus to be presented on subsequent trials, counterbalancing should not be used.

A further illustration will be considered. Suppose we had used only two interval durations, say, 8 seconds and 17 seconds. If we block-randomized with 32 trials, there would be 16 blocks. It seems quite likely that the subject would soon come to predict the interval (short or long) which would occur on some trials. By block-randomization a given stimulus can follow itself only once in any two successive blocks. Therefore the subject might pick up the pattern so that if he has two long intervals on successive trials he knows that the next one will be short, and that two short intervals in a row will be followed by a long interval. If this would indeed happen, it would recommend against the use of block-randomization. As a substitute we would use complete randomization of the two intervals, perhaps imposing only the restriction that each must occur equally often over all trials. There are other possibilities. If we are really interested in only two particular intervals (used here merely to illustrate the general case involving two conditions), we might occasionally insert intervals of other durations so as to prevent expectations from being developed.

We have seen that in the case of a variable like line drawing versus circle drawing, expectations would seem to be of no consequence. So why not block-randomize L and C rather than use counterbalancing? There would be 16 blocks, with L and C in each block, ordered randomly. If the randomization for L and C and for the four intervals were carried out independently, it would be quite accidental if the number of trials given each interval under L and C were equal. To have them equal is a convenience. By modifying this plan just slightly, we can have a design which essentially results in block-randomization for each variable. All we need to do is make sure that L and C occur once with each of the four intervals across each block of eight trials as follows:

Trial:	1	2	3	4	5	6	7	8
Interval:	5	14	8	23	14	23	5	8
L or C:	L	C	L	C	L	L	C	C

Matters of convenience will sometimes dictate the balancing method to be used providing there is a choice among the alternatives which are equally good for handling the balancing. For example, having the subject interchange line drawing and circle drawing frequently (as required by the eight-trial block given above) may be judged to be inconvenient. Instructions would have to be given for every change. In more severe cases, the conditions may require appreciable change in the apparatus, so that it becomes convenient to use blocks of trials under the same condition, and to use ABBA to balance across blocks.

Finally, it may be noted that either counterbalancing or block-randomization can be used for each variable within an experiment when there are more than two variables. A scheme can be worked out for any number of independent variables, although after three or four the interlocking becomes rather severe, and a large number of trials is required. The basic idea does not change: each condition must be represented equally often at each stage of practice.

Why Not Always Use This Design?

It is probably correct to conclude that the complete within-subjects design is less likely to give us an erroneous conclusion than is the independent-groups design. Why not always use the within-subjects design and forget about the use of independent groups? In answer to this question, a number of matters will be discussed, some representing basic considerations, some matters of convenience.

1. There are certain independent variables that cannot be effectively manipulated by a within-subjects design. As a general statement, it may be said that any type of an instructional variable cannot be effectively handled by giving all of the conditions to the same subject. Suppose we want to investigate the effect of a certain strategy on anagram solving. To make it simple, let us say we have only two conditions, a control (in which no strategy is imposed) and a strategy condition (in which the subject is told how to go about efficiently solving the anagrams). For a within-subjects design we would have a subject go back and forth unsystematically between the two conditions. Could (or would) the subject "turn off" the strategy when he is given the control condition? Probably not. Consequently the measurements might show little difference between the two conditions.

2. The complete within-subjects design is ideally suited for research in which a measurement under a given condition requires only a few seconds, and where the effect of one condition has little if any influence on the behavior under another condition. It is a remarkably efficient design for many studies in perception, psychophysics, reaction time, and in other areas. All of these involve trials or measurements which are accomplished quickly, the same condition can be given many times, and very stable data can be obtained from a single subject. One can hardly imagine the use of the design if the independent variable represents different curricula and the behavior of interest is arithmetic skill. Not only is the behavior irreversible (we cannot take away the arithmetic skill that a subject learns under a given curriculum), but it would take years to run a series of "trials."

3. For completeness sake, we should note here that if we are going to investigate the influence of a subject variable, we must necessarily use different groups. Suppose the independent variable is age—no one has yet discovered the means by which to change an eight-year-old into a six-year-old and then back to an eight-year-old. Subject variables which are developmentally based are irreversible, and many traits not tied to age are difficult if not impossible to change from moment to moment.

4. Finally, there are certain types of experiments where it is necessary to use a within-subjects design. Consider, for example, doing a study of the

estimation of interval duration in which drawing horizontal lines is used to express the judgment. If we use independent groups, we would have a different group for each interval. We would tell our subject that he is to draw a line to represent the length of the interval. Although he might be led to believe that different intervals would be presented, the lines he would draw probably would all be fairly equal in length. Furthermore, the group given a 5-second interval to judge might have a mean length that would be the same as the group given the 23-second interval. It is the contrast in the duration of the presented intervals, hence in the lines drawn to represent these durations, that makes this procedure "work."

A general principle may be stated: whenever several stimuli are to be evaluated on some characteristic, each stimulus being contrasted in a relative manner against the others, the complete within-subjects design is to be used. For example, in scaling stimuli by any of a variety of techniques in which relative judgments are required (e.g., method of rank order), the complete within-subjects design would be used. On the other hand, if we require absolute judgments (along a well-known physical scale) of the characteristic possessed in varying degrees by the stimuli, we have a choice. Thus, if we wanted subjects to make absolute judgments (in seconds) of the duration of four different intervals, we could use four independent groups, one for each interval. That we would choose instead to use a within-subjects design would probably be based on other considerations, such as convenience.

There is a problem for special types of within-subjects manipulations that is of such basic importance that it will now be described under a separate heading.

Special Cases

The results of accumulated work over the past several years have made it evident that in some areas of research the effect of certain variables may differ markedly if studied by a within-subjects design as opposed to being studied by an independent-groups design. The type of within-subjects design in question is not exactly the same as the one we have been discussing (as will become apparent shortly), but the logic underlying the two is equivalent. The fact that the influence of an independent variable will be quite different depending upon the design of the experiment used is both distressing and revealing. It is distressing because it emphasizes how closely behavioral laws may be tied to the design exhibiting them, but it is revealing because it may provide insights into processes which might otherwise have been overlooked.

We may initiate the exposition by looking at a particular task with which we are already familiar: the simple, free-recall learning task. Let us assume that we wish to study the learning of abstract versus concrete words, using this task. One way to design the experiment is to construct two different lists, one consisting of abstract words, the other of concrete words. One list could be given to one group, the other to a comparable group (random-groups design). Or we could give both lists to the same person at different times, using a design to be discussed shortly (incomplete within-subjects design). But there is still a third choice which is essentially a complete within-subjects design. We could randomize the positions of the abstract words and the concrete words in a single list and have a single group of subjects learn this list. This meets the requirement of a complete within-subjects design. Each subject's data are complete. If we give the subject a single trial on the list we have only a single trial on each word, as opposed to the usual within-subjects design where multiple trials are given. However, because there are several concrete and several abstract words in the list we have multiple trials on the same type of item even with a single trial on the list as a whole.

Suppose we use 16 abstract words and 16 concrete words, and we assign them to positions in the list randomly. We may think of these 32 successive positions in exactly the same way as we would the 32 trials in Figure 4.1. We have clearly balanced the abstract-concrete variable against progressive error. Of course, if we give multiple trials on the list, the randomization will be different for each trial, and we will simulate almost perfectly the usual complete within-subjects design where multiple trials are given on the same stimulus. A design such as this has great attraction for an experimenter for the same reason that the within-subjects design has proven attractive in studying problems in perception, psychophysics, et al.

As a next step, let's dig into the subject's mind. He is presented this rather long list and he knows he cannot learn all of the words in one trial. The assumption might be that the subject tries equally hard to learn each item as it is presented. But, suppose he thinks to himself: "This is tough; I think I will try to learn all of the concrete words first, then after I learn those I'll spend more time on the abstract." Therefore, when the abstract words occur on the early trials, he spends his time thinking about or rehearsing the concrete words he has already seen on that trial. The consequence of such a "strategy" would be that the abstract words would appear to be more difficult to learn than would the concrete words; that is, if the experimenter counts up the number of concrete words correctly recalled across trials, and the number of abstract words recalled across trials, the former will be greater. Conclusion: concrete words are easier to learn than abstract words. In fact, however, if the subject did what we are supposing he did, the evidence does not tell us anything about the differential difficulty of abstract and concrete words. The data tell us only that, for whatever reason, the subject decided to allot his time differentially to the two classes of words. The only requirement needed to produce the result leading to the false conclusion (that concrete words are easier to learn) is that a preponderance of the subjects follow the same strategy.

Consider next a more extreme case. Suppose the free-recall list consisted of eight consonant syllables, such as KVG, and eight three-letter words. Suppose further that most subjects decided to spend their initial efforts on learning the words (because they appear easier to learn) and then turn to the syllables. Again, a conclusion from this experiment might drastically overestimate the influence of the variable.

The question is: do some such selection strategies actually occur? Do subjects establish priorities when faced with a task where it is possible to establish them? The evidence is quite clear that something like this can happen. The proof is in comparing mixed lists (so-called because they contain at least two distinct classes of materials) versus unmixed lists (those containing only one distinct class). There have been a number of reported cases where an independent variable, inferred to be highly potent in a mixed list, has no effect when unmixed lists are used. In the unmixed list the subject cannot establish priorities for a class of items because they are all of the same class. Still, there are other cases where the estimate of the influence of a task variable is quite comparable for unmixed and mixed lists. In the illustrations given above, it was mentioned that the subjects might choose to learn first the items in the class perceived as being more readily learned. This is not known to be a general strategy; some subjects might in fact choose to learn the items in the class they perceived to be the more difficult. The only certain conclusion is that the mixed list introduces a very complex situation.

We have persistently emphasized that an experiment is executed to obtain an answer to a question. The purpose of studying various types of designs is to allow informed choice of a design that will have the highest probability of giving an unambiguous answer to the question posed. Thus if we want an unambiguous answer to a question about the influence of a task variable in a learning experiment, we do not use a mixed list. On the other hand, if our question pertains to the functioning of selection strategies or priorities (about which we know little), then the mixed list might well be used in the experiment.

So far as can be determined, this problem has arisen only in learning experiments, although not exclusively in experiments using verbal material. It is particularly critical when task variables are being manipulated, but it need not be limited to these variables. For example, suppose we wished to study free-recall learning as a function of time of presentation of each item. Again, a mixed list, hence a complete within-subjects design, is a compelling one. With the use of appropriate apparatus we could program the list so that some items are presented for two seconds of study, others for four seconds, others for six seconds, for as many intervals as we wished to use. But just suppose that during the longer intervals the subject rehearses items which had been presented for a short interval. We might still get an effect of study interval, but the results might reflect an underestimate of the true effect of this variable.

The facts are compelling enough to insist that in studying task variables with human subjects in learning tasks we should never use the complete within-subjects design as exemplified by a mixed list. Even if we wish to use it for other classes of variables, we ought to be extremely thoughtful about the matter before deciding to do so. Research has not told us as yet just why certain priorities are established by subjects (if that is what happens, which seems likely), but the research does make it clear that we may misrepresent the influence of variables by this within-subjects design. There is no reason not to use independent-groups designs or incomplete within-subjects designs, and there are established facts which tell us not to use the complete within-subjects design.

INCOMPLETE WITHIN-SUBJECTS DESIGN

With this design, each subject serves in all conditions of the experiment. It follows, therefore, that we eliminate completely the potential for subject variables being a source of confounding. The basic difference between the incomplete design and the complete within-subjects design is that in the former a subject is given each condition only once. The upshot of this restriction is that each subject's data are thoroughly confounded by stage of practice and are worthless for estimating the effect of the independent variable. We eliminate differential effects of progressive error by combining the data for the various treatments across subjects. Just how this is accomplished is the critical issue in understanding the design.

In ABBA counterbalancing, a subject is given a series of trials under Conditions A and B, e.g., ABBA ABBA ABBA ABBA ABBA. With the incomplete design, each subject is given A and B, but each only once. Obviously, the order in which these two conditions could be administered to a subject is either AB or BA. If there is progressive error, it will fall more heavily on B than on A when the order is AB. If, on the other hand, the order is BA, the progressive error will influence A more than B. If the change in performance due to progressive error is exactly the same for both subjects, and if we give one subject AB and the other BA, the two conditions will be equally influenced by progressive error when summed across the two subjects. If one subject puts five cents in bank A and ten cents in bank B, and the other subject puts ten cents in A and five cents in B, each bank contains the same amount.

It would be unreasonable to assume that two subjects, chosen at random, would have the same progressive error. But if we assigned, for example, 40 subjects to two subgroups of 20 each, it would not be unreasonable to assume that the progressive error for the two subgroups would not differ appreciably. Thus if one of the subgroups was given AB, the other BA, we would expect that the component of the performance attributable to progressive error would be equivalent for the two conditions.

Perhaps we should remind ourselves that the intent of an experiment is to determine the effects of Conditions A and B. We are not usually interested in progressive error; it is simply a pesky source of concern when we design our experiment if the same subject serves in all conditions. We must arrange the conditions of interest so that the effects of progressive error will be distributed equally over the measurements taken under Condition A and Condition B.

The one critical rule we follow in arranging the order of conditions for an incomplete within-subjects design is that each condition must occur equally often at each stage of practice of the experiment when viewed across all subjects. Each condition given a subject defines a stage. If there are only two conditions there are only two stages and, as we have seen, Conditions A and B are made to occur equally often at both stages. If there are eight different conditions there are eight stages and we would have to arrange the design so that each condition occurred equally often at each stage. A corollary which emerges when we carry out the rule is that the number of subjects required is always some multiple of the number of conditions. If we have eight conditions we must use 8, 16, 24, 32, . . , or 1200 subjects to meet the rule that each condition occurs equally often at each stage of practice.

Before getting enmeshed in some of the details of laying out a matrix for the design, we may ask about the sorts of experiments for which we might employ the design. Generally speaking, we use this design when each condition of the experiment requires an appreciable amount of time to gather the data. This is in contrast to the complete within-subjects design where perhaps only a few seconds are required to obtain a measurement. Suppose we wanted to study free-recall learning as a function of the level of concreteness of the words. We would construct, let us say, three lists within each of which the words are homogeneous with regard to level of concreteness and which represent, across lists, low, medium, and high concreteness. Perhaps we might choose to give five trials on each list, with each trial requiring three or four minutes to complete. It would involve the better part of an hour to test the subjects on all three lists. Many experiments using the incomplete design have given a single condition a day, so that the subject would appear at the laboratory for as many days as there were different conditions. Basically, the complete within-subjects design and the incomplete within-subjects design are interchangeable as far as the logic and the dos and don'ts of the designs are concerned. We tend to choose one over the other because of convenience. For experiments in which a considerable amount of time is required to obtain the measurement for a condition it is inconvenient to use the complete within-subjects design.

Order of Conditions

We have seen that each condition must occur equally often at each stage of practice, and that the number of subjects required to accomplish this is always a multiple of the number of conditions. How do we arrive at the particular orders of the conditions to be used for each subject? With two conditions there are only 2 possible orders, so we use these equally often. With three conditions there are 6 possible orders, with four there are 24, with five 120, and so on ($n!$, where n is the number of conditions). Normally, if we have four or fewer conditions we use all possible orders, assigning each subject randomly to a particular order.

When all possible orders of the conditions are used, we sometimes speak of the conditions as being completely counterbalanced. Using all orders equally often assures, of course, that each condition occurs equally often at each stage of practice. In addition, complete counterbalancing results in each condition preceding and following all other conditions an equal number of times. This latter characteristic is probably not an important one to impose, for reasons which will be discussed at a later point. That is to say, if we have three conditions in the experiment there is no particular advantage to using all six possible orders (ABC, ACB, BAC, BCA, CAB, CBA) over using three orders (ABC, BCA, CAB). Nevertheless we normally use complete counterbalancing if we have four or fewer conditions.

We may turn to the case where more than four conditions are involved. Assume we have five conditions and that we have decided to use 25 subjects. This will be viewed as five blocks of five subjects each. First randomize the order of the five conditions. Then for the next four subjects in the first block, simply move all conditions one stage to the left for each successive subject:

Subject #1	C	B	E	A	D
Subject #2	B	E	A	D	C
Subject #3	E	A	D	C	B
Subject #4	A	D	C	B	E
Subject #5	D	C	B	E	A

For the next five subjects, start with a new random order (for Subject #6) and repeat the process of moving one stage to the left. For Subject #11 a new random order is used, and so on. Again, the reasons for these procedures will become apparent later. The same plan may be used for six, seven, eight, or more conditions; the only thing that changes is the block size.

Class of Variables and Data Analysis

A contrast must be made between task variables and other classes (excluding subject variables, of course, for which this design cannot be used) when we draw up the matrix of conditions and stages and when we ask about the information which can be extracted from the data obtained. For illustrative purposes we will use three conditions and complete counterbalancing, although the principles which evolve hold for all matrices.

We may return to the study on free-recall learning as a function of concreteness. The lists may be designated as consisting of words of low concreteness (LC), medium concreteness (MC), and high concreteness (HC). The experiment will have three stages, and the matrix may be set up as follows:

	Stage 1	Stage 2	Stage 3
Subject #1	LC (10)	MC (8)	HC (4)
Subject #2	LC (12)	HC (7)	MC (7)
Subject #3	MC (10)	LC (10)	HC (5)
Subject #4	MC (6)	HC (2)	LC (3)
Subject #5	HC (5)	LC (7)	MC (5)
Subject #6	HC (4)	MC (5)	LC (6)

For the moment ignore the numbers in parentheses. The matrix gives the orders of administering the conditions to each subject. Each condition occurs equally often at each stage (twice) so the results cannot be biased by progressive error. We would probably run more than 6 subjects; perhaps 18 or 24 would be more appropriate. For each successive group of 6 subjects the above matrix would simply be repeated.

The numbers in parentheses are imaginary, indicating the number of trials required by each subject to learn each list to the point that all items could be given correctly. In order to determine if concreteness is related to the mean number of trials to learn, we need to form a new matrix in which the scores for each condition are arranged in columns:

	LC	MC	HC
Subject #1	10	8	4
Subject #2	12	7	7
Subject #3	10	10	5
Subject #4	3	6	2
Subject #5	7	5	5
Subject #6	6	5	4
Sums	48	41	27
Means	8.0	6.8	4.5

We would conclude that rate of free-recall learning was directly related to concreteness.

In the complete within-subjects design we saw that the progressive error, per se, could be determined from the data of any experiment. Does the present design allow a comparable determination? All we have to ask is whether or not stage is confounded by type of list. Since each list occurs equally often at each stage, we would conclude that there is no confounding, so the magnitude of progressive error across stages can be determined. If we simply add the numbers in the columns in the original matrix we get an unbiased estimate of progressive error (frequently called practice effects in such experiments). The mean values for stages 1, 2, and 3 are 7.8, 6.5, and 5.0, respectively, indicating that the subject becomes more and more proficient in learning with each successive list.

The general principle that evolves from this illustration is that whenever a task variable is manipulated in the incomplete within-subjects design, the magnitude of the progressive error can be determined. When we turn to other variables, this statement cannot be made. To illustrate this for a nontask variable, we will choose time of day. Further we will assume that we are going to test the idea (voiced by many students) that learning rate varies as a function of time of day. We choose three times: 7:00 A.M., 12:00 noon, 5:00 P.M. To avoid being distracted by discussing new tasks, we will continue with the free-recall illustration. Each subject will be given a free-recall list at the times noted. We can see immediately that we cannot do this experiment with a single list. If we give the list to a subject at 7:00 A.M., we cannot give him the same list at 5:00 P.M. This is an irreversible task in that once learning has occurred there is no way to "set" learning back to zero for the list. The solution is to employ three different lists, one for each stage. Therefore, this design simply is inappropriate unless we can form different tasks from a specified class of materials.

A second consequence of manipulating this particular independent variable is that we can only give a single session a day. If a subject had the order of conditions as 7, 12, 5, we could give the three sessions on the same day, but only one out of every six subjects would have this order. If the order is 5, 12, 7, we would be in trouble, since time too is irreversible. Therefore, Stages 1, 2, and 3 become synonymous with three successive days. We have three lists, so the matrix of condition orders may be described as follows:

	Stage 1	*Stage 2*	*Stage 3*
	List 1	*List 2*	*List 3*
Subject #1	7	12	5
Subject #2	7	5	12
Subject #3	12	7	5
Subject #4	12	5	7
Subject #5	5	7	12
Subject #6	5	12	7

Numbers have been arbitrarily assigned to the lists; List 1 is learned by all subjects during the first stage, List 2 during the second, and List 3 during the third stage. After the data are collected, we would bring the appropriate scores together under three columns labelled 7, 12, and 5.

Let us suppose that the three lists differed in difficulty. Would the design still be adequate? To answer this question we need to ask whether each list occurs equally often with each condition (each level of the independent variable). They do, and so we would conclude that even if the lists differ in difficulty no bias will result. Each condition (7, 12, 5) occurs equally often at each stage of practice and each condition occurs equally often with each list. In neither case, therefore, can a bias be present.

A further question is whether or not we can determine the magnitude of the progressive error across stages. As a reminder, we must treat stage (which reflects progressive error) as an independent variable. Consequently we must ask whether the measurements at each stage are confounded by another independent variable. An inspection of the matrix produces the conclusion that stages and lists are confounded; we cannot sum the scores by stages without including in those sums differences in learning produced by differences in list difficulty. The principle is that we cannot determine the progressive error when a variable other than a task variable is being manipulated. If we want to make this assessment, our design must be slightly more complicated, as will now be described.

We must balance the order of the lists in addition to the order of the conditions. If we want to use 36 subjects, we can completely counterbalance both lists and conditions. In the matrix given above, the lists are in the order 1-2-3. For the next block of 6 subjects we could have the order 1-3-2, then 2-1-3, and so on, for six blocks. Under each of these six list orders, we would have 6 subjects with the conditions completely counterbalanced as described earlier. We could also accomplish the appropriate balancing by using 18 subjects and incomplete balancing of the order of the lists: 1-2-3, 2-3-1, and 3-1-2. If we used incomplete balancing of both condition order and list order, the minimum number of subjects required would be nine.

The consequence of any of these schemes is that each list occurs at each stage of practice an equal number of times, so if the scores are summed for each stage the values would be an unbiased measure of progressive error. Furthermore we can tell whether the lists did in fact differ in difficulty. Each list will have occurred equally often at each stage of practice and equally often with each condition. Lists, therefore, are not confounded with either of the other two independent variables (stage of practice and conditions). By bringing the scores for each list together any differences in difficulty implied by the differences in the mean scores can be unambiguously interpreted.

In discussing the complete within-subjects design we noted that an investigator frequently gives practice or warm-up experiences to reduce the variability among his scores within a condition. These considerations also apply to the present design. We might, for example, give the subject several practice lists before beginning the experiment proper. Also, if we are using three different lists for each condition of our experiment, and if the three lists differ in difficulty, it will increase the variability of the scores within each condition, so we might want to try to get three lists which are known to be about equal in difficulty. It should be clear that use of practice lists, or the use of lists of equal difficulty, has nothing to do with removal of confoundings. Such uses will reduce variability which, of course, has statistical implications, but this has nothing to do with confounding.

Restrictions and Cautions

In the discussion of the complete within-subjects design, we saw that if an instructional variable is involved we should never use a within-subjects design. The rule still applies for the incomplete design. More generally, we say that we must be alert to the possibilities of differential transfer. If in going from Condition A to Condition B, the carry over of skills or habits or sets or expectations is different from the carry over from B to A, we have differential transfer. We may think of this in another way, assuming three conditions. If we have any reason to believe that the performance under Condition C will differ more when preceded by Condition A than when preceded by Condition B, we would again speak of differential transfer.

The possibility of differential transfer when an instructional variable is manipulated is quite apparent. For other classes of variables such possibilities are far less certain. It would not be unreasonable, however, to suppose that in any within-subjects design there would be small amounts of differential transfer. Condition A may have a small positive effect on Condition C, whereas Condition B may have a small negative effect on Condition C. We might anticipate that such "chaff" in the system would not bias the results if we used a good sampling of the possible orders of the conditions. This is accomplished in complete counterbalancing by using all possible orders. When five or more conditions are involved we try to use a number of different sequences so that each condition will precede and follow every other condition an approximately equal number of times. This is the reason why, in discussing the matrix for a five-condition experiment, it was proposed that we use a different random order for each block. We could carry this to the extreme by choosing a different random order for each subject and then making adjustments in a few of the orders to meet the requirement that each condition occur equally often at each stage of practice. Indeed this would be recommended when we have, let us say, eight or more conditions.

After an experiment is complete, we might want to examine the results to find out if differential transfer did occur. Unfortunately this cannot be handled adequately except in a few cases. The basic idea would be to "pull out" scores for subjects who had a given condition at the same stage of practice, but preceded by different conditions. When three conditions are used with complete counterbalancing, any block of 6 subjects will give us, for example, two cases in which C was preceded by A and two in which C was preceded by B, with stage of practice neutralized. If we had 36 subjects in such an experiment we could have scores on 12 subjects under each of the two sequences. Thus looking for differential transfer in this design would be a meaningful occupation. But as the number of conditions increases beyond three, we would seldom test a sufficient total number of subjects to make such post hoc assessments reliable. In effect, then, for most of our experiments our decisions about differential transfer and its potential disturbing effect must be made by a thoughtful evaluation of the possibilities. But, to repeat, a small amount of potential disturbance should not be of concern.

There is one final matter. We assign the subjects at random to the various sequences of conditions in the matrix of an incomplete within-subjects design. It can be seen that we have a random-groups design when only the conditions given on the first stage are considered. With a constant total number of subjects, the number assigned each condition on the first stage decreases as the number of conditions increases. If we run a total of 48 subjects for three conditions, 16 subjects are represented in each condition for the first stage. With four conditions, 12 subjects are represented at the first stage. With designs of this type, we could look at the results for these random groups to see how the effects of our independent variable compare with those when the results for all stages are combined. Unless there is heavy differential transfer, we would expect the two sets of scores to reflect the same relative influence of the independent variable. This is to say again that if we want to get the maximum information out of the data from an experiment, we need to cut and slice the data in as many different ways as possible.

MIXED DESIGNS, INTERACTIONS, AND SUBJECT VARIABLES

The four basic designs used for experiments have been discussed in their relatively pure forms in Chapters 3 and 4. In the initial part of this chapter we will recognize explicitly that in many experiments mixed designs are used. An experiment set within a mixed design involves the manipulation of at least two independent variables, a procedure that is not new to us. The experiment by Guzy and Axelrod on click counting involved three independent variables. What is new in the mixed design is that one independent variable is handled by one type of design, and a second independent variable is handled by a a different type of design. This language may be a little confusing in that we are talking about two different designs to be used within a single experiment. We must remember that when two independent variables are manipulated we are in effect conducting two experiments simultaneously; therefore it becomes meaningful to talk about two different designs within a single experiment. In fact, if we were manipulating three independent variables within a single study we could use three different designs, a different one for each of the three independent variables.

MIXED DESIGNS

Types of Mixed Designs

Limiting the discussion to the manipulation of two independent variables, we may see what the possibilities are for a mixed design. We have not included the natural-groups design in these possibilities.

		Variable A			
		RG	MG	IWS	CWS
	RG	1	2	3	4
Variable B	MG	5	6	7	8
	IWS	9	10	11	12
	CWS	13	14	15	16

RG = Random Groups
MG = Matched Groups
IWS = Incomplete Within-Subjects
CWS = Complete Within-Subjects

The above matrix shows 16 cells, which have been numbered arbitrarily. Four of these cells represent unmixed designs, namely, the 4 cells in the left to right diagonal (1, 6, 11, 16). This leaves 12 cells representing true mixed designs. But there are really only 6 unique cells because cells 2 and 5 represent the same mixture, 3 and 9 the same mixture, and so on. The 6 unique cells are RG-MG, RG-IWS, RG-CWS, MG-IWS, MG-CWS, and CWS-IWS.

It is not known that all six of these combinations have in fact been represented in published experiments but there is no apparent reason why each could not be used. Each combination will be examined, using the simplest two-variable experiment, the 2x2 design, in which each independent variable is represented at two levels.

RG-MG. We initially "sort" our subjects into two random groups. One group is to receive Variable A1, the other A2. We proceed to break down the A1 subjects into two matched groups, and we break down the A2 subjects into two further matched groups. One of the subgroups under A1 receives B1, the other receives B2. The same is true for the two groups under A2. Obviously, our matching procedure must not be such as to destroy the original randomness of the groups. It can be seen that this design is not likely to be used in practice; if we are going to match at all we might just as well match four groups, thus meeting the requirements of an unmixed design (Cell 6 in the above table).

RG-IWS. Again the first step would be to form two random groups, one to receive A1, the other A2. The two levels of the other variable (B) are given to all subjects in both groups by any method whereby the progressive error will be neutralized when the data are combined across subjects. As an example, assume we wish to determine the memory span as a function of the rate of presentation, for example, one second-per-unit versus two seconds-per-unit (A1 and A2), and as a function of the type of material, such as digits versus consonants (B1 and B2). The two random groups represent the rate variable, while all subjects within these two groups receive both digit and consonant memory-span trials. These are given in counterbalanced order in that half the subjects receive all digit trials prior to the consonant trials, and half receive the reverse order.

This design may be related to several of the experiments we have already discussed. For example, assume that Sharma and Moskowitz wanted to ask about the influence of the speed of marihuana intake on the autokinetic illusion in addition to asking about the influence of the amount of marihuana. In their study 20 minutes were allowed to smoke the cigarettes before testing was initiated. They could have used another group in which the subjects were required to smoke the cigarettes within a 10-minute period. Had this been done, rate of intake would have been represented by random groups. The amount of marihuana would still be represented by an incomplete within-subjects design just as in their published experiment.

RG-CWS. This combination is very much like the RG-IWS design except that the within-subjects variable is scheduled so that each subject's data are balanced against progressive error. The study on memory span could be modified slightly to fit this design. Rather than having all digit strings given prior to the consonant strings for half the subjects, with the reverse order for the other half, we would give the digits and consonants in ABBA order, or in random order to each subject. This would neutralize the effects of progressive error. In the previous chapter, a study was reported in which subjects indicated the duration of a temporal interval in one case by drawing a horizontal line, and in another case by drawing a circle. This was a complete within-subjects design for both variables. However it might have been wiser to have used the RG-CWS design, in which one group would draw only the horizontal lines and the other only the circles. It is possible that when a subject interweaves both tasks he may tend to draw a circle with a given diameter (matching the horizontal lines) rather than a circle with a given area.

MG-IWS. With this design two groups would be matched initially. One would be assigned to A1, the other to A2. Then B1 and B2 would be administered to both groups. The discussion above for RG-IWS would apply here, once the initial matching of the two groups had been done.

MG-CWS. This is comparable to the MG-IWS design except that the B1 and B2 conditions would be given for multiple trials with provisions made for handling the progressive error within each subject's sequence of trials.

IWS-CWS. In this final mixed design, both variables are manipulated within subjects, hence only a single group is involved. To pursue the illustration used above in which memory span was the response measure of interest, we might study memory span as a function of auditory versus visual presentation (A1 and A2) and digits versus consonants (B1 and B2). A1 and A2 could be administered as an incomplete within-subjects design. That is, half the subjects would receive the auditory strings first followed by the visual strings, and half would have the order reversed. The digits versus consonants would then be given by a complete within-subjects design, with progressive error being neutralized by any of the various techniques discussed in Chapter 4. In the current illustration, the assignment of the variable to a given design was quite arbitrary, and could be reversed, i.e., the consonants versus digits might be given as the incomplete design with the auditory-visual variable being administered by the complete within-subjects design.

Why Mixed Designs?

In the presentation of the four designs in their pure forms, a number of cautions were advanced about when and when not to use a particular design. For example, an instructional variable almost demands an independent-groups design. The same cautions must be weighed when designing an experiment in which two or more independent variables are manipulated. Nothing in the multiple-variable experiment abrogates the need for such caution. We must continually remind ourselves that when we manipulate two variables within a single study we are essentially doing two studies concomitantly. Any rules or cautions that apply to an experiment in which a single variable is manipulated also apply to one in which two or more variables are manipulated. Recognizing this fact, why would anyone choose a mixed design? Why not always use the diagonal cells? Why not always use the same design for each variable? The answers to these questions can almost always be reduced to a very unprofound level, a level at which matters of convenience and economy of time are involved. If only a few seconds or a few minutes are required to determine the influence of one variable at each of its levels, it would be quite uneconomical to use random groups, one for each level. However, the other variable may not be one that should be administered to the same subjects. Therefore independent groups would be used. There are times when a within-subjects design would be quite appropriate as far as design considerations are concerned, but matters of convenience might recommend the use of random groups. For example, if a within-subjects procedure requires three hours to complete, and if subjects are available for only one hour, we simply must use independent groups or we cannot do the experiment.

It can be seen that we work at two levels in deciding whether or not to use a mixed design for an experiment. First, we see if the variables involved require a particular design for effective manipulation, e.g., an instructional variable requires a between-subjects design. If we still have a choice, we move to the second level, looking to matters of convenience, economy, and sometimes statistical precision for the final decisions.

INTERACTIONS

A primary purpose for undertaking an experiment with two independent variables is to determine if the two variables interact in their influence on behavior. As we have pointed out several times, an interaction is present when

the magnitude of the influence of one of the independent variables on behavior differs as a consequence of the level or setting of the other independent
variable. Contrariwise, if the magnitude of the influence of one independent
variable is uninfluenced by the level or setting of the other, we say that the
two variables do not interact. These verbal statements need elaboration and
illustration.

Let us assume we do the simplest of all two-variable studies, one fitting the
2x2 matrix. We will continue calling the two variables A and B, with the
two levels of each indicated by 1 and 2. Assume we have completed the
experiment and have obtained the means for each of the four cells. One
possible outcome is plotted in two ways on the left side of Figure 5.1. This

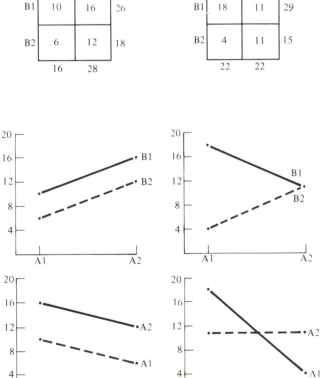

Fig. 5.1. Two possible outcomes of an experiment using a 2x2 design. The
entries in the cells are assumed mean values, and the figures show two different methods of plotting the results.

outcome leads to the conclusion that the two variables do not interact. We conclude this because in the upper left figure the effect of B (B1 versus B2) is the same for both A1 and A2; the influence of one variable is not changed across two levels of another. The lower figure on the left must lead to the same conclusion because the same data are used. Another verbal statement of the lack of an interaction would be that the magnitude of the difference between A1 and A2 does not change as we move from B1 to B2. In general, when the lines within the graph are parallel the lack of an interaction between variables is indicated.

In the matrix the sums of the columns and the sums of the rows represent the influence of Variable A and that of Variable B, respectively. These sums are often spoken of as the marginal totals, or main effects. As pointed out in Chapter 1, to get the best estimate of the influence of Variable B we collapse across or over Variable A. Because the marginal totals represent the influence of one variable summed across two settings of a second variable, the conclusion concerning the influence of the variables has greater generality than would be the case with a single-variable experiment. Both variables influenced performance. Referring again to the left panel of Figure 5.1, it can be seen that as we move from A1 to A2, performance increases; as we move from B1 to B2, performance decreases. In plotting the results of a two-variable experiment, either variable may be assigned along the baseline, with the other identified as a parameter within the body of the graph. The response measure is always plotted on the ordinate.

The results shown in the matrix and in the accompanying two graphs on the right in Figure 5.1 present quite a different picture from those on the left. Under A1 there is a large difference in performance for B1 and B2, but under A2 there is no difference in performance for B1 and B2. Thus, the magnitude of the influence of one variable (B) depends upon the level or setting of another (A). The two variables interact in influencing performance. The lack of parallelism in the lines of the graph provides the visual index of the interaction. Again, since the two graphs on the right are based on the same data points, they are transmitting exactly the same information, although the visual picture may appear to be quite different.

The Implications of an Interaction

In developing the implications of an interaction, we will continue to refer to the right-hand display in Figure 5.1. Suppose that we had done an experiment in which only the single variable B had been manipulated? In doing such an experiment, variable A becomes a static variable in that it would be held constant (at a fixed level). It can be seen that if A were held constant at level A2 we would conclude from the experiment that B was not a relevant independent variable, since the response measure did not differ for B1 and B2. On the other hand, had we happened to have chosen A1 as the level at which A would be held constant, we would have concluded that B was a highly relevant independent variable. More explicitly, suppose two experiments had been done on the influence of B, the two being carried out in two different laboratories. In one laboratory, A was held constant at the A1 level, in the other laboratory A was held constant at the A2 level. The results for the influence of B would have been in flat contradiction and a source of puzzled expressions in the two laboratories.

It is this type of apparent empirical contradiction which may lead to a two-variable experiment. The two single-variable experiments would be examined in detail to see just where the procedures differed. Very likely they would differ in a number of ways in addition to the level at which A was held constant. The time of year each experiment was performed was likely different. The subjects most assuredly were not the same, nor were the experimenters. These examples serve to point out a few of the inevitable diversities. The experimenters would weigh the likelihood that each of the differences between the two experiments might have been responsible for the different outcomes. Particularly, emphasis would be placed on variables which might be involved in an interactive relationship with Variable B. If the best guess is that Variable A is the critical one, a subsequent two-variable experiment in which A and B were both manipulated should give a confirming answer. We will return to this situation for further discussion in a somewhat different context in a later chapter.

The above discussion should not be taken to mean that multiple-variable experiments are performed only to clean up contradictions, albeit such experiments can produce some tidiness in an otherwise messy area. A theory may predict an interaction and this will lead to the appropriate experiment. The investigator may make more or less casual observations which lead him to believe that two variables will interact. This belief may lead him, in turn, to an experiment. Some experimenters simply take the position that interactions are very important kinds of knowledge in an area and so perform multi-variable experiments as a matter of course. All of this is to reiterate that there is no one path which leads to an experiment.

Once more we need to refer back to Figure 5.1 for the interaction shown on the right. The marginal totals in the 2x2 matrix show that Variable A had no influence on behavior when considered alone; the sum of the two cell values is 22 for both A1 and A2. Are we to conclude, therefore, that Variable A is irrelevant? This would seem to be a very inappropriate conclusion. We must break the findings down and examine the effect of A separately for B1 and B2. The difference is that with B1 performance decreases from A1 to A2, whereas with B2 performance increases from A1 to A2. Because this decrease and increase are of the same magnitude, they offset each other when summed across B1 and B2. Had we done two experiments, both examining the influence of A, but one with B set at B1, and one with B set at B2, both experiments would have prompted the conclusion that A was a relevant variable, but the nature of the effect would have been in direct contradiction. Once more the puzzled expressions would seek a resolution.

Figure 5.1 and the attending discussion dealt with the 2x2 design. It is customary in drawing line graphs for the results of such studies to connect the two points for a given level of one variable by a straight line. We should not take these straight lines too seriously. As we know, to establish the nature of the functional relationship we must have a minimum of three levels of a variable and these should be chosen to represent the full range of the variable, when that is possible. Thus we might conceive of a 3x3 design to be the minimal requirement for determining whether an interaction exists, and if it does, what its gross quantitative characteristics are. There is obviously no requirement that both variables be represented by the same number of levels. We might have a 2x4 design, a 3x6 design, or any other combination which suits the requirements of the investigation.

The results of an experiment using a 2x2 design can produce results of some complexity as we have seen. In fact, it takes rather careful preparation to state verbally just exactly what a particular interaction represents. The complexity increases by several steps when we move to a three-variable experiment in which there is an interaction among all three variables. We will return to such outcomes in the next section. If we do an experiment with four variables, which is quite possible, and if we get an interaction among the four, the minds of most of us become horribly boggled as we try to determine the exact nature of this interaction and what it may mean with regard to the interpretation of behavior.

Some interactions are products of a limited scale of measurement. These are sometimes spoken of as "ceiling effects" or "basement effects," implying that the interaction results from the fact that performance reaches a maximum (ceiling) for one variable so that measurement of further increases is not possible. Such an interaction may be reliable statistically but it has little meaning psychologically. Assume that we have a 2x3 design and that we get the results shown in Figure 5.2. Visually, the two lines are not parallel and we might conclude, therefore, that there is meaningful interaction. However, the B1 curve simply cannot rise further because of a ceiling effect—the limit of the scale is 100 percent correct. It can be seen that if we "turn the curves over" so that the scores approach zero as a limit (such as zero errors), we would again have an interaction, this time being due to a "basement."

Experimental psychologists sometimes make vocal their despair at the slow progress being made toward understanding behavior even in a relatively small area of research. As a result of these moments of despair, or even after a period of thought about the matter, it has been remarked that the progress is as slow as it is because the behavior is so complex. How can we interpret the meaning of "complex" as used in such statements? One interpretation might be that many, many independent variables influence the phenomenon under

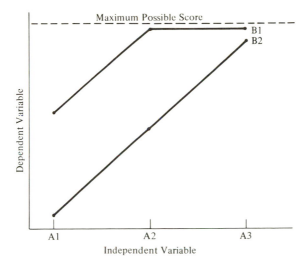

Fig. 5.2. Illustration of an interaction between two variables which results from the limits of the measuring scale.

study. However, were this the only meaning of complexity the path ahead might be long, but it would be clear and certain. The second meaning of complex as used in this context is probably more compelling, namely, that it is the interactions among variables which cause the strong men to weep. Interactions, it is believed, make the explanatory problems far more difficult than would be true were interactions not present. If the relationships between relevant independent variables and behavior were all linear and there were no interactions among variables, the explanatory problems would be quite simple (or so some believe). Indeed some might suggest that there are no explanatory problems under such circumstances unless one wishes to relate the behavior to a lower level of explanation, e.g., the physiological level. Such an idyllic dream cannot stand—one does not have to pursue the psychological literature very extensively before realizing that interactions are here to stay.

It is obvious that we must accept the interactions as they are discovered and then try to develop explanatory systems into which we may fit them. Indeed, as will be proposed in a later chapter, it seems that our most useful explanatory attempts will include processes which themselves interact as a consequence of the manipulations of one or more independent variables. For the time being we are going to look at another "use" of interactions. This view starts with the assumption that interactions are useful, if not necessary, in solving conceptual problems associated with empirical relationships involving subject variables. Working from this point of view, we find that interactions become analytical tools for testing theoretical propositions about individual differences. In the following section the discussion will build gradually toward a description of the use of interactions in their role as analytical tools.

INTERACTIONS AND THE NATURAL-GROUPS DESIGN

In an earlier chapter the natural-groups design was identified as the one in which groups of subjects, differing on some characteristic, were selected and used as the independent variable. Thus Jones selected groups of subjects differing on age and on vision. In the language we have been using, his design was a 2x8, there being two levels of vision (blind and sighted), and eight age levels. We spoke of the logic of this study as that of selecting subjects to represent "points" or levels of the two independent variables as opposed to the logic used for other designs where the independent variable is manipulated or administered. When subjects are selected, nature has administered the variable prior to the experiment. The central issue in the natural-groups design is how to determine cause-effect relationships. Can it be done? In other words, can we arrive at a way of thinking about subject variables which approximates the sureness with which we accept the cause-effect relationships when the independent variable is administered?

Developmental Variables

Jones reported very marked changes in kinesthetic positioning performance as a function of age. This is merely to say that something correlated with increasing age results in better and better positioning performance. Changes associated with increasing age cannot always be accepted for what they are presumed to show. Suppose we measure the learning ability of a group of subjects who are 30 years of age and that of another group of subjects who are 60 years of age. All of the subjects in both groups reside in the same relatively isolated community. What are we to make of any differences that might be found by these measurements of learning ability? Essentially we have no conclusion of substance which can be drawn about the relationship between age and learning ability. To understand why this is true, we may imagine an impossible situation as a means of establishing the source of the problem.

In a small, isolated town, the 200 babies born during a given year are assigned randomly to one of two groups. One group is tested for learning ability at the age of 30, the other group at the age of 60. All subjects had remained in town from birth and all had lived to at least the age of 60. The cultural-social-educational environment of the town had remained constant throughout the 60 years and changes in the world outside did not penetrate the isolated community. If all of these conditions were met, and if we then found a difference in learning speed between the two groups, one measured at 30 years of age, the other at 60, we could truly say that this difference is meaningful. It is a difference that could not have been produced by any confounding. We could then begin to search for an explanation in terms of changes (processes) which may be correlated with age.

The absurdity of the requirements just described highlights the problem involved in accepting a conclusion about the influence of age changes when these requirements are not met. If we simply measure a group of 30-year-olds and a group of 60-year-olds living in a town at the moment, we have not the faintest idea what a difference means—nor for that matter, what the lack of a difference means. The groups may have differed initially on genetic factors; deaths produce a selection process, and if longevity is in any way associated with learning we clearly have subject selection. There is no simple way to conduct this type of an experiment and expect a meaningful answer. Even the Jones experiment is not without some problems, although the selective loss which occurs at the younger ages is likely to be less severe than that which may occur at the older ages.

Selecting groups of subjects differing on a developmental variable (such as age) at a given point in time and measuring the groups on a given skill is spoken of as cross-sectional analysis. Such measurements may have some practical value but they are essentially useless if one is interested in establishing the existence of a phenomenon for which one seeks causal agents. The problems are so insuperable in cross-sectional analyses that another option has been gradually introduced. This option, called true developmental analysis, measures the same people at different ages. A little thought will show that a true developmental study is expensive and time consuming, but it does solve many of the problems intrinsic to the cross-sectional approach. In effect a within-subjects design is used. Problems remain, however. First there will be loss due to subjects dying, moving away from the geographical area, or perhaps refusing to continue to serve in the study. It is possible to determine if this loss is selective with regard to (correlated with) the measurements of interest because initial measurements (pretests) on all subjects are available and appropriate adjustments may be made. The second problem has to do with the successive measurements which are made on each subject over the years. Perhaps the successive measurements serve essentially as practice trials (sources of progressive error) and performance will improve as a consequence. Estimates of changes associated with age per se would be contaminated. But this problem too can be solved by including groups which are measured varying numbers of times so that the effect of testing can be determined. It is therefore possible to do a first-rate study of changes associated with age, although the investigator himself must have tenacity, patience, and longevity.

Static Variables

Jones showed that blind subjects could more accurately estimate and reproduce the extent of a movement of the arm than could sighted subjects. We would like to think that this results from the fact that a blind child, in order to move about safely or cope with his spatial environment, must depend heavily upon information from kinesthetic and tactual cues. The blind child, it could be argued, becomes more practiced in estimating distances in space by using kinesthetic cues than does the sighted child. Why should the blind child not be more skilled than the sighted child? Yet if we think about the results of this study (and others like it) in a dispassionate way, we realize that the study tells us nothing about the causal conditions for the differences observed between the blind and sighted children in positioning skill. In fact, we have no substantial evidence that the differences between blind and sighted children as observed by Jones have any generality. Several cases will be examined to direct the thinking about this matter.

We should first remind ourselves that we could take any large group of normal, sighted children, measure the positioning accuracy of each, and then "pull out" two groups which differ in the same amount as the sighted and blind children differed in the Jones experiment. This would surely lead us to recognize that if practice alone is responsible for producing the difference, factors other than blindness can lead to differential practice. If this matter is pursued, we would probably reach the conclusion that there are some unknown differences among children which will result in differential performance even if the same amount of practice were given. So the fact that the blind subjects tested by Jones did better than sighted subjects does not mean that the cause for the better performance was blindness. The blind subjects might have shown the same superiority over the sighted subjects had the former never been blind.

Suppose Jones had found no consistent differences between the blind and sighted subjects on accuracy of positioning? Or suppose the blind children had performed more poorly? The same reasoning must apply. We would never know what role (if any) blindness per se played in the outcome. The problem of drawing cause-effect conclusions from the natural-groups design is a general one. Whenever we identify two or more groups differing on some subject variable, we are faced with the devastating fact that these groups may also differ on one or more other characteristics. It is devastating because if we get differences when we test the two or more groups on some common task, we are unable to identify the causal agent. Division of subjects into groups on one factor may also be dividing them into groups on several other factors.

Extroverts and introverts may be identified reliably. Given that we formed two groups, one of introverts and one of extroverts, we might test them on a perceptual-motor task. If we get differences in performance on the task are we to say this was caused by differences in extroversion and introversion? Not at all, for performance might have differed for the two groups even though the subjects in one group had not become introverts, and those in the other had not become extroverts. Or, in the more extreme case, the performance might have differed even though the extroverts had become introverts, and the introverts, extroverts. The only condition which must prevail is a positive or negative correlation between extroversion-introversion and whatever characteristic is responsible for performance on the perceptual-motor task. Given this situation, a conclusion that performance on the task is determined by introversion-extroversion simply cannot be defended.

Next consider a somewhat more blatant case. In learning a paired-associate list of words, subjects differ in their tendency to produce overt errors. It is as if some subjects will not respond unless they are quite sure that their response will be correct. We will call these conservatives. Other subjects seem unconcerned about making erroneous responses—they say whatever comes to mind. We will call these subjects radicals. Of course there are other subjects who fall in between the extremes so we may speak of a conservative-radical dimension or continuum. We give a large number of subjects a paired-associate list to learn, and from the results we identify a small group of conservatives and a small group of radicals. As the next step we test these two groups on a different type of learning task, but still one in which the subject has an option to make or not to make overt errors. We find that those we have called radicals make far more overt errors than do those we have called conservatives. While these data show that we have found a reliable way to identify two groups of subjects, it would be nonsense to say that the error differences on the second learning task were caused by differences on the radical-conservative dimension.

One more: We take a group of schizophrenic patients and a group of normals and test them on a common illusion, such as the Müeller-Lyer illusion. We find that the average extent of the illusion is much greater for the patients than for the normals. To say that the illusion is greater because of schizophrenicity is a delusion. Again, the illusion differences might have been the same even if the one group of subjects had not become schizophrenic. If this is the case, we do not even have to speak of a correlation between schizophrenicity and whatever characteristic(s) is responsible for the illusion. However, if in general (across many patient and normal populations) the diagnosed schizophrenics consistently show a greater illusory effect than the normals, we would have to assume some correlation. We would also have another diagnostic tool in that the magnitude of the illusion could be used to help diagnose schizophrenia. But to speak of either as causing the other is not admissible. Both may have been caused by a common factor—a factor which results in both schizophrenia and susceptibility to illusions. The data we have do not tell us about this.

Can we circumvent these very serious roadblocks in our attempt to understand the basic factors involved in producing individual differences in performance? Can we bring individual differences (subject variables) into a causal framework as we believe we can for variables in the other classes (environmental, task)? That is the question to which we must address ourselves. As will be seen, it appears that greater leverage can be obtained on the issues than has been normally true heretofore. Indigenous to the thinking is the interaction between variables.

Interactions and the Elimination of Competing Hypotheses

In the illustrations given above, factual-like statements were made. It was stated that patients diagnosed as schizophrenics show greater illusory effects than do normals. The question we are posing is whether the observed difference is in any way the result of or a concomitant of being a schizophrenic. The solution to the problem (according to the approach to be taken here) lies initially in the development of a theory about a process (or processes) influencing performance on a task. Further, the theory must state how two groups, differing on some subject variable, also differ in the critical process. The nature of theory will be discussed in later chapters; for the time being, we will let the usual meaning carry the burden.

The first illustration of the approach is hypothetical. Assume we have identified two groups of third-grade students, one a group of poor readers, another a group of good readers. In examining the nature of the errors made in identifying words, an investigator notes that certain letters are frequently confused by the poor reader. More particularly, a C is often said to be O, an R is frequently called B, an F is called P. It was as if the poor reader sees nonclosed letters as closed. There is a phenomenon called closure which is defined as the tendency to see nonclosed figures as closed. For example, the figure to the left below may be perceived as a circle, the figure to the right as a triangle:

Suppose, the investigator thinks, that the poor readers have a stronger tendency toward closure of letters than do the good readers.

The investigator might then proceed as follows. First he constructs a test (in which letters are not used) to measure closure thresholds. The results show that in fact the poor readers do have much stronger tendencies to see incomplete figures as complete than do the good readers. At this point we are in possession of an empirical relationship: poor readers have stronger closure tendencies than do good readers. The presence of this inverse relationship between reading ability and closure gives the investigator a hunting license to continue. Had he not found the relationship, he would need to start anew with another notion about the critical characteristic underlying the difference between good and poor readers. Although it might seem that the closure differences (which were demonstrated on the test) are also involved in the reading differences (because of the nature of the errors made by poor readers when they read), a very good hypothesis in competition with closure differences is that the poor readers are poor because of a failure to discriminate among similar letters. This alternative hypothesis assumes that closure differences are not involved; rather, poor readers are poor because they have not learned to attend to small differences in the perceptual configuration of the letters. Other competing hypotheses might also be offered. We need, then, to devise situations which will make such competing hypotheses difficult to maintain. One way to do this is to try to show that under certain circumstances differences in closure tendencies will enhance performance; that is, we try to devise a situation in which poor readers will perform better than good readers.

A letter recognition test is constructed in which closure tendencies would facilitate recognition. This is done by printing letters in incomplete form:

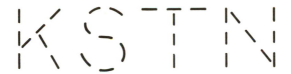

We will also have complete letters on the same form, including those on which the poor readers normally make errors (by theory, errors produced by strong closure tendencies). Letters are presented singly with the subject's task being that of naming the letter as quickly as possible. Let us say that the response measure is the number of errors made in naming. The outcome is as depicted in Figure 5.3, where the interaction is obvious. The finding is quite

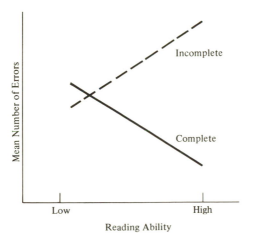

Fig. 5.3. Hypothetical results relating number of errors made in naming complete and incomplete letters by good and poor readers.

in line with the hypothesis that the two groups differ in their tendency toward closure. Other competing hypotheses might still be offered, but the basic point is that the moment we can produce an interaction we eliminate any number of hypotheses based on simple correlational thinking. For example, it cannot be argued that some factor correlated with, but not responsible for, poor reading is producing the so-called closure effects. This argument will not stand because we have shown that under certain circumstances the poor readers are better than good readers in a reading activity. Whatever we are dealing with is intimately associated with reading performance.

We might wish, and would probably be advised, to take another step. Some may complain that the identification of individual letters cannot be considered to be the crux of reading and that to bolster the point, the critical unit should be the word. Therefore we decide to expand the experiment. At the same time we see a way to make it even more difficult to suggest reasonable alternative competing hypotheses. Our first step is to find words in which all of the letters making up the words are closed letters. We find another group of words in which most of the letters making them up are unclosed. If closure tendency is a fundamental cause of poor reading, the poor readers and good readers should differ little on the words made up of closed letters. On the other hand, the poor readers should be much worse on the words made up of many open letters. Note that if these two outcomes are produced in the study the result is an interaction. The interaction is one which other hypotheses, for example, the failure of discrimination hypothesis, would be hard pressed to accommodate. The reason for this is that many closed letters are quite similar. Therefore discrimination should be difficult and the poor readers should be inferior to the good readers. The closure theory predicts there will be little difference in reading words where all of the letters are closed. We have two variables, reading level and words made up of open and closed letters. We add a third variable, namely, the printing of the letters in continuous versus discontinuous lines (or as it was called earlier, complete printing versus incomplete printing). We may now review the expectations from the theory that poor readers have stronger tendencies toward closure than do good readers:

Words with closed letters:
    Complete: No difference between good and poor readers
   Incomplete: Poor readers better than good readers
Words with unclosed letters:
    Complete: Good readers better than poor readers
   Incomplete: No difference between good and poor readers. This prediction is based on the assumption that the tendency toward closure, while helping in detecting the incomplete letters, will produce closure errors for the unclosed letters.

When all of these are put together the expectation is a three-way interaction, sometimes called a triple interaction among the three variables.

These expectations are graphed in Figure 5.4. A triple interaction can be shown in a three dimensional figure under appropriate circumstances, but perhaps it can be more readily inferred from a two-panel graph as in Figure 5.4. A verbal statement of a three-way (triple) interaction can be formulated by building upon the statement used to describe the interaction between only two variables. A triple interaction is present when the nature of the interaction between two variables differs as a function of the level of a third independent variable. In Figure 5.4 this generalized statement is given specific illustration: the nature of the interaction between two variables (poor readers versus good readers; complete versus incomplete letters) differs as a function of a third variable (closed versus unclosed letters). Thus if the influence of three variables is displayed in two panels as in Figure 5.4, we know that there is a triple interaction if the two-way interactions in the two panels differ. If the interactions in the two panels are visually similar, it signifies the lack of a triple interaction.

If the effects of the three variables are as depicted, it gives strong support to the hypothesis that the process involved in closure is an important one for reading performance and that poor and good readers differ in the degree to which they possess closure tendencies. With a triple interaction, alternative competing hypotheses become very rare indeed.

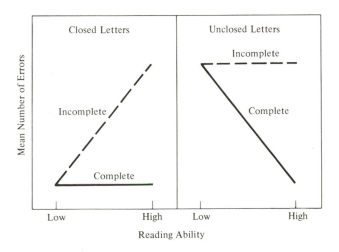

Fig. 5.4. Interaction among three variables: (1) low versus high reading ability; (2) complete versus incomplete letters; (3) closed versus unclosed letters.

Yet the whole issue is not nailed down beyond doubt by the triple interaction and further work would probably be undertaken. We might, for example, put the strong closure subjects through a training program in which the objective of the program is to reduce the strong closure tendency which developed in these subjects (for reasons not known or not covered by the hypothesis). We would obviously use materials other than letters for this training, but after the training it would be important to test reading performance to see if the training had transferred to letter identification. A positive outcome would give a further boost to the basic hypothesis.

A further illustration. A college student, when presented single words to memorize (as in a free-recall list) will often spontaneously produce implicit associative responses. The word *heavy* may produce the implicit response "light"; the word *tiger* may produce "animal." In a published study the hypothesis prompting the experiment was that a fundamental difference between mental retardates and normals was that the retardates rarely spontaneously produce implicit associative responses of a conceptual nature. Thus the hypothesis stated that retardates would rarely produce "animal" (implicitly) to the word *tiger*, nor would they produce "bird" to the word *robin*, when these words appeared in a learning task. The hypothesis simply asserts that there is a contrast between normals and retardates in their tendencies to produce conceptually implicit responses to other words spontaneously. Intuitively this might seem to be a reasonable hypothesis, but since it is possible that normals and retardates differ on other mental characteristics which might be correlated with the tendency to produce conceptual responses implicitly, the design problem was once again that of devising situations in which competing hypotheses about correlated characteristics could be dismissed. More particularly, it was necessary to choose independent variables (specifically task variables) for which the presence or absence of implicit conceptual responses would produce interactions in the learning performance of retardates and normals.

From previous work it was known that, for normals, a free-recall list made up of conceptually related words would result in faster learning than would a list of words not conceptually related. An interpretation of this finding in terms of implicit conceptual responses is generally accepted. At the same time it was known that if conceptually related words were arranged in certain ways within a paired-associate task, learning would be impeded as compared with a list in which the words were not related conceptually. To say this another way, with normals it was known that there was an interaction between type of task and words which were related or not related conceptually. The interpretation is that in both cases the spontaneously occurring implicit conceptual responses are responsible.

If the hypothesis that mental retardates do not spontaneously produce implicit conceptual responses is to have staying power, a clear prediction of a triple interaction emerges. Retardates will be essentially uninfluenced in their learning when a free-recall task has instances of concepts within it; they will also be uninfluenced when the instances are in a paired-associate list. Relative to normals, retardates should not be facilitated in free-recall learning when related instances are used, but they should also not be inhibited when the related words are used in a paired-associate list. Thus:

Free-recall list:

  Conceptually related versus unrelated:

    Normals facilitated by conceptual relations

    Retardates uninfluenced by conceptual relations

Paired-associate list:

  Conceptually related versus unrelated:

    Normals inhibited by conceptual relations

    Retardates uninfluenced by conceptual relations

The results were essentially as predicted. Again, there may be other hypotheses which could predict these findings, but certainly many simple correlational hypotheses would fall by the wayside. One alternative explanation is that retardates simply do not have the ability to group instances under the relevant concept. Obviously if this were the case it would not be expected that they would spontaneously produce category or concept names when the instances were presented. This alternative hypothesis was eliminated by including in the experiment only those retardates who could assign the instances to appropriate categories when asked to do so. Thus the hypothesis is that the retardates do not *spontaneously* produce the category name implicitly when the instances are given as words in a learning task.

Our aim has been to show that interactions among variables provide a very powerful technique for eliminating many potential explanations when questions about subject variables are being asked in an experiment. It should not be inferred from the illustrations that we always need a triple (or higher) interaction to make progress. In many cases an interaction between two variables may eliminate a number of alternative explanations for the effect of a subject variable on a certain task. Perhaps a final illustration of this point will be useful. Suppose we develop a scale to measure the emotional responsiveness of individuals and that with this scale we form two groups, one high and one low on the scale. We then construct a list of words all of which have strong emotional implications, words such as *love, murder, thrill*, and so on. Both groups learn the list and are tested for recall after one week. We find that the group with high-emotional responsiveness has better recall than the group with low-emotional responsiveness. We might then want to dash off a theory about how the emotional words fit into the emotionally charged associative network of the subjects in one group, and how they do not fit into the network of the subjects in the other group. An immediate competing hypothesis is that the subjects with high-emotional responsiveness simply have better memories than do the subjects with low-emotional responsiveness. Back in the laboratory we now give both groups a list of words with neutral affective connotation and again the recall of the list is measured after a week. If we get the same effect as we did with the emotionally loaded list of words, the competing hypothesis (the people with high emotional responsiveness have better memories than those with low emotional responsiveness) is quite tenable (and might be preferred on grounds of parsimony). But if we get any type of interaction between the two variables we can at least conclude that differences in memory per se are not the entire story. And if we find a symmetrical crossover interaction, we would conclude that differences in memory in general have nothing to do with the original outcome. For the time being, then, we may hang on to the hypothesis relating the consonance between the emotionally loaded words and the emotional responsiveness of the subject.

We may summarize the approach which we judge to be most fruitful in dealing with subject variables. First, we do not deal theoretically with the surface behavior or evidence which leads to the identification of many subject variables. Rather we ask about differences in what we presume to be fundamental processes which underlie the surface behavior. We then try to devise situations in which the fundamental processes will facilitate performance in one case, and situations in which the processes will inhibit or retard performance in the other. The choosing of subjects who differ widely on surface manifestations is merely a way of identifying subjects in whom the assumed process is strong or weak, of a large magnitude or of a small magnitude, or merely present or absent. If the outcome of our manipulations fails to show the expected interactions, we start over again. If the outcome is compatible with expectations we may do further experimental work in attempts to modify the process. In the meantime we hang on to the hypothesis until an equally attractive alternative is proposed. When this occurs we try to devise new situations which will arbitrate between the two. If, however, we are able to carry our hypothesis to the point of predicting an interaction among three variables, the likelihood of a reasonable competing hypothesis coming along is very low. We may even begin to believe that our hypothesis represents a truth; it is no longer to be viewed as a theoretical notion.

HERE-AND-THERE DESIGN PROBLEMS

Let us take stock. Thus far we have discussed all of the basic designs. In addition, in the previous chapter we saw how two (or more) designs could be used in combination to produce mixed designs. With this background we are prepared to evaluate some special problems which sometimes arise in planning experiments. These problems usually, although not always, are related to the scope of the factual conclusions used to summarize the findings of an experiment.

CONTROL GROUPS

In describing studies which meet the minimal requirements of an experiment (at least two treatments), we often refer to one of the groups as the C Group (in the between-subjects design) or to one of the conditions as the C Condition (in the within-subjects design). For both situations the generalized term is C Group. If we were to scale terms used in psychological research along a dimension of affectivity it would probably be found that "Control Group" would elicit high positive affect. It connotes the feeling of goodness, perhaps even righteousness. This may be quite proper, for we have never heard of an experiment which was criticized for having a C Group although, as will be seen, C Groups may be useless or inappropriate.

The reasons for calling a particular group a C Group may seem to be quite varied, although in most cases where this label is used there is a common denominator. A C Group may be thought of as a normative group; it is a group which provides the baseline performance against which the performance of groups given special treatment (E Groups) is assessed. Yet we must realize that there are certain independent variables which logically cannot include a C Group and that to identify one of the groups as a C Group would lead to confusion. If we study free-recall learning as a function of word familiarity, there is not a group of words (to give to a C Group) which can be thought of as normative in nature. Even a low-familiarity list is a treatment which may be of as much interest to the investigator as a high-familiarity list. So to identify the group given either the high- or the low-familiarity list as a C Group would not seem appropriate.

One-Treatment Experiment

For the following discussion we will use as a reference point the simplest of experiments, that including only a C Group and an E Group. The question we ask is whether there are circumstances under which the C Group is unnecessary; that is, using only the E Group, are there circumstances under which we can reach a firm conclusion concerning the influence of the treatment. There are some such cases, but in dealing with them we do not ignore or dismiss the idea of a C Group. Rather, the C Group is not used whenever it is possible to predict with high accuracy the performance which would have been shown by a C Group had one been used. Several different illustrations will be given.

If two lines of the same length are shown, one with a vertical orientation and the other with a horizontal orientation, and if the subject is asked to choose the longer of the two lines, he will usually choose the one with the vertical orientation. This phenomenon is known as the horizontal-vertical illusion. Suppose that we were the first investigators ever to ask whether such an illusion did in fact exist. Suppose further that in planning the experiment we asked ourselves what an appropriate C Group would be. What would this C Group be asked to do? It would seem that the subjects in the C Group should be asked to select the longer of two lines of the same length when both are presented vertically, and when both are presented horizontally. We immediately see, however, that the results of such procedures are foreordained; the subjects will perceive the two lines to be equivalent in length. If we force them to choose one we can be sure that their choices would not be based on perceived differences in length but upon irrelevant factors, such as position. Evidence for the existence of the illusion is produced when the vertical line is selected more frequently than is the horizontal line by the subjects in the E Group. A C Group is not necessary. It is assumed that without the differences in orientation both lines would be perceived to be of equal length. Hence control measurements are inferred because they are quite predictable.

For a second illustration, we will once again turn to the free-recall task. Suppose we wanted to define learning for this task and we decided to use very difficult consonant syllables, e.g., KFQ. We would give the subjects in the E Group a study trial and then we would ask them to write as many of the syllables as possible. Our treatment for the E Group, it can be seen, is provided by the study trial. Therefore, for a C Group we must omit the study trial. But again, what do we ask the subjects in the C Group to do? We might tell them that other subjects had been shown a list of consonant syllables for a study trial and that these subjects tried to recall as many syllables as possible. "So, (we continue in our instructions to the subjects in the C Group) we want you to recall as many of the syllables as you can in spite of the fact that you have not been shown the syllables." Our control subjects would undoubtedly view this as a preposterous request, which it is. Even if we persuaded them to write as many syllables as had the average subject in the E Group, the probability of any of the syllables being ones which were in the list presented to the subjects in the E Group would be essentially zero. Again, therefore, we assume a value for the C Group because this value is highly predictable. Thus the mean number of syllables recalled by the subjects in the E Group represents directly the amount of learning resulting from a single study trial.

The third illustration represents a somewhat different case but still meets the general principle, namely, that a C Group need not be used when the performance it would show, if tested, is quite predictable. Assume that a series of performance measures are available for an E Group over trials, and that these successive measures are very stable. It will be assumed in addition that the performance has plenty of "room" to increase or decrease from the stable level it has achieved. A performance curve of this type is illustrated in Figure 6.1. Now assume that at a given point along the time course of the performance curve (arrow in Figure 6.1) we introduce the treatment of interest. As a result of this treatment, the performance of the E Group shows an abrupt, marked increase and then continues at this new level over further trials. Can we attribute this change in performance to the treatment change? Normally we would insist that we should have a C Group which is not given the treatment change. In this case, however, it can be seen that had no change been introduced the performance of the E Group would be highly predictable beyond the point at which the treatment was administered; it is predictable

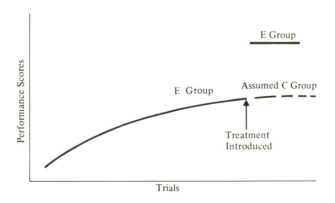

Fig. 6.1. Illustration of a situation in which the performance for a C Group may be accurately predicted from the projection of the performance curve for an E Group.

by simply extrapolating the performance curve. Or to say this another way, it seems highly unlikely that any abrupt shift in the performance level would have occurred had not the treatment change been introduced. In brief, we can infer with high precision what the mean performance of a C Group would have been had one been used.

The situation as depicted in Figure 6.1 may seem idealized, but in fact for certain types of performance curves it is not, particularly if the number of subjects used in the E Group is substantial. Perceptual-motor tasks may show such stable curves, and the use of a separate group as a C Group seems quite unnecessary. Consider another illustration. Investigators in the animal laboratory do not normally use a C Group in studying extinction. Given that an acquisition curve is rising, or has reached a stable asymptote, it does not seem necessary to use a C Group (receiving continued reinforcement) when the treatment change (removal of reinforcement) is introduced. If performance starts decreasing, it must be due to the treatment change.

There are some fairly obvious sensitive matters which must be taken into account if we are not to bungle inferences concerning projected C Group performance. Obviously, the more unstable the initial performance curve the less precise the extrapolation of the scores. This would be particularly troublesome if we wished to project to a single trial. At the same time, the greater the number of trials across which the performance curve is extrapolated or projected, the greater the likelihood of an error in the conclusion that the treatment change was responsible for the change in performance. There are certain tasks, such as learning to typewrite, in which performance may increase rather sharply following a series of trials on which little performance increase had been observed. It would not be advisable to use the projected-score technique when such tasks are employed. Nevertheless, a judicious implementation of the logic behind the single-treatment experiment is quite justified.

The fact that stable measures over time or trials allow a projection of scores which will approximate the values of a C Group had one been used may be of primary importance in the laboratory because it is economical. In other settings the technique might allow a conclusion concerning the influence of a treatment change under circumstances where it would not be possible to use a C Group. In an earlier chapter we pointed out that there are many experiments which in principle can be performed to study educational or social problems but which for a variety of reasons cannot be carried out in practice. There are other such problems which may be investigated by introducing a treatment change but for which it is impossible to use a C Group to determine the effects of the treatment change. If the projected C Group technique is applicable, a firm conclusion can still be reached concerning the influence of the independent variable. An illustration will be given.

Assume that in a certain school in an impoverished area the public health officials believe that a general upgrading of the health status of the children would occur if more of the children could be induced to drink milk as a part of the school lunch program. A campaign is undertaken through letters to parents, through signs placed around the school, through contests among home rooms, and so on; all are directed toward producing an increase in milk consumption. It can be seen that it would not be possible to have a C Group at this school, a group that was not exposed to the Let's-all-drink-milk campaign. But it is quite likely that the lunchroom records show the amount of milk which has been consumed week by week for the past few months prior to the initiation of the campaign. This "performance" curve could be projected with some accuracy to indicate the likely consumption to be expected for at least a few weeks beyond the point at which the campaign was launched. If the actual consumption records rise appreciably above this projection following the start of the campaign, it would be reasonable to conclude that milk consumption had been influenced by the treatment.

The above conclusion may seem straightforward. Notwithstanding, we must emphasize the need for caution in all studies in which the projected-score technique is used. It is always possible that the changes observed following the treatment were due to events other than the treatment. The likelihood of this occurring is maximized when the treatment extends over a long period of time (as did the milk campaign), and is minimized when the treatment is of relatively short duration (as in the usual laboratory study). It is possible to imagine that an event other than the drink-milk campaign was responsible for the increased milk consumption. Let us suppose that most of the boys in the school read a particular sports magazine. At about the same time that the drink-milk campaign was initiated, the sports magazine carried an article describing the childhood experiences of several current sports stars. All of the stars asserted that their careers had been successful because of their healthy physical development as children, and that the development was in large part due to having drunk lots of milk. Given this event, it is possible that the increased consumption of milk at the school was not produced by the campaign at all. To say this another way, the increased milk consumption would have occured even without the campaign. Had it been feasible to use a C Group in the school, we would have found that the increase in milk consumption was equivalent for both the E and C Groups. Again, therefore, we emphasize that the use of the one-treatment experiment must be accompanied by careful thought if false conclusions are to be avoided.

The use of projected C Group performance scores is possible only under rather limited situations. This limitation results because the procedure is applicable only when the independent variable is introduced after a series of performance scores have been obtained. It is a far more frequent case to introduce the independent variable at the outset of the measurements. There-fore we will still frequently need to question ourselves and others by asking: "What would a C Group have done?"

E Groups Only

Experiments are frequently carried out in which two or more E Groups are used, but no C Group. These studies clearly meet the requirements of an experiment because at least two different treatments are involved. For ex-ample, we might conduct an experiment in which the interest is in the in-fluence of audience size on learning a complex motor skill. There might be three conditions in which the audience sizes are one person, three people, or five people. It would be quite feasible to have a C Group for which there was a zero-sized audience, but the investigator chooses not to include this C Group. We cannot fault the investigator for this so long as he fully realizes the very limited nature of the conclusions which his experiment must necessarily produce. Two of several possible outcomes are illustrated in Figure 6.2. The solid line in each panel represents the obtained findings, the dotted lines the possible outcomes had a C Group been used. In the left panel the results show that for the three E Groups the performance did not differ as a function of size of audience. Indeed, this is all that can be said by way of

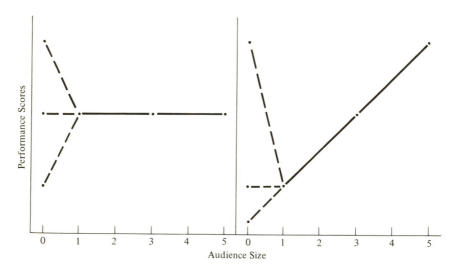

Fig. 6.2. Two possible outcomes of an experiment in which the influence of size of audience (one person, three or five people) on performance is deter-mined. The dotted lines connect different possible performances of a C Group (no audience) had one been used.

summarizing the results: "Performance did not vary as a function of audience size when the size ranged from one to five." The three dotted lines connect points representing three possible performances of a C Group with the point representing the performance obtained when an audience of one was used. The use of a C Group would allow a far more extended conclusion; it would allow the investigator to conclude whether an audience of any size (from one to five at least) inhibits, facilitates, or has no influence on the performance on this task.

In the right panel of Figure 6.2 the results are plotted so that the performance for the three E Groups increases directly as audience size increases from one to five. Again, the conclusion must be limited to such a statement. However if a C Group is used (for which three possible different findings are depicted) a conclusion has much more breadth. The reference condition (no audience) again allows statements about the role of an audience per se in facilitating or inhibiting performance. It seems that the marked increase in information resulting from a C Group would make it most worthwhile. If this is true, why would an experiment such as this ever have been done without including a C Group? There are justifiable reasons.

We must not be trapped into viewing each experiment as an isolated, abstract entity upon which we impose our thinking without considering the background work which is available to the investigator. There are at least three reasons why an investigator might deliberately choose not to include a C Group when we, viewing the experiment in abstract isolation, might feel that he should have. First, he may be concerned with an applied or real-life situation in which an audience of at least one is always present. He sees no reason to include a C Group because it has no representation in the situation in which he is interested. Second, the investigator may have an enormous amount of data on the performance on this task with a zero audience size and therefore knows that he can make a reasonable conclusion as to whether the presence of an audience is facilitating, inhibiting, or having no influence on performance. Third, the theory he has about the influence of audience size on performance on such tasks may not involve an audience of zero size. If he is interested only in testing his theory, the C Group adds nothing to the test. Thus it becomes important to know the background thinking which led an investigator to choose not to use a C Group when its inclusion, viewed in the abstract, would allow a much broader conclusion. This does not mean we will always find a satisfactory rationale in the background thinking as given in the introduction to a report of the experiment. It is quite possible that the investigator saw the restrictions he had placed on his conclusions only after the experiment was completed, and that our view in the abstract should have been his initial view, too.

The general point to be made is that in designing an experiment we should always ask ourselves if a C Group is necessary to arrive at the answer to the question we are giving to the experiment. As we said earlier, our experience has never shown anyone being criticized for including an appropriate C Group. In fact, we may want to include more than one C Group.

Appropriate C Groups

The treatment given the E Group (or groups) is frequently of a gross nature. This means that there are several distinguishable components or subtreatments involved in the overall treatment process, and there is no way to avoid it. If the experimental treatment is to produce a lesion in the frontal lobe of an animal, at least three steps can be identified, namely, the administration of the anesthesia, the operative procedures allowing access to the frontal lobe, and finally the production of the lesion. Let us say that the portion of this gross treatment which is of interest to the investigator is the lesion effect on the performance on some task after recovery from the operation. What is the appropriate treatment for the C Group? Frequently the experimenter speaks of a nonoperated C Group. This C Group consists of animals randomly formed into a group at the same time that the E Group was formed, but which were given no operation before being tested on the task on which the E Group was tested following the operation. In the abstract this would not be an appropriate C Group. The proper treatment for the C Group would be to give the anesthesia, to undertake the operative procedures necessary to reach the frontal lobe, but not to produce the lesion.

As stated, in the abstract a nonoperated C Group is inappropriate. In fact, it may not be if there is information from other experiments that neither of the two initial steps has any influence on subsequent performance on the task. But unless such knowledge is available, we must take the position that every part of the treatment given the E Group must be given the C Group except that part which is the focus of interest. If the investigator is planning a series of studies on the effects of lesions, he might choose to explore systematically the effects of each component of the treatment given the E Group. For example, he might use three C Groups: C1, no treatment; C2, anesthesia only; C3, anesthesia plus the operative procedures necessary to expose the frontal lobe. Furthermore, if the investigator has a theory which relates performance to lesions produced only in the frontal lobe, he probably should use a C Group in which lesions were made in a different lobe.

Let us look at another illustration. In paired-associate learning there is a transfer paradigm or relationship known as A-B, A-D. This indicates that the stimulus terms in the two lists are identical (e.g., the same words), but the response terms are different. Normally it is expected that interference or negative transfer will be produced by this paradigm. That is, the learning of the second list will be inhibited or interfered with because of the contrary associations developed in learning the first list. What is the appropriate C Group? The answer depends upon the question asked by the investigator. Several alternatives will be developed.

Assume that the question to which the experiment is addressed is: "Is there negative transfer?" To answer this question, we would use the following E and C Groups:

	A-B	A-D
E Group	Yes	Yes
C Group	No	Yes

If the performance of the E Group on A-D is poorer than the performance of the C Group, an affirmative answer is given to the question. It might be noted that if it were known that the two lists, symbolized by A-B and A-D, were equal in difficulty, a C Group would not be needed. A direct comparison of the performance of the E Group on the two lists would give an appropriate answer to the question.

When a subject is given practice on successive lists made up of unrelated items, there is usually an increase in the rate of learning of each successive list. This is a progressive error often referred to as learning-to-learn. It can be seen that the performance of the E Group (in the above design) on A-D would be positively influenced by learning-to-learn; that is, having learned A-B, the learning of A-D may be positively influenced by learning-to-learn. If there is also interference from A-B to A-D, it becomes clear that the gross transfer effect obtained using the above design consists of at least two components (learning-to-learn and interference). Therefore the question may be more analytical: "How large is the negative component produced by this paradigm?" This question implies that our C Group must be one that will "remove" the learning-to-learn component, leaving only the negative component to influence the performance difference between the E and C Groups. The following procedures would seem to be appropriate:

E Group:	A-B	A-D
C Group:	C-B	A-D

The reasoning is that the performance of the C Group on A-D will be influenced positively by having had C-B and that this positive component will be equal in magnitude to the positive component resulting from the E Group learning two lists. Therefore, insofar as the performance of the E Group on A-D is inferior to that of the C Group, it would seem that this deficit is due to interference of A-B on A-D. Furthermore, if the reasoning is correct it follows that the difference in performance of the two groups on A-D in this design will be greater than the corresponding difference in the earlier design.

An examination of the design just described may lead to the conclusion that we are still not getting at a pure measure of the negative effects of the paradigm, A-B, A-D. It might be argued that in learning A-B the E Group develops a familiarity with the A terms and that this provides a positive factor in learning A-D. If this is true, we would not have a pure measure of the negative effect produced by the learning of the first list by the E Group. We might choose to use a C Group which, in some way, was given equivalent familiarity with the A terms before A-D learning but without having learned associations to them. Actually, this problem has not as yet been satisfactorily solved. Sometimes we can see the need for a given kind of control group but we may lack the techniques for implementing the procedures.

There is no area of psychological experimentation where the choice of an appropriate control group is not of fundamental importance. The isolation of the critical part of a gross independent variable is necessary if we are not to draw false conclusions concerning the influence of the effective component of the independent variable. If the implementation of an independent variable in the animal laboratory inadvertently leads to differences in the amount of handling of animals in the E and C Groups, the independent variable is contaminated by the effects of handling. We cannot prejudge such matters with confidence. That is, we cannot arbitrarily say that handling should have no influence and proceed to ignore it. If we were possessed of such wisdom we would probably not need to do an experiment. Whenever we can detect that an independent variable has multiple components, we must be sure that our C Groups are going to strip away all components except the one of interest.

Yoked Controls

It will be remembered that in free-recall learning a subject is allowed to recall the words in any order he chooses, and that the order of presentation for study changes on successive trials. Assume that we have a theory which predicts that the subject uses a certain order of recall because it makes the list of words easier to remember—perhaps because in that particular order the words are associated, one with the next. How would we test such a theoretical notion? On first thought we might say that we would use a C Group for which the words were always presented in the same order on all study trials and the subject was required to recall them in that order. But we see that subjects in the C Group would have extra memory requirements in that they would have to learn a particular order of the words. The subjects in the E Group, on the other hand, had been allowed to determine their own order which might vary in part from trial to trial but which gradually would become stable, particularly on later trials. The theory says that this ultimate order represents an easy ordering because each word tends to suggest the next word in succession.

What we need to do is determine if the final order of recall of all items is in fact an easier order than is a random order. In such circumstances the yoked-control technique may solve the problem. It is said to be a yoked technique because the task given a control subject depends upon the performance of a particular subject in the E Group. It should be obvious, therefore, that the observations made on a control subject must always follow those made on a subject in the E Group. In the present case the yoking would be carried out as follows: We would use a form of block-randomization in which there are three subjects in each block, one E subject and what may be called two C subjects. The first subject will always be an E subject. This subject is given the list of words to learn by usual free-recall procedures until all words are given correctly on a single recall trial. The theory says that this particular order is an easy-to-learn order. Knowing this order, we can then give it to a control subject (C1). Now we present the list in the same order on all study trials (the order as determined by the E subject), and we require the subject to recall the words in the presented order. A second control subject (C2) is presented the same words in a random order, with this random order being used on all study trials and with the subject required to recall them in the order presented. Thus both C1 and C2 subjects are given the same words, but the C1 subject must learn the order which is predicted to be easy while the C2 subject must learn the random order. Of course each successive C2 subject gets a different random order to guard against the possibility that a single random order would not be representative of the difficulty of all possible random orders.

We continue testing subjects across blocks with the E subject always tested first followed immediately in time by the C1 and C2 subjects in random order. To support the theory, the C1 Group must show more rapid learning than the C2 Group. If the two C Groups do not differ the hypothesis would be rejected. If it is said that the order of recall developed by the different E subjects is completely idiosyncratic and therefore should not facilitate the learning of subjects in the C1 Group, the hypothesis is not testable. It also follows that if the subjects in the C1 Group find the list easier to learn than do the C2 subjects, a careful inspection of the orders "given" to the C1 subjects by the subjects in the E Group would show that the orders were quite similar.

The yoked-control technique is not widely used but is sometimes absolutely necessary to test certain notions or to derive appropriate control groups. One further illustration will be covered briefly. Retroactive inhibition is defined by using the usual E and C Groups. The E Group receives Task A followed by Task B and then recalls Task A. The C Group is given Task A, but not Task B, and then recalls Task A. Of course, for the subjects in the C Group there must be a delay between the learning and the recall of Task A to correspond to the delay required by the E Group:

	Task A	Task B	Recall Task A
E Group	Yes	Yes	Yes
C Group	Yes	No	Yes

If the recall of Task A is better for the C Group subjects than for the E Group subjects, retroactive inhibition has been demonstrated. Now assume that the subjects in the E Group must learn Task B until a specified level of performance is achieved. Because these subjects will differ in their rates of learning Task B, the interval between learning Task A and its recall will be variable across subjects. There are several solutions to this problem, one of which is to use the yoked-control technique. The rest interval given to a subject in the C Group would be the length of time a yoked subject in the E Group needed to reach the level of proficiency required for Task B. Thus, although the interval between learning and recall of Task A will differ across the control subjects, the mean time and the variability will be exactly the same as for the subjects in the E Group.

PROBLEMS IN MULTI-STAGE EXPERIMENTS

A multi-stage experiment is one in which there are distinct changes in the conditions at various points in time, these changes being necessary to "get to" the phenomenon of interest. Retroactive inhibition, as defined above, is a three-stage experiment for the E Group. This phenomenon involves recall as the third stage following two earlier stages (learning of Task A followed by the learning of Task B). The study of the spontaneous recovery of a conditioned response also requires three stages; the conditioned response must be acquired and then extinguished before spontaneous recovery can be studied. The usual transfer experiment consists of two stages.

Certain problems of method may arise in multi-stage experiments. These problems will become manifest when the independent variable is introduced during one stage in order to determine its influence on the performance at a later stage. In contrast, the same problems are not likely to arise when the independent variable is introduced during the same stage at which the phenomenon of interest is measured. These two cases will be illustrated. A study of experimental extinction requires two stages. We might do an experiment in which the variable is introduced during the second stage (the extinction phase) with the interest being in the effect of this variable on extinction. On the other hand, we might introduce the independent variable during the learning stage to determine its influence upon the later stage—upon rate of extinction.

As noted above, no new problems of method arise when the independent variable is inserted during the stage in which the phenomenon of interest is measured. Problems of method may arise if the independent variable is inserted during one stage to examine its influence on the performance on a later stage. As we will see, these problems are conceptually the same as those present in the confounding of two independent variables, although the genesis of the confounding may be seen as being different.

Assume that we do a study on the role of magnitude of reward during learning on the extinction of a turning response of rats in a T maze. Note that the phenomenon of interest is not the influence of magnitude of reward on the acquisition stage—on the learning of the habit. Rather, the interest is on the role of the magnitude of reward during acquisition on the subsequent rate of extinction. Suppose, therefore, we gave a constant number of acquisition trials for the different groups, each group receiving a different sized reward in the goal box on each trial. After the acquisition trials are completed we give a constant number of extinction trials (on all of which the reward is omitted). Assume that our measure of extinction is the latency of leaving the starting box, and assume further that we find that the average latency for the extinction trials is inversely related to the magnitude of the reward during extinction. That is, the animals which had large rewards during acquisition have shorter latencies across extinction trials than do the animals which had small reward magnitudes.

It is quite clear from this experiment that there was a relationship between magnitude of reward during acquisition (first stage) and rate of extinction (second stage). Let us assume, however, that the magnitude of reward influenced acquisition performance; the larger the magnitude the better the performance (less time to leave the starting box). It is a well known fact that (under most circumstances) the higher the performance level at the end of acquisition the slower the rate of extinction. In other words, degree of acquisition is an independent variable influencing rate of extinction. We have a confounding, therefore. At the start of extinction our groups are not equivalent on all characteristics except the one of interest. The groups differ both on the level of learning at the end of acquisition and on the magnitude of reward given during acquisition. Which is responsible for the differences in extinction performance? At this point we establish empirical priorities for the interpretation. Had a single magnitude of reward been used for all groups but with the groups having been given differing numbers of acquisition trials so that the performance levels differed at the termination of acquisition, the outcome would have been, or could have been, the same as was found with a variation in reward magnitude. The differences in extinction may be accounted for by differences in level of acquisition alone. Thus it is not appropriate to interpret the differences in extinction as being due to an additional carry-over of some other influence (reward magnitude).

For this specific experiment, there is probably no satisfactory solution for the problem. If there is one, it is not a simple one and we prefer not to pursue the matter to its resolution. One rather obvious possible solution should be discussed briefly, however. Could we not solve the problem by carrying acquisition to the same level for all reward magnitudes before introducing the extinction trials? Probably not. If the rate of acquisition is related to reward magnitude, the groups would differ on the number of trials required to reach a specified level of acquisition. Simultaneously, the number of times rewards were given would also differ, and this factor may contaminate the effect on extinction of reward magnitude per se. Therefore this would not seem to be an adequate solution.

We might ask why an investigator would want to do such an experiment. What was the background thinking which led him to ask about a carry-over effect of reward magnitude from acquisition to extinction? Perhaps he had a theory which led to the articulation of the question. The theory may have predicted a carry-over because of a contrast between the conditions of acquisition and extinction. If the magnitude of the reward was large during acquisition, the contrast at the start of extinction between a large reward and no reward would be greater than the contrast when the magnitude was small during acquisition. The theory may further state that the greater the contrast the more rapid the extinction. Actually, a crude test of this proposition could be made by proceeding with the experiment as originally described (a constant number of acquisition trials for all reward magnitudes). If it was found that extinction was more rapid following a large reward during acquisition than following a small reward, the theory would be supported because the results are exactly opposite those to be expected if level of acquisition alone was determining the rate of extinction. Of course the exact magnitude of the carry-over effect could not be determined, but that something was carrying over would seem evident. Thus, in certain situations we can test a theoretical notion without solving a design problem.

Perhaps the design issue will be illuminated by a somewhat contrived analogy. A fisheries expert was interested in factors which influence mortality when fish produced in the hatchery are transferred to a natural habitat. More specifically, he had the hypothesis that the larger the hatchery pond (first stage) the greater the likelihood that the fish would survive when moved to the natural habitat (second stage). He reasoned that the number of different conditions to which the young fish had to adjust would be greater the greater the size of the hatchery pond. Therefore, assuming these adjustment habits would serve to increase life expectancy, survival rate in the natural habitat would be directly related to the size of the hatchery pond.

Three hatchery ponds were constructed, small, medium, and large in size. Into each pond the investigator placed 100 male fingerlings, each fingerling being tagged as to pond size. After one month, the 300 fish (all miraculously having survived) were placed in a small lake (natural habitat) which had been cleaned of all other fish. One year later the small lake was drained, and the number of fish remaining in each group was counted. The number was directly related to the size of the original hatchery pond.

The results would seem to support the investigator's thinking. A variable introduced during the first stage influenced performance in the second stage, the conditions for the second stage being constant for all groups. Actually, had the investigator been alert he would have noted that when the fish were transferred to the small lake their mean size was directly related to the size of the hatchery pond. A difference in size would be anticipated because the larger the pond the greater the opportunity to supplement the food provided by the investigator (with insects, worms, and whatever else fish eat). Thus, the three groups were not "equal" when transferred to the lake, and it could be anticipated that the larger the fish the greater the likelihood of obtaining food in the small lake. The larger fish would survive at the expense of the smaller. In effect, then, the "performance" on the second stage may not at all have been due to adjustment habits acquired in the first stage and carried over to the second stage; second-stage performance resulted from size differences produced by the variable introduced during the first stage. Size should have been equalized for the three groups before placing them in the second stage. Or, to state the matter in one final form, the same results would probably have been found had the investigator merely varied size of fish in the second stage without ever having had a first stage.

Leaving the psychology of hypothetical fish, we will turn to another illustration of the point that two-stage experiments can be troublesome. Meaningfulness (defined broadly) influences the rate at which free-recall lists are learned. If we are interested in long-term retention as a function of meaningfulness, we cannot give a constant number of acquisition trials before introducing the retention interval, for most assuredly performance for the different lists will differ at the end of learning. Since long-term retention is acutely influenced by level of learning, we cannot tell whether any differences observed in retention are due to differences in level of learning or to differences in the rate at which forgetting occurs for the different levels of meaningfulness. In order to avoid this confounding, we must be sure that the level of learning achieved is the same for all levels of meaningfulness before the retention interval is introduced.

In summary: if we are interested in the carry-over of the presumed influence of an independent variable from one stage to another, and if that variable has an influence on the levels of performance on the first stage which will influence the second stage, we have a confounding. The cause of differences which occur in the second stage becomes indeterminate. We eliminate this confounding when possible by equalizing performance on the first stage across all levels of the independent variable. This is not always possible, particularly if the performance differences are very great during the first stage. We sometimes have to admit that the appropriate experiment cannot be done in a manner that would yield an unambiguous interpretation. Multistage experiments multiply the possibilities of confounding, and we must be alert to this fact.

REACTIVE MEASURES

In an early chapter a description was given of an investigator standing by a stop sign, holding a clipboard, with the intent of observing differences in stopping behavior as a function of the cost of the automobile. He found that all cars stopped. His presence undoubtedly influenced the behavior of the drivers. This is spoken of as a reactive measure in the sense that the act of measurement influenced the behavior being measured.

In a general sense, many experiments may involve reactive measures. A naive subject serving in a learning experiment may not behave in a perfectly natural way simply because he knows his performance is being monitored. If certain measurements, such as respiration rate, psycho-galvanic response, blood pressure, finger tremor, and so on, are taken by extensive equipment strapped on the subject, these measurements may be influenced by the newness of such a situation to the subject. Even mild anxiety may be elicited. Of course investigators are normally aware of such possibilities and may go to some length to remove the newness before introducing the independent variable. In the learning laboratory the subject may be given practice trials before being given the task of particular interest to the investigator. Reactive measures become of concern when the independent variable has an influence only under reactive conditions. In the usual laboratory study this is not likely to happen, but there are cases where it may. We need to illustrate reactive situations and to ask how we determine whether a measure is reactive.

A few pages back we gave an illustration of an experiment in which the independent variable was a campaign to increase milk consumption at school lunches. The measure was the amount of milk consumed as determined by records of purchases from week to week. Imagine that instead of using this measure we had stationed a large, fierce-looking man with a clipboard at the milk counter. Because the student had been exposed to the campaign to drink milk it would probably be quite apparent to him that this man was counting the students who took the milk. The mere presence of the man may therefore have increased the number of students who took milk. We are interested in the campaign as an independent variable, and not in the effect of a fierce-looking man, but we would not know where to place the cause for the increase in milk consumption. Perhaps the campaign would have had no influence were it not for the method of measurement. Therefore it was a completely reactive measure.

Let us consider another illustration of this type of measurement, one which is somewhat more subtle. Assume that we have developed a scale which measures political attitudes. Let us assume further that we want to discover if certain experimental procedures will change these attitudes. Finally, let us say that this was studied as a natural part of a course in political science. A classical way of doing such a study is to use a pretest-posttest design. The subjects are given the attitude test (pretest) and then, following the treatment, are tested again (posttest). Equivalent forms might be needed to avoid a memory effect, but we will not worry about the mechanics of actually carrying out the study. Of course, any changes between the pretest and the posttest are not clearly interpretable as being due to the treatment, so a control group given the pretest and posttest but not having the treatment is used as a reference point. Changes must be greater for the E Group than for the C Group to conclude that the treatment had an effect. We will assume that this was in fact found, and so we conclude that our experimental treatment instruction and readings during the political science course had caused the change in political attitudes. It just so happens, however, that we included another E Group in the study, a group which did not have the pretest but did have the treatment and the posttest. Upon examining the posttest scores for these subjects we find that they do not differ from either the pretest or posttest scores of the C Group. How can this be?

What seems to occur in such situations is similar to what we assumed to have occurred in the lunch room when the fierce-looking man was used to count the number of students who chose milk. If there had not been a campaign to drink milk there would be no obvious reason why a man would be counting something, and even if he were, there would be no reason to believe that what he was counting was of any special importance. In the case of the political attitudes, it appears that the pretest sensitized the subject to the particular area (political attitudes) to which hitherto he had given little thought. When the treatment was given he began to look at this information in the light of his original attitudes as expressed on the pretest. Consequently he was "sensitized" to a change in his attitudes. We see that we are dealing with a reactive measure because the influence of the independent variable was dependent upon the measurements of the pretest.

It can be seen that there is no fundamental reason why a pretest should have been used in the above study. Two random groups could have been employed, both being given the posttest, but with only one of the groups being given the treatment. However, we have observed that pretests are sometimes useful devices if we want to be sure that the E and C Groups do not differ prior to the treatment. The thinking therefore fits into the thinking of the matched-groups design. Nevertheless, as has been indicated, a phenomenon may occur only because this design is used.

In dealing with reactive measures we are not dealing with a completely new concept of measurement. We should note that if we extend to an experiment the question of whether a measure is reactive we are asking whether there is or is not an interaction between the two independent variables which are involved. One variable is the treatment, the other variable the pretest, with the response measure for all groups being the common final test (posttest). The matrix is as follows:

Pretest

		Yes	No
	Yes	1	2
Treatment	No	3	4

In this matrix the numbers are used merely to identify the cells. If the difference on the posttest between the groups in cells 2 and 4 is less than the difference between those in cells 1 and 3, the pretest would be judged to be reactive. The difference between these differences, of course, represents the interaction of the two variables. If the column totals do not differ (the sum of 1 and 3 does not differ from the sum of 2 and 4), the pretest would be judged not to be a reactive instrument.

At this point we will repeat the basic concern attending a reactive measure: with a reactive measure the independent variable has an influence different from that with a nonreactive measure. This represents another situation in which the degree of generality of a particular finding is of moment. An empirical finding may become very trivial under conditions where reactive measurements are involved. Therefore it should be given little weight in stating the generality of the effect of a given independent variable. The investigator with the clipboard, standing openly by the stop sign, was quite as effective as a uniformed policeman in influencing stopping behavior, so nothing of substance could be learned about the problem he set about to investigate until he removed himself from the scene and made his observations. If we had a hypothesis about frequency of eyeblinks during an auditory discrimination task, and if we tested this by positioning ourselves squarely in front of the subject and making a mark or pushing a counter every time the subject blinked, we would be very likely to get a reactive measure. A minimum amount of good judgment would eliminate reactive measurements as obvious as this.

STEPS TOWARD THEORY

When an experiment is reported we usually try to fit the results into a perspective that is more general than the particular findings. Almost any dedicated researcher will at first secretly conclude that his results represent the greatest step forward since Teflon. It is somewhat unfortunate that in the process of giving the results their needed perspective he is led to conclude (secretly, again) that it will be his next experiment that will cause the Nobel Prize Committee to call an alert. As was discussed briefly in the first chapter, there are a number of steps which may be involved in establishing a perspective for the results of an experiment. Grossly, these steps have to do with an empirical assessment and a theoretical assessment. There is no sharp division between the empirical and the theoretical, although at times we may seem to behave as if there were. The plan for this chapter is to proceed from the empirical through the theoretical in characterizing the modes of thinking which may be involved in fleshing out a report in the discussion section. In the following chapter the emphasis will be on the description of dimensions along which theoretical approaches may differ.

EMPIRICAL EVALUATION

Here is where we stand: we have analyzed the data for an experiment in which a given independent variable has been manipulated. We have confidence in this analysis so that statements concerning the outcome are not in doubt. We are ready to undertake the task of giving a perspective to the results. Since it is highly unlikely that this represents the first time in history that the influence of this particular independent variable has been investigated, our first step is to view the past findings in conjunction with the present ones, assessing the correspondence between them.

It is not inappropriate to ask why an investigator might study the effects of an independent variable when it has been studied in earlier experiments. Why should we find ourselves in a position of needing to establish an empirical perspective when others have investigated the same independent variable? Why was the experiment done in the first place? There are a number of reasons why this situation is a common one. Some of the reasons have been alluded to in earlier discussions, but we will repeat them here for completeness.

1. Occasionally a study is reported which some other investigator may find difficult to believe. The disbelief may be based on something as vague as an intuition (the results are counter intuitive). At the other extreme, the results may be discordant with an established theory. Still, why would we question the findings from this study? Three possibilities will be identified.

First, there is always a chance that a statistical aberration occurred. If a two-condition random-groups design is used there is the possibility that the random assignment of subjects to the groups went awry. Of course, if the experiment in question involved several different levels of the independent variable and the results are systematic with respect to these levels, the possibility of a statistical fluke is essentially nonexistent.

The second possible cause for questioning the results of a study is that a confounding of the independent variable was perceived. The new experiment is conducted to remove the confounding and to see if the finding remains.

The third possibility is that the previous result is viewed as being reliable, but quite specific to the static conditions of the experiment. That is, the result may be thought to be specific to the particular level or levels of other relevant variables which were held constant in the true sense. Perhaps the instructions given to the subject were such as to produce the outcome almost necessarily. Perhaps the rate of presentation was very fast or very slow and the belief is that the finding would only occur under these extreme conditions. In terms of the language with which we are familiar, two variables may interact sharply and the particular result in question may be thought to occur only with extreme combinations of the two variables. This alternative accepts the results as given, but questions their generality. In any event, for these three reasons or others, it is not uncommon to find investigators rushing to the replication laboratory when a novel finding is reported in a journal.

2. Some investigators believe that all experiments showing a relationship between an independent variable and behavior should be replicated as a routine matter. This point of view assumes that until a result has been found twice, we should not concern ourselves with it. It has even been proposed that replication of past experiments should be carried out as a matter of routine by candidates for the Master's degree. This approach toward the development of a body of knowledge seems difficult to defend. In the first place, replication for replication's sake is about as exciting as ordering a boiled egg in a gourmet restaurant. For a student who is developing his skills as an experimentalist in order to push the frontiers of knowledge ahead, replication can

seem a bit deadening. Any experiment involves much routine, even boring, work, but the anticipation of a new finding provides an affective level which in turn produces considerable staying power.

More importantly, replication (in whole or in part) of the conditions of a previous experiment will normally occur as a consequence of the orderly development of an area of research without replication being the only goal. Suppose an earlier experiment had shown that there was a difference in behavior produced by Variable A when manipulated at two levels, A1 and A3, with Variable B static at B1. In a subsequent experiment, another investigator studies the influence of two independent variables A and B, each at four levels. Details of the experiment (the task, the setting of static variables, and so on) are much the same as those of the earlier experiment. This would be a 16-condition experiment, with A being represented at A1, A2, A3, and A4, and with B being represented at corresponding levels. This design includes the conditions of the earlier experiment, as well as having the benefit of pushing much further ahead by asking about both A and B and their interaction.

When an area of research has a long history and a voluminous literature we may sometimes replicate a previous study without being aware of it. This means that our homework has not been done properly. The senior author once reported the outcome of an extensive experiment at a meeting. The report was given with great emphasis on the novelty of results and on their relevance to a particular theoretical position. At the conclusion of this oral presentation a member of the audience arose and informed the speaker that he and a colleague had reported essentially the same experiment some ten years earlier. And indeed they had. The embarrassment of the speaker could not be easily assuaged under such circumstances. Replication does occur unknowingly sometimes.

3. The final point repeats and extends the discussion of an issue introduced in an earlier chapter. An independent variable, although already studied in several previous experiments, may be manipulated in a further experiment in order to help establish the generality of its effects. We must remember that the generality of the influence of a variable can only be established by many experiments in which its influence is assessed across different tasks, across different classes of subjects, or across some sampling of different variables in all classes. This means that the levels of the static variables may change markedly from experiment to experiment. If it is found that the influence of a specific independent variable is maintained across these changes in the levels of the static variables, we may come to speak of the relationship between the variable and behavior as representing an empirical generalization. Some might choose to call it a general law. The relationship between amount learned and study time is a broad empirical generalization or a general law.

The empirical evaluation of a given set of results will almost always involve the assessment of the degree of correspondence of the findings with all of the previous findings. We will normally develop our knowledge of previous findings before we do the experiment; therein will usually lie the reason for undertaking it. We are frequently aided in our acquisition of background knowledge by periodic reviews which essentially tell us the empirical status of the influence of a given independent variable (along with others) in a given domain of research, e.g., problem solving. The value of these stock-taking reports cannot be overemphasized.

Each experiment we do will usually have empirical ties with the past. Like all knowledge, experimental knowledge is an accumulation of the efforts of many. It is our responsibility to use the products of these efforts to give an empirical perspective to the outcome of our particular experiment. We do not leave our results simply lying there, unattended by the past.

Interactions Again

Suppose that our finding for a given independent variable does not correspond with those found by several previous investigators. What are we to make of this? Given that our experiment has been carried out with meticulous attention to method (which, of course, will be the case), the empirical contradiction may represent a discovery of importance. It can mean only one thing, namely, that the independent variable interacts with some other variable. Our task is then to survey the previous studies in an effort to determine which static variable may have differed in level from that used in our experiment. There may be several such variables. We then try to make a decision as to which particular one is likely to be the critical one. Theoretical thinking may be involved in this decision, but in some way we try to arrive at a best guess as to the likely interacting variable. We then proceed to design a new experiment which will make a direct test: an experiment with two variables, the independent variable of interest and the one we believe is involved in the interaction.

The above approach may be illustrated by a situation existing in our laboratory at the moment. In an earlier study, subjects learned two paired-associate lists which formed an A-B, A-D interference paradigm. One group learned A-B on Monday and A-D on Thursday, then recalled A-D on Friday. Another group learned both lists on Thursday and, as had the first group, recalled A-D on Friday. The recall of A-D by the first group was far superior to that of the recall of the second group. It was as if the separation of the learning of the two lists by three days had provided some sort of temporal discrimination which minimized the interference between the two lists at the time of recall.

Given this finding, we set about to explore systematically the temporal separation of the two lists. To do this, we used four groups:

	Monday	Tuesday	Wednesday	Thursday	Friday
Group 1	A-B			A-D	Recall A-D
Group 2		A-B		A-D	Recall A-D
Group 3			A-B	A-D	Recall A-D
Group 4				A-B, A-D	Recall A-D

There was also another variable (length of retention interval) which need not concern us for the point to be made. We had anticipated, on the basis of the previous finding, that the recall of A-D would decrease systematically from Group 1 through Group 4. Note that Groups 1 and 4 are an ostensible replication of the earlier study. When we examined the results of this second experiment we found no difference in recall for the four groups and the level of recall was about the same as that shown by the group learning A-B and A-D on Thursday in the earlier experiment.

Once the gnashing of teeth had run its course, it seemed apparent that the two experiments must have differed on one or more variables which interacted with the temporal-separation variable. The original finding could have been a statistical "fluke" but the magnitude of the difference was so large that we chose not to use this "out." We could identify five differences between the two experiments.

1. The subjects, although college students in both experiments, could have differed in some critical way.

2. The lists were constructed of different materials in the two experiments, although in both cases the A-B, A-D relationship was present.

3. Different experimenters were used in the two studies.

4. The first experiment was done during a presidential election year, the second during a nonelection year.

5. The number of trials on A-B in the first experiment was 32, in the second, about 10 trials on the average. The level of learning of A-D was the same in both experiments, about 10 trials on the average.

For reasons which would take us too far afield if we detailed them, we reached the conclusion that the likely interacting variable was the fifth listed above—the number of trials on A-B. This supposes, therefore, that the temporal separation of the two lists will have an influence only when there is also some minimum unknown difference in the number of trials on the two lists. An experiment now underway varies both the temporal separation and the number of trials on the A-B list. In general summary, it may be repeated that the inability to replicate a previous result is valuable insofar as it leads to the identification of an interacting variable.

There is an odd counterpart to the discovery of interacting variables when replication fails. This usually occurs when we try to bring a theoretical understanding to the influence of a given independent variable. Sometimes investigators try to find situations in which the effect of a given independent variable will be destroyed, or at least, grossly changed. To say this another way, they may try to find a situation in which the levels of the static variables are such as to destroy or blunt the influence of the independent variable of interest. This type of finding would identify an interacting variable. It is assumed that such knowledge would help us understand how the independent variable of central interest produces its effect. There is a current illustration of this situation.

If an item in a free-recall list is presented twice within the list on a single study trial, its recall will be much lower if these two occurrences occupy adjacent positions than if they are separated by other items. Attempts to get a theoretical purchase on this phenomenon have been hampered by the fact that no investigator has been able to find a situation in which the magnitude of the phenomenon varies appreciably. The difference has been found in experiment after experiment across all types of subjects, materials, and so on. Theoretical accounts (it is believed) would be more easily formulated if a situation could be found in which the phenomenon was no longer present.

The material covered so far in this chapter is related to a single matter, namely, that the report of an experiment will usually include an assessment of how the results have changed (if at all) the empirical status of the effects of the independent variable or variables manipulated in the experiment. If one has been so fortunate as to discover a truly new phenomenon, this part of the discussion section is, to say the least, abbreviated.

EMPIRICAL STATEMENTS

Research is commonly built up around broadly conceived phenomena. Visual illusions as a class would be an example of this kind of phenomenon; forgetting would be another, as would classical conditioning. These gross phenomena are usually given more specific operational representation in subphenomena which evolve from frequently used procedures (paradigms) for experimental study. Visual illusions are represented by a number of different specific illusions, such as the horizontal-vertical illusion, the moon illusion, or the Müeller-Lyer illusion. Any one of these might engage the attention of an investigator for several years as he worked out the influence of specific independent variables on the magnitude of the illusion. The study of forgetting has revolved around procedures believed to vary interference, the two common paradigms being called retroactive inhibition and proactive inhibition. Classical conditioning procedures may be broken down into key subphenomena such as acquisition, extinction, and spontaneous recovery.

The empirical base of a discipline rests on the experimentally discovered relationships between dependent and independent variables. These are customarily organized around key phenomena such as those noted above. We may see how this might work out for a particular case, retroactive inhibition. This generalized phenomenon was given operational definition in the immediately previous chapter, but we will repeat it here:

	Task A	Task B	Recall Task A
E Group	Yes	Yes	Yes
C Group	Yes	No	Yes

This diagram, plus a verbal statement to the effect that retention of List 1 must be less for the E Group than for the C Group, constitutes the operational definition of retroactive inhibition. An operational definition is a statement of the conditions needed to demonstrate a phenomenon. Note that the critical defining procedures are two in number. First, the E Group is given a second task (commonly called interpolated task) that the C Group is not given. This specifies the critical independent variable. Second, behavior must differ in a specified way following the two differential treatments.

This is a very general operational definition in the sense that it can accommodate enormous variations in detail. There are many, many independent variables which can be studied within this paradigm. We would still speak of them all as dealing with retroactive inhibition because they all fit within the paradigm. We can ask about the influence of different kinds of materials or tasks, different levels of training on both tasks, different temporal relationships between the tasks, different types of retention measurements, and others. The body of experimental facts which has developed over many years as a result of such manipulations is said to constitute the empirical knowledge about retroactive inhibition. Similarly, bodies of evidence like those noted earlier will grow up around other gross phenomena.

In principle it would be possible at some point in time to judge that we have learned at the empirical level about all we are ever going to learn about a given gross phenomenon. This would imply that all relevant independent variables influencing a phenomenon had been discovered and that the empirical relationships between these independent variables and the phenomenon of interest (e.g., retroactive inhibition) and their interactions give a sum of this knowledge. What this means is that based on past findings we could predict with great accuracy what is going to happen for any manipulation within this key paradigm. In this accumulation of knowledge as described we have attributed no cause for the phenomenon other than that implied in its definition, e.g., the interpolated learning is responsible for retroactive inhibition.

Is it satisfactory to be content with empirical statements? When you make your empirical evaluation in the discussion section are you, or should you, be done with the report? On this matter some will answer yes, but many more will answer no. We count ourselves among the latter group. We believe that theoretical thinking must be brought to bear on our data whenever possible. Predictions may come from massive amounts of data built around a given phenomenon but both prediction and economy in research may arise from theoretical thinking. Theoretical thinking also leads to something which, for the moment, we will call better understanding. Theory can serve as a vehicle to bring together a host of apparently discrete empirical statements into a common framework. But this is getting ahead of our plan. At present we are simply asserting that we do not believe we should be entirely content with the empirical.

From empirical evidence we can predict without hesitation that if a subject learns a paired-associate list and if his memory is tested for it one week later, there will be forgetting. Indeed, we could predict within a very small margin of error how much the average student will forget over that period of time. Theory should tell us what, correlated with the passage of time, is responsible for the loss. Based on available evidence we can predict with high confidence that in almost any situation (nontrivial in nature) an item repeated in adjacent positions in a free-recall list will be remembered less well than one for which the two occurrences are separated by other items. This ability to predict has not satisfied most investigators; they have been most persistent in their search for a theoretical perspective that will suggest a cause for this phenomenon, a cause which is stated at a different level of discourse from that given by the procedures defining the phenomenon. Prediction is a very important product of massive empirical research, but it is not what we mean when we say we search for an understanding at a different level of discourse. This different level of discourse is inherent in most forms of theoretical thinking.

The operationally defined phenomena in a given domain are viewed here as something to explain. We try to explain them by a variety of means, all of which are said to involve theoretical thinking of some sort. We are approaching these forms of thinking by very small steps.

EMPIRICAL RESTRICTION

It would seem axiomatic to assert that the fewer the number of distinctly different empirical phenomena with which we have to deal the easier it would be to reach an understanding of them or to explain them. When we define phenomena operationally in terms of basic key paradigms used to demonstrate them, we are attempting to keep the number of distinctly different phenomena needing explanation to a minimum. Suppose, for example, that for any minor change of an independent variable within the retroactive-inhibition paradigm we assert that we are dealing with a new phenomenon. In one experiment we give five trials on Task 1 and in another we give eight trials, with all other procedures comparable. The difference in the retention of the E and C Groups in the two cases would probably differ. We surely should not conclude that we are dealing with two distinctly different phenomena. Otherwise logic would lead us to believe that every experiment produces a unique phenomenon since it is doubtful that two identical experiments have ever been performed.

In fact, we have already made a theoretical decision of sorts when we ask about the generality of the effects of an independent variable across experiments. In so doing we have made a judgment about nature; we have judged that superficially different situations should not be taken to mean that there is complete independence in the factors underlying the behavior. All of the behavior observed in the different situations may stem from the same factor or factors. If every experiment is assumed to involve a factor that is qualitatively different from the factor involved in every other experiment, we might as well close up shop. We cannot presume that nature would be so constituted. Rather, we proceed on the assumption that the number of different factors underlying the behavior we measure is sharply limited. We legislate economy in our thinking when we try to arrive at empirical generalizations.

The necessity of economy in thought is not new to us when we set about trying to determine basic factors underlying behavior. We go through this form of thinking whenever we produce an abbreviated description of a set of data, i.e., when we state the empirical relationship between an independent variable and behavior for a single experiment. Guzy and Axelrod had 9600 observations. No mind can comprehend these without abstracting commonalities. This reduction process is accomplished by determining values which are representative of all observations under common conditions, the common conditions being the different levels of the independent variables. When we arrive at empirical generalizations across experiments we are going through the same processes insofar as we try to arrive at a simple, direct statement that reflects the commonality of all of them.

As we push toward theoretical thinking we do not change this; we try to abstract commonalities underlying empirical generalizations. Empirical restriction is such a step. In carrying out empirical restriction we try to see if we can bring together ostensibly different phenomena by observing the common properties involved in the procedures used to study them. If we are successful we have reduced the number of different phenomena which need independent explanation. This is not an easy matter, for there are no set criteria which can be imposed to determine what we mean by same and different phenomena. We will return to this later. We first need some illustrations of the thinking involved in empirical restriction.

Guzy and Axelrod believed that interaural shifts in listening, required by the fact that the signal alternated rapidly between the two ears, were to be viewed as motor responses. Therefore, as with rapidly produced motor responses, fatigue occurs. These investigators further believed that independent variables which produced decrements in motor responding would likewise produce decrements in interaural shifts. They studied factors influencing performance on click counting and on a more obvious motor task, looking beyond the differences in procedural details involved in studying each. They suggested that the underlying factors between the situations must have commonality. Click counting was not viewed as a unique phenomenon which should stand apart from work in an ostensibly different domain. It was perceived as being analogous to the rapid responding required in many motor tasks; rapid shifts in responding were seen as the common procedural requirement in both. This form of operational envelopment will serve to reduce or restrict the number of independent empirical generalizations with which we have to deal. If Guzy and Axelrod are correct in their analogical thinking, a theory which explains the performance in the one situation should explain it in the other.

Consider another case. Suppose we are going to study attitude change. The procedure might be as follows. We first measure the attitudes of the subjects on a given topic or area of interest. Then for the E Group we undertake some instructional program designed to change the attitude in question. The C Group is not given the instructional program. Sometime later we measure both groups to ascertain if a change has occurred for the E Group that is greater than the change for the C Group. These procedures, it can be seen, are quite commensurate with those used in studying retroactive inhibition. If an attitude is thought of as a learned disposition, then changing it requires training in a new, different disposition. Then the paradigm of attitude change and the paradigm of retroactive inhibition may have not only high operational comparability but also the same underlying factors producing the behavioral changes.

These illustrations suggest that when we do an experiment in a relatively new area of research we should be sensitive to the possibility that we may be using procedures that have also been used in other superficially different domains of research. To identify our so-called new phenomenon with an old one is, if correct, an economical step in that it restricts the number of distinctly different phenomena which would require explanation. The critical question which must be asked and then answered, is whether or not the identification is appropriate. We do not want to dismiss one phenomenon as being merely a special case of another if they are not related in a fundamental way. How do we tell? It is probably necessary to take two steps, although some might be satisfied with one. First, the two phenomena (the old and the new) should be related in the same way to common independent variables. But how many independent variables do we have to manipulate before we reach a decision that the operational identification was or was not appropriate? Suppose we test five independent variables and find that four of them produce the same results but that the other one does not. There is no pat answer to the handling of these findings. This is why the second step may be necessary. The second step is that of seeing if a single theory can handle the empirical facts in both domains. Even a difference in the effect of some independent variables may not require us to abandon the identification if these discrepancies can be given a theoretical rationale.

The attempt to unify two or more areas of research as a consequence of the correspondence in the procedures used to demonstrate the phenomena in the two areas is frequently productive of disagreement. One such disagreement has been in full bloom for some time in memory research. This disagreement pertains to short-term memory versus long-term memory. Procedurally, short-term memory is arbitrarily identified as dealing with retention intervals up to (let us say) 30 seconds and long-term memory is identified with intervals longer than 30 seconds. Several independent variables (although not all) are known to have essentially the same influence on performance in the two situations. Still, there is some resistance to the acceptance of the notion that basically the two paradigms tap the same processes. In this case some believe there are theoretical reasons for keeping them separate, in contrast to the point made above where a theoretical rationale may also be used as a means of unification. However this may be, the basic point is that we should be alert to operational restriction as a means of economizing. This cannot be done hastily; success in the endeavor usually requires not only subsequent research but also theoretical leverage. We do not lightly collapse two domains of research into one.

INTERVENING PROCESSES

We are considering matters which might govern a person's thinking in giving a perspective to a particular experiment. Thus far we have been pressing strongly on empirical matters. We have talked about the need to fit our results into those previously obtained by other investigators. This recognizes the importance of arriving at empirical generalizations, statements which represent the relationships between an independent variable and performance which are not limited to a highly specific set of conditions. In effect, we try to state what it is that a theory needs to explain if we choose to go beyond this empirical level. In a further effort to restrict the number of different empirical generalizations, it has been suggested that we look across ostensibly different domains of research to see if we can merge them because of the operational comparability involved.

In discussing ways of reaching empirical generalizations we have not found it possible to avoid completely what might be said to be theory-like language. We have, for example, talked about underlying factors. Although this is relatively neutral language, it does have theoretical overtones because it implies a different level of discourse from that implied by empirical statements. We are now prepared to consider these matters directly.

Empirical statements can be made in such a manner as to remain entirely "outside" the organism. In a manner of speaking, we feed independent variables into the organism and observe the corresponding behavior. Our statements are limited to the relationship between these two sets of events. Although we know the organism is an intermediary, we do not let this influence our statements. We may now start, gingerly, to remove ourselves from this empirical position and to take the initial steps toward more obvious theoretical or explanatory thinking than has been manifest thus far. The first step involves the "insertion" into the organism of certain intervening processes.

We know that in the animal laboratory, following removal of reward or following removal of the unconditioned stimulus, a previously acquired response will more or less gradually cease to occur. There are two ways in which investigators may think about the term involved (extinction) which identifies these operations. If we want to remain strictly at the empirical level we simply identify the stimulus manipulations and the performance differences which are necessary to demonstrate the phenomenon. This implies no causal process other than the independent variable (removal of reward). Some investigators, however, may choose to think of this in a second way. They will say that the observed relationship between reward removal and cessation of responding was caused by a process called extinction. In other words, a process "inside" of the organism, a process produced by the removal of the reward, in turn produced the cessation of responding. This may be schematized:

Removal of Reward $[\rightarrow$ Extinction Process $\rightarrow]$ Cessation of Responding

To internalize processes in this manner really has not changed anything. It is the mode of thought which leads to such internalization that is important. Very shortly we will find that we may wish to insert intervening processes which are further and further removed from the empirical. For the moment, however, we must realize that in principle any operationally defined relationship may be thought of in terms of an intervening process. We could say that retroactive inhibition was the cause of the difference between the E and C Groups; we could say the same about generalization, altruism, and learning.

There are certain phenomena which by their nature almost seem to demand being thought of in terms of internal processes. Learning is one of these; so is motivation. We could operationally define motivation, for example, by the relationship between differences in the monetary value given for successful performance and the correlated change in performance on a task. But it seems quite natural to think of motivation as an internal process which changes as the amount of incentive changes and thereby influences the performance:

Incentive Magnitude [→ Motivation →] Performance Differences

Personal-like phenomena seem difficult to keep out of the organism—but (we repeat) to internalize them, and to do that only, has not really changed the empirical or increased our understanding. It is, however, the beginning of a mode of thought that can readily accommodate theorizing which involves internal processes. We will proceed to the simple case in which the internal process becomes a theoretical tool.

ASSUMED INTERNAL PROCESSES: EMPIRICALLY DERIVED

In this form of theorizing the investigator uses an empirically demonstrated fact about behavior derived in one situation as a part of a theoretical system in another situation. In Chapter 5 we evaluated the use of theoretical notions to obtain a meaningful interpretation of the influence of subject variables. As one illustration, the empirical phenomenon of closure was used as a theoretical device in an attempt to understand differences in reading performance. This illustration (which was hypothetical) represents in minimum form the use of an empirical phenomenon as a theoretical intervening process. Also in Chapter 5 an illustration was given which involved the use of implicit verbal responses as a theoretical tool. We will now extend this idea as the first of two illustrations of the theoretical use of an empirical phenomenon.

In word-association procedures subjects are presented one word at a time under instructions to say or to write the first word they think of as each word is presented. From the results of these procedures, using a number of words and many subjects, tables can be prepared showing the number or percentage of subjects who gave the same word as a response to a presented word. For example, to the stimulus word "lemon," the word *sour* may be given by about 45 percent of college students. Perhaps 12 percent may produce *yellow*, 8 percent *juice*, and so on. To the word "black," perhaps 70 percent will respond with *white*. Of course, there are words for which there is very little convergence on the response; the most frequently given responses to the word "fear" are *hate* and *afraid*, but these are given by only a small proportion of the subjects. Whatever is responsible for these differences is not of importance here; we know we can examine word-association tables and can find a number of stimulus words to which the same response was given, for example, by at least 50 percent of the subjects. As will be seen momentarily, data of this type have been used as the basis of a theoretical development.

A simple technique for studying recognition memory may be carried out as follows: The subject is presented a long series of more or less unrelated words, each for, let us say, five seconds. As each word is presented the subject must decide whether the word had (YES), or had not (NO), been presented earlier in the series. Two types of errors are made. There will be some misses which consist of saying NO when in fact the words had been presented earlier. The other type, called false positives, involves saying YES when the words had not been presented earlier. What would produce false positives?

One theory that has been proposed to account for at least some of the false positives is known as the implicit associational response theory (IAR theory). This theory makes two assumptions. First it assumes that the associational responses which are overtly produced under instructions in word-association procedures are also produced implicitly in a situation in which the subject is asked to remember words. In word-association procedures, "black" produces *white*; if "black" were a word in the recognition task, it is assumed that many subjects produce *white* implicitly. The second assumption is that the subject cannot discriminate between the words actually presented in the recognition task and the words he produces implicitly. Therefore, if "black" occurs in the recognition task, 75 percent of the subjects should produce *white* implicitly. If subsequently "white" is actually presented for the first time, the subject will respond YES—a false positive.

If a number of false positives occur in a predictable fashion, and if the frequency with which they occur is greater than that for control words, the theory would seem to be useful in helping to account for false positives. A theory which accounts for only one phenomenon is not helping matters; it would not be economical to have a different theory for each phenomenon. There are a number of additional predictions which follow from the theory, one of which will be described.

Suppose we present the subject a list of words for free recall, and in the list both the words "black" and "white" occur, although separated by other words in the list. The theory presumes that when "black" is presented for study the subject produces *white* implicitly. Furthermore, because the two words are associated in both directions, when "white" is presented for study we may expect that *black* will occur implicitly. Each word will then have occurred once as a presented word, and once as an IAR. Assuming, finally, that increased frequency of occurrence increases learning, we would expect these two words to be better recalled than would control words (words which are not benefited by the IARs).

Another theory which uses empirically derived assumptions is known as frequency theory and it has been found useful in accounting for various phenomena associated with recognition memory. We will again examine the empirical basis first. It can be shown that all of us carry with us as adults an enormous amount of relative-frequency information of recurring events. Some examples: we are able to make quite accurate discriminations of differences in the frequencies with which different words occur in books, newspapers, and magazines. We just seem to know that we have seen the word *cat* more frequently than the word *cad*, *wall* more frequently than *wail*, and *ambitious* more frequently than *ambergris*. So too, we would probably be correct if we judged that we had seen more gas stations than floral shops in the USA, and that there are more potatoes than artichokes eaten in the western world.

The ability or skill we possess in assimilating frequencies of recurring events can be studied directly in the laboratory, using neutral stimuli if necessary. We would present squares, circles, triangles, and other figures with varying frequencies (in such a way that direct counting is not possible) and then ask for judgments concerning either relative or absolute frequencies. Studies of this kind show this skill to be quite highly developed. Frequency theory uses this skill as an internal process; it internalizes the "counting" and assumes that the discrimination of apparent frequency differences is responsible for the performance on certain tasks in which the frequency discrimination is not at all apparent in the overt behavior. We will examine the application of the theory to one task.

In the verbal-discrimination task the subject is presented a series of pairs of words, one member of each pair having been arbitrarily designated as the correct word (C word), the other as the incorrect word (I word). The subject's job is that of learning to identify the correct word in each pair. Frequency theory aims at a description of how this is accomplished. There are several assumptions. In presenting the pairs the subject is shown a pair, A-B, and then is shown the correct word, in this case A, alone. Thus A has been presented twice, B once on a single trial. The first assumption, therefore, is that this objective frequency differential has a representation in the subject's memory. The second assumption is that the subject performs by trying to apply a rule which is applicable to all pairs. The third assumption is that the rule most applicable is "choose the word in each pair with the higher frequency." The fourth assumption is that over trials the apparent frequency grows more rapidly for the C word than for the I word. There are a number of possible reasons for this that need not concern us.

This relatively simple theory has led to a number of predictions, predictions concerning the relevance of independent variables which had not been manipulated prior to the formulation of the theory. The basic idea in making predictions is that of "thinking of" procedures which will change the frequency differential between the right and wrong words in each pair. More elaborately dressed, these are called deductions from the premises or axioms of the theory. For example, if each word is used as a C word in one pair and an I word in another, the task should be impossible to learn. There is no rule which can be followed because the frequency of both I and C words will be equivalent. Tests confirm this expectation. As a further illustration, suppose an I word is used in two different pairs, with each C word being used only once. This procedure would also tend to equalize the frequency for I and C words and make the task difficult. On the other hand, if all of the C words were given several trials of free-recall learning prior to becoming the C words in a verbal-discrimination task, performance should be essentially perfect after one trial because the free-recall learning has already given the C words high situational frequency.

The theory assumes that the subject applies a rule. In the usual verbal-discrimination task there is no rule that applies to all of the pairs other than differential frequency. However, if we printed all the C words in red ink and all of the I words in black ink, the rule applied would certainly be a color rule rather than a frequency rule.

One of the values of theorizing at the level illustrated by IAR theory and frequency theory is the obvious possibilities present for correcting details of the theory. For example, frequency theory, as stated above, assumes a two-to-one ratio between the C and I words in a pair after one trial. Suppose, however, the subject implicitly rehearses the C word twice to himself. Does this increase the apparent frequency of the word correspondingly? To make such a determination we can return to the procedure wherein frequency judgments are requested directly. We manipulate the independent variable in question, determine the consequences for apparent frequency, and modify the theoretical expectations for verbal-discrimination learning accordingly.

This ability to correct and refine, if successful, is a very valuable and necessary adjunct for the development of any theory. At the same time we are constrained in this type of theorizing by the known empirical relationships we are using theoretically. The characteristics assumed for the intervening processes are identical to the known empirical relationships as derived from studies in which frequency discriminations are examined directly. If, in a frequency-judging test, we find that a difference of three-to-one in the frequency of two events is perceived 95 percent of the time by our subjects, we assume that this same proportion will hold in applying the frequency rule by our subjects in verbal-discrimination learning. It should be apparent that if there were obvious reasons why this correspondence should be modified, modification would be permissible, but any appreciable number of such modifications may begin to change the nature of the theorizing. It would be moved toward the type of theory in which we postulate intervening processes, a type to which we will turn momentarily. There is one further matter that should be mentioned about the use of assumptions based on empirical data.

As frequency theory was presented above, it may have seemed that we already had at hand a large body of data concerning frequency discriminations. This was not the case. The theory merely assumed originally that a subject could make the frequency discriminations required because it was known that some level of frequency difference did yield a discrimination. Adequate development of the theory required a corresponding development in the manipulation of variables influencing frequency discriminations per se. The two areas, unified by the theory, have grown hand in hand. Nevertheless, one could imagine a situation in which a body of relationships, thoroughly developed in one area, could be applied theoretically in another new area and thus hasten and systematize the development of the new area.

ASSUMED INTERNAL PROCESSES: POSTULATED

Earlier it was noted that investigators differ in the way they think about operationally defined phenomena. Some, it was noted, may think of extinction not as merely a name for a phenomenon but as an internal process which is responsible for the behavior change. For the development of this section we need to remove or externalize the name again. In the case of extinction we simply identify the difference between E and C Groups as the phenomenon called extinction. Then as a theoretical venture we postulate a process to account for extinction. By postulation we mean only that as a theoretical device we are going to assert the existence of a process, X, which causes or is responsible for the phenomenon we call extinction. Or, we might give X some physiological flavor by saying that extinction is caused by a neural inhibitory process.

As another illustration, consider retroactive inhibition strictly as an empirical phenomenon. We might propose (postulate) that retroactive inhibition is caused by interference. A single postulated process used as a causal mechanism must vary precisely in amount or magnitude as the empirical facts demand. If retroactive inhibition increases as the degree of interpolated learning increases, it must also be said that interference varies accordingly. It is perhaps obvious that to postulate a one-to-one relationship between the magnitude of a single assumed process and the magnitude of the empirical relationships for which it is presumed to account does not advance our understanding. We have gotten nowhere. It is not possible to predict any new phenomena.

No approach has explanatory value unless at least two processes are involved. Furthermore, in addition to the two processes being postulated, either one or both of two additional requirements must be met. First, the magnitude of the change in the two postulated processes must differ for at least one independent variable. Second, the influence of the assumed processes on the response measure (performance) must differ for comparable changes in the magnitude of the two processes. Either of these will fit the general case that the two assumed processes must interact in their influence on the response measure. This is a bit complicated because we are dealing with several sources of variation. We know what an interaction is between two independent variables when the response measure is used as a basis for indexing the interaction. To understand the theoretical interaction of postulated processes one may think of two internal processes that show different relationships as a function of a given independent variable or that show differential influence on the response measure as they vary in magnitude.

It was stated above that we must have at least two intervening processes if a theory is to have explanatory value. With certain approaches this requirement may be viewed in a different way. One could assume a single intervening process which has different relationships across the levels of one independent variable as a function of a second independent variable. Frequency theory, as described earlier, might be said to fit this type. The growth of apparent frequency over trials was assumed to be less for incorrect items than for correct items. On the other hand, we could view the growth of apparent frequency for incorrect items and the growth for correct items as representing two different processes. In any event, the critical objective in constructing a theory is to insert assumed interactions among the intervening processes.

To illustrate the necessity of assuming such interactions if the postulational approach is to be serviceable, let us first consider an impotent case. Two intervening processes are assumed, X and Y. These two processes are assumed to change in precisely the same way for each independent variable and they combine in a simple additive way to determine performance. Given these assumptions, there can be no interaction; it is like dividing a single postulated process into two subprocesses with exactly the same properties. X and Y have no independence under such circumstances and a theory couched in this manner would have no predictive capacity. On the other hand, if for one or more independent variables the changes in X and in Y are assumed to differ, we no longer have a simple matching of the internal processes with the measured behavior. Such an approach may well have predictive power. Let us illustrate this.

Theorists using the postulational approach in learning theories have frequently made use of an interaction between a process which is assumed to produce an increase in performance and process which is assumed to inhibit performance. This is illustrated in Figure 7.1. The independent variable is along the baseline with some magnitude measure (of hypothetical processes marked off in arbitrary units) along the ordinate. Assume a theory is stated so that the growth in the positive process is as indicated, a process which stands in a one-to-one relationship with performance. As postulated, the inhibitory process is much less in magnitude than the positive process, and it increases at a slower rate than does the positive process. The negative process is assumed to depress performance in a one-to-one relationship. Thus, the two assumed processes interact as a function of the independent variable, but the positive and negative effects on performance are equivalent for each unit of each process. These two assumed processes predict performance as indicated; the negative component is simply subtracted from the positive component to obtain the expected performance relationship.

A system somewhat similar to the one just described has been used in accounting for certain facts in learning motor skills. It could be assumed that each trial (in this case an independent variable) increases the positive or learning component. Practice, however, is assumed to produce a negative factor, such as fatigue, which depresses performance while having no influence on the positive or learning component that "really" exists. It "subtracts" from the performance as determined by the positive or learning process. Some independent variables will be particularly critical in causing the magnitude of the inhibitory process to vary. If practice periods are very short, and long rest periods intervene, the magnitude of the inhibitory process would be kept at a minimum, and the performance would be essentially in a one-to-one relationship with the learning component. One prediction that is repeatedly confirmed is that if practice proceeds without rest periods for some time, and if then a rest period is inserted, performance will literally jump when practice is resumed. This prediction is based on a further assumption that with rest, the negative process dissipates or disappears whereas the positive process does not.

Let us return to the statement made earlier that to have predictive power the two processes must interact for at least one independent variable. It was stated that unless the theory includes this provision, true prediction (hence, a test of the theory) is not possible. A further elaboration of this point may be useful. Suppose, for example, that the positive and negative processes in Figure 7.1 always grew at the same rate for any independent variable which influenced them at all. If this situation existed, the prediction would always be that performance would be a constant. That is, given that the two lines are

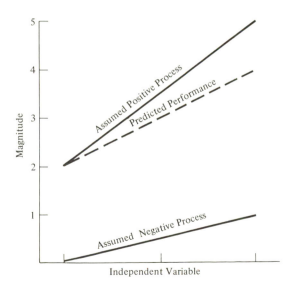

Fig. 7.1. An illustration of the postulation of two intervening processes and their interaction. See text for complete explanation.

parallel, the difference between them at any point along the baseline would be the same. Even if performance was shown to be constant, the assumption of the two processes is not necessary to mediate it. We may just as well assume a single process and then we do not have a theory because the assumed process would mirror performance exactly. On the other hand, we could still have a predictive theory even if we assume equal rates of change for the positive and negative processes by assuming in addition that the two processes have differential rates of decay, as might occur over an interval of relative rest. However the theorist chooses to accomplish it, there must be an interaction between the changes in the postulated processes for at least one independent variable if the theory is to show life.

Of course, the postulational approach is governed initially by available facts in the research domain for which it is applicable. The postulated processes are assigned characteristics (relationship with at least one independent variable plus its relationship with performance) required to mediate the known facts. Having made these initial assignments, novel predictions may emerge. But, as new facts are obtained which do not quite fit the expectations, it may be necessary to change the original assignments in order to mediate the new facts. All theories, it seems, require this corrective process to remain serviceable.

Theories using postulated processes can become complicated, sometimes beyond easy comprehension. We might assume three or four intervening processes which interact in various ways depending upon the independent variables being manipulated. Without help, under these circumstances, the mind becomes boggled. The help must come from mathematical expressions of the relationships and thence from equations which will coordinate the expressions to allow predictions.

Computers have been attractive to many theorists and not only because of the enormous help they give in solving mathematically-expressed theories. Some choose to identify intervening processes with certain of the capabilities of the computer. There is an input and an output (independent and dependent variables), and the transformations which may be programmed into the computer between the input and output may be given psychological meaning.

As will be discussed more fully in the next chapter, the mathematically oriented theorist, whether computer referenced or not, must be quite unambiguous in his assumptions concerning the intervening processes he postulates. The virtues of this are unquestioned—if it can be done.

Theoretical thinking is frequently guided by what might be called flow diagrams. These diagrams show the assumed flow of events and the "structures" which are assumed to play roles in the area of behavior under investigation. The many flow diagrams which have been proposed in the areas of information processing and memory usually reflect a minimum of three structures, as shown in Figure 7.2. The stimuli from the outside world must somehow enter the system if they are to have an influence. This fact is reflected in the interface structure which may be likened to the visual or auditory modalities. The neurally transformed stimuli (transformed by the interface) then enter the short-term system and may, under certain situations (differing for different theorists), be transferred to long-term memory. Figure 7.2 does not show an arrow leading to the dependent variable because behavior presumably can be "requested" at any point in the sequence. A simple reaction-time experiment would tap behavior at the interface. A vocabulary test would involve all three structures.

These diagrams must be viewed as heuristic devices, devices which help orient the reader to the thinking of the theorist. The diagrams per se do not represent a theory. As will be discussed more fully in the next chapter, they represent examples of pretheoretical assumptions. They provide the orientation within which the theory will be developed. The developed theory must tell us how particular independent variables are handled in the system and thereby how they influence performance. The theorizing will adhere to the basic premise that to be useful there must be interactions somewhere in the assumptions that are made to give psychological meaning to the system.

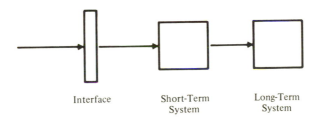

Interface   Short-Term   Long-Term
                 System   System

Fig. 7.2. A simplified flow diagram frequently used in the area of information processing and memory.

8

DIMENSIONS OF THEORY

In the previous chapter, as some of the steps leading toward theory were described, the progression was essentially from the relatively safe and secure empirical or data level to the abstract level where we were "putting" imaginary processes or mechanisms inside the organism. A distinction was made between empirically derived processes and postulated processes. As would be expected, theories frequently represent a mixture of empirically derived and postulated processes. Furthermore, when we start to analyze theoretical proposals, we find a number of different dimensions or characteristics which may be used to describe theories in addition to those given in the previous chapter. A more comprehensive understanding of theoretical approaches requires that some attention be paid to these further characteristics.

Theory building, when viewed broadly, is a very free-wheeling enterprise simply because theories can differ in so many ways. It is probably proper to say that any discipline imposed on theory-building activity should be minimal in amount. Theories are usually described as being useful or not useful in doing the job for which they were intended. Still, there may be some gross rules we might follow in order to increase the likelihood that a theory will be useful. Some of these will arise as the discussion proceeds. Finally, after examining some of the dimensions along which theories may differ, we will get back to the working situation and see what guidelines might be used as the beginning student in experimental psychology begins to practice theory-like thinking when he has a particular set of data before him.

EXPLICITNESS-TESTABILITY

Both of these terms should produce nods of approbation and might seem to deny the need for discussion. The critical question, however, concerns the manner in which we make our theories explicit, and thereby insure that they are testable. Some background comments will help lead toward an answer. Specifically, the issue of explicitness necessitates an examination of the notion of a model.

145

A model is a known system of relationships in one area of discourse which is used as an explanatory system in a different area of discourse. We may first relate this form of theorizing to previous discussion. Assume that we had available a rather well worked out set of relationships between independent variables and frequency assimilation. If we used these laws or relationships as an explanatory system in recognition memory, it would be a form of modeling. As discussed earlier, frequency theory did not develop in this way; the laws of frequency assimilation and their application to recognition memory have developed simultaneously. But it would have been possible to have had a fairly well developed set of laws for frequency assimilation which was used as the model for a theory of recognition memory. In this case, the area of discourse from which the model came and the area for which it was used as an explanatory model are not far removed inasmuch as they are both psychological in substance. But this need not be the case. We might take the system of relationships existing in a telephone system and use it as a model to understand the relationships known as memory. The idea would be to see if the functioning of memory could be understood by applying a known set of laws which exist within the telephone system. One might even model memory in terms of the plumbing system in a home; there are clearly inputs, outputs, and storage in both systems so the idea might not be as farfatched as it seems initially.

What we should emphasize about modeling of this sort is that when we postulate such a correspondence between, for example, the telephone system and memory, we are also bringing with it particular known properties or relationships within the telephone system. If we started our theory from scratch, we would have to postulate or guess at the relationships within memory. If these interrelationships are already known (in the telephone system), we have an initial economy. Furthermore, when the basic features of the telephone system are identified with the presumed corresponding features of memory, a very explicit theory results. The laws of the functioning of the telephone system must hold for the memory system or the analogical venture is denied its usefulness.

At somewhat the opposite extreme, we might start with a certain gross metaphorical relationship between a physical structure and memory and then gradually develop a theory. Assume that we choose to think of memory as consisting of an enormous number of storage bins. Whenever we learn something new, the memory for it goes into a new bin, this bin being determined randomly. Repetition of the same event will, we may assume, result in an increase in the number of memory units in the appropriate bin. Given these initial assumptions, we may begin our initial tests of the adequacy of the theory thus far. How do we retrieve a memory? Should we assume that we randomly sample the bins until we find the appropriate one (how we would know it was appropriate is ignored)? A little thought will show that this will never do; there are thousands of bins and to sample randomly until we hit the correct bin would take hours and hours. We then return and change a basic assumption. We now assume that memories are not stored randomly but rather they are stored in some organized fashion. Still we find this will not do alone, for when we have a retrieval inquiry, there must be some way of shunting the inquiry to a particular area in which the memory is stored. We might postulate a "master shunter" which handles this function. As we pursue the development of a theory using this gross mechanical model we will probably soon find that it just is not going to work because within any reasonable bounds of simplicity we cannot make it explicit enough to mediate predictions.

The more abstract forms of modeling use a mathematical system as the model. The system contains postulates built around certain terms and their relationships which in themselves have no relationship with behavior. However, the theorist may assume a correspondence between the terms and particular psychological events, such as the stimulus. Given this identification, the logic inherent in the set of postulates allows for deductions which become testable because of the identification between the terms and behavior. Because of the mathematical expression involved, these theories are as explicit as it is possible to make them with current tools. Nevertheless, as is the case with any other theoretical approach, the initial use of a mathematical model represents an approximation. Widely erroneous models can be ruled out before they become formalized. But given a model that provides an approximate accounting of certain behavioral phenomena, the pattern of development is the same as with any other theoretical approach, namely, test, revise, test, revise, and so on. The mathematical model has the great virtue of forcing the theorist to be explicit, thereby removing the fuzziness or ambiguity from his thinking. Assumptions which may be hidden in theories stated verbally are brought to light by these models.

Given the merits of explicitness and testability of the mathematical model, we may wonder why all theories are not given mathematical expression. Some investigators prefer to work with gross theoretical formulations initially to determine the feasibility of their application. Predictions are made in terms of "greater than" or "less than." If these work out, the assumptions of the theory may be refined until eventually they may be given mathematical expression, if not by the original theorist then by others. The likelihood of a theory being successful in detail rests to some degree on the amount of empirical knowledge available, and the development of this knowledge may be prompted by less precise theoretical thinking than that inherent in a mathematical model. Verbally-stated theories need not be completely impotent because of ambiguity. They may lead to unambiguous predictions of "greater than" or "less than" relationships which can be given definitive tests. Theories stated in gross quantitative forms have their value in the scheme of things, and they may be responsible, in part, for the usefulness which a mathematical model may subsequently demonstrate. There are many experimental psychologists who do not have the necessary mathematical skills required to work constructively at the mathematical level. There are others who have the skills but who seem to believe that more rapid progress can frequently be made without an initial concern for mathematical precision in theorizing. Nevertheless, it seems beyond reasonable doubt that mathematical modeling will become more and more dominant within a domain of research as the empirical base of the domain expands.

The Independent Variable and Testability

In the discussion of theory thus far we have consistently stated that assumed intervening processes are tied to independent variables. That is, the postulated processes are assumed to vary in such and such a manner as the independent variable changes. The reason for this deliberate stance needs to be explained.

Assume that we have a given set of phenomena within a domain of research. Being theoretically inclined, we decide to postulate mediating processes to account for the empirical relationships. However, suppose we postulate a process or agent which is in no way related in its magnitude of change to any independent variable. Every time an experiment is performed which results in a change in the dependent variable, we say that our postulated agent obviously changed to produce the observed effect. In fact, given this lack of constraint in theorizing, we do not need to postulate two intervening processes or agents; one will do. We can assign all of the needed characteristics to a single process. This is comparable to the situation described in the previous chapter. There we said that retroactive inhibition could be attributed to interference, and every time retroactive inhibition changed in magnitude it was "caused" by corresponding changes in the amount of interference. Fulfillment of prophecies is guaranteed by such circular attribution of causal agents. A postulated process must be said to be related in some manner to at least one independent variable; otherwise, the possibility of deriving a prediction which will test the theoretical formulation is not present. Explicitness, thence testability, requires that theoretical processes be tied directly or indirectly to independent variables. Any exceptions to this principle are so rare that they need not enter our thinking.

Kinds of Predictions

It is said that a theory, to be useful, must predict new phenomena. A theory is initially formulated by "making" it account for known facts, but its staying power rests on its capacity to predict new phenomena within the domain for which it is intended to apply. In the scheme of events, these predictions may be one of three kinds.

First, a theory may make a prediction which has never been tested, but it is a prediction that seems so intuitively reasonable that so-called common sense would expect it. In addition, if there are other theories in the same domain, they would make the same prediction. If a theory predicted that, on the average, three-letter consonant syllables should be more difficult to learn than common three-letter words, the number of lifted eyebrows would be at a minimum. The confirmation of such a prediction is necessary, but not very exciting. The excitement would be much greater if the prediction was not confirmed.

A second type of prediction might be called a counter-intuitive prediction. As its name implies, this prediction runs counter to common sense or against the half-formulated theoretical ideas which prevail at the time. This may be illustrated by reference to frequency theory and a particular prediction made for verbal-discrimination learning. Suppose we arrange a 12-pair list so that only 2 different right words are used (each occurring in 6 different pairs), with 12 different wrong words. Similarly, in another list we use only 2 different wrong words (each occurring in 6 pairs) and 12 different right words. If we examine these lists, it would seem perfectly reasonable to conclude that they will be learned with equal facility. In the first list, the subject merely learns that when either of two words occurs, he must respond with that word because these two words are the correct words. For the second list, the subject again merely learns that whenever either of two words occurs in a pair, he is *not* to respond with that word because these two words are the wrong words. However, frequency theory predicts (and the data support the idea) that the first list (two different right words) will be learned more rapidly than the second. The theory predicts this because the frequency difference between the two words in each pair will be greater in the former case than in the latter.

The third type of prediction is one which differs from the prediction made from another rival theory. This type of prediction is similar to the one called counter-intuitive but is more formal. Some believe that such head-on meetings are the most productive types of experiments that can be arranged. The outcome of an experiment of this kind, while disconfirming one theory, leaves the alternative theory as a viable one. Theories which may be disconfirmed, or at least not supported consistently by experiments, have a disconcerting habit of hanging around when no satisfactory alternative theoretical approach has been proposed.

REDUCTIONISM

This term, as it is usually used in psychology, means that theoretical processes are stated as physiological processes. Rather than proposing theoretical processes which are impalpable and which exist only as a statement of a relationship, reductionism uses physiological processes as the mediators. As can be seen, this is the application of a physiological model to explain behavior. This position is easy to defend. We would all accept the proposition that the observed relationship between the independent variable and behavior is mediated by physiological processes, with the nervous system being particularly involved. Then why not tie the behavioral observations directly to the neural level of functioning? The basic reason is that the physiological model is far from complete, so that the application of the model requires the postulation of hypothetical neural functions to round it out. Nevertheless reductionistic theoretical thinking is quite prevalent and will undoubtedly become more so as discoveries at the physiological level are made.

Those who study sensory functions (vision, audition, and so on) rarely use behavioral concepts in their theoretical formulations. Indeed, the research is closely tied to neural functioning. Experiments are done on neural functioning to try to understand certain behavioral facts, e.g., how we experience the taste of sour. Physiology and behavior are so closely entwined in these areas of research that one does not think of one without the other. Reductionism can proceed still further. Neural functioning may be best understood by chemical analysis and theories. Thus the search proceeds onward, but downward, as the causal agents are sought at what are believed to be more and more fundamental levels of discourse and analysis.

The fact remains that many, many experimental psychologists work entirely at the behavioral level and their theorizing has no contact with neurophysiological notions. Yet within the behavioral level there are reductionistic-types of analyses and theorizing with which we should be acquainted. An illustration will be given of the type of thinking involved.

A paired-associate list would not seem to offer a very complex learning task for the subject. He simply has to learn to produce a response term to each of several different stimulus terms. Logically the overall task can be broken down into subtasks, and we might speak of subprocesses which underlie each of the subtasks. Several such subtasks have been identified, but for our purposes two will be sufficient to illustrate the point of interest. One subtask is that the subject must learn to be able to produce the response terms per se. The other is that he must hook up or associate a given response term with its appropriate stimulus term. These are reductionistic, theoretical-like statements in that it is asserted that two more or less independent processes underlie the overall performance on the paired-associate task. However, both subtasks may be investigated directly by appropriate arrangement. Thus free recall of a list of words may simulate the response-learning stage of paired-associate learning. Associative learning can be studied directly without the requirement that the subject must produce the response terms, hence circumventing the response-learning stage. In turn, if we study these subtasks we might find that they could be logically broken down into further subtasks or subprocesses, each of which could also be studied in isolation. What we mean by studied, of course, is the examination of the role of certain independent variables.

The above approach, the approach by which a given task is broken down into the components or elementary processes underlying it, is a common one in many areas. It is a reductionistic approach in that it seeks to establish empirically the most elementary behavioral processes which underlie performance on complex tasks. These elementary processes, their relationships with independent variables, and their interrelationships, become the theoretical underpinning. They are like empirically derived postulates. From them, ostensibly we should be able to predict not only phenomena associated with a particular complex task, such as paired-associate learning, but also the phenomena associated with all tasks that are seen to involve the elementary processes of the theory.

INDIVIDUAL DIFFERENCES CAPABILITIES

One of the great sources of variance in experimental research is that attributable to differences among subjects. In most domains, very few independent variables produce as large a difference in mean scores as is present in the distribution of individual scores at any given level at which a mean is calculated. At the same time, it is probably correct to say that no variable has been so consistently ignored as has the individual-difference variable in theory construction within experimental psychology. The intent of this section is to point out that (1) certain theoretical approaches allow individual differences to be an integral part of the theoretical thinking, and (2) this capability gives an immediate test of the adequacy of the theoretical notions being employed.

The use of individual differences as a theoretical tool emerges most clearly in theories in which the postulated processes are empirically derived. Again we will turn to frequency theory as an illustration. The theory assumes that correct recognition memory as exhibited in the usual verbal-discrimination task is based fundamentally upon a frequency discrimination between the correct and incorrect items in each pair. When the frequency difference is of such magnitude as to be discriminated, and when the choice rule is applied, performance will be correct. It must be assumed that individuals differ in their ability to discriminate frequency differences of the same magnitude. In fact, this is demonstrated when frequency judgments are requested. Thus the theory has a self contained individual-difference assumption: subjects with good frequency discrimination must perform better on a verbal-discrimination task than subjects with poor frequency discrimination. Furthermore, unlike most theoretical assumptions, this one may be tested directly. First, we test the capacities of a group of subjects to discriminate frequency differences directly. We derive a score for each subject to represent his relative ability to discriminate frequency differences. If the idea that verbal-discrimination performance is based on frequency discrimination is sound, it must be predicted that the scores on the frequency-discrimination task will be correlated with scores for verbal-discrimination learning. We may now examine the conclusions we reach depending upon the magnitude of the correlations.

First, assume that the correlation found was zero. The conclusion is that we must abandon the theory. As we will see, we can stand some chaff in the system, but a complete lack of relationship as indicated by a zero correlation must force us to give up the theory. (How nice it would be if all theoretical proposals which eventually prove to be of little use could be nipped in the bud by this individual-difference approach.)

Assume next that the obtained correlation is moderate to high; perhaps .60 to .75. The relationship should probably not be expected to be perfect. Another postulate in the theory is that a rule is applied which covers all pairs. The discovery of the frequency rule, or the rate at which rule-applying behavior is instituted, may not be correlated with the ability to discriminate frequencies. A less than perfect correlation should not be upsetting, but it might be improved had we the means to measure rule-applying behavior independently, and then to calculate a multiple correlation based on a measure of frequency discrimination and a measure of rule-applying speed. In any event, knowing only the individual differences in frequency discrimination, what does a strong positive correlation mean with respect to our subsequent theorizing? All it provides is a license to proceed with the testing and development of the theory experimentally—that and no more. In no sense is the theory given any proof. The reason for this is that the verbal-discrimination task may be mastered by a skill which is correlated with the skill involved in making frequency discriminations but which is not this skill as such. So, we see, a low correlation puts the theory out of business; a substantial correlation keeps it in the business of subsequent experimental testing.

When the intervening processes used theoretically are not empirically derived, the individual difference capabilities of a theory are difficult to determine. What we would have to do is somehow externalize a postulated process and see if we could get a direct measure that is assumed to reflect the essence of the postulated process. When the postulated process is strictly abstract in nature, perhaps identified only as X, one cannot even contemplate measuring it directly. Sometimes, however, surplus meaning may be ascribed to a postulated process and this might allow our so-called externalization. Thus, a process characterized as inhibitory in nature might be judged to be amenable to some form of measurement directly or indirectly. But generally speaking, individual-differences capabilities are initially present only in theories which are based on empirically-derived assumptions.

OTHER DIMENSIONS

Other characteristics or dimensions along which theoretical formulations may differ will now be presented with a minimum amount of discussion.

Scope

Theories may be developed to account for a sharply limited domain of research. The phrase "miniature theories" has been used to describe these formulations. In essence, the theory specifies the boundary conditions within which the theory is held to be relevant. A theory might be formulated to account for the acquisition and extinction of classically-conditioned responses, but it might be held to be inappropriate for instrumental-avoidance learning. A theory might be developed to apply to paired-associate learning with any pertinence to serial learning being disavowed. One can be fairly confident, however, that if a theory is found useful in the limited domain for which it was intended, an attempted conquest of a larger domain may be expected. This is as it should be; if a theory is successful in a given domain, it should be pushed beyond that as far as it can be before breaking down. The notion that we will have a grand theory of all human behavior in the near future does not at all seem realistic. A useful theory within a limited domain is an attainable goal. The more global theory may gradually come by unifying the theories in adjacent domains.

Simplicity

It seems that frequently, rather than being satisfied with a simple theory that is useful for a limited domain, we tend to start adding postulates to encompass larger and larger domains. As a consequence, a theory with a few simple assumptions initially begins to gather a complexity that may eventually cause its demise. Although it has been argued that because behavior is complex our theories about it must be complex, there remains a natural elegance about simplicity in theoretical formulations that is difficult to deny. Clearly, if we have two or more theories with equal explanatory usefulness, preference would be given to the one with the fewest assumptions. Parsimony remains a worthwhile basis for helping choose among theoretical approaches.

Pretheoretical Assumptions

Almost any theoretical formulation is based on certain assumptions which, while not entering directly into the theory, influence its development. For example, in developing a theory of memory we might assume that nothing which has been learned is ever forgotten. This assumption is not a part of the theory which explains so-called forgetting by making assumptions about conditions which lead to failure in retrieval of memories. The pretheoretical assumption helps us to understand why the theory was developed in the way that it was. It also helps explain why experiments of certain types are performed as tests of the theory. Frequency theory is worked out within a broad conception of memory which holds that there are various types of information which constitute a memory, of which frequency information is only one. This clearly limits the domain of applicability of the theory, but it did not influence the formulation of frequency theory per se.

SOME WORKING GUIDELINES

The survey of modes of theoretical thinking and the identification of some of the characteristics of theories which result from such thinking may seem a little far removed from the working situation of the usual student who, perhaps, has been involved in only one or two experiments. We are quite aware of the fact that for the initial experiments done by any student the mere task of data reduction and the statistical analysis may constitute formidable hurdles. An investigator needs first to discover what the data mean with regard to the question posed by the experiment, and this determination is not one which can always be made easily in the beginning. To expect that on top of this a student may propose an original theory, with some degree of completeness, is unrealistic to say the least. Still, after the empirical conclusions are drawn, including an assessment of the results in light of previous research, something more may need to be said in trying to establish a perspective that goes beyond the empirical. We will suggest various guidelines which might help at this level. In so doing we will necessarily consider both the background thinking which led to the experiment and the outcome.

Intent and Outcome

Test of available theory. The experiment that has been performed may have been designed to make a test of a specific deduction from an available theory. Under these circumstances, of course, the introduction to the report will show precisely how the experiment is viewed as a test of the theory. We need to discuss the two possible outcomes of such an experiment, and to see how these may influence the discussion in the final section of the report.

The finding of the experiment may be positive in the sense that the obtained differences among conditions are as predicted by the theory. We frequently have a strong urge to say that the experiment proves that the theory is correct. *Prove* is considered a strong word. Supposing two quite different theories predicted the same result. Does the experiment prove both theories? The results may be said to confirm or support the deduction from the theory, or they may be said to be consonant with theoretical expectations, but a theory is never said to be proved by a result.

The other alternative is, quite obviously, a negative finding with respect to the theory. The theory may have predicted that a given independent variable would produce a difference when none was found, or it may have predicted an interaction between two independent variables when none was found. In the most extreme case the results may be opposite to theoretical expectations, e.g., an inverse relationship was found between the independent variable and behavior, but a direct relationship had been predicted by the theory. Something is wrong with the theory in either case. Suggestions for revision of the theory may be made, these being such as to accommodate the new finding. Other theories might be examined to determine their success in predicting the obtained results. In any case, negative results are said to disconfirm the expectations from the theory.

Whenever an experiment is designed to test a theory, it is perhaps wiser not to make the test of theory the sole responsibility of the experiment. Many theoretical expectations can be tested by a two-treatment experiment. Except insofar as the data from such an experiment provide a test of the theory, they do not contribute much to the empirical base of the domain of research. We may even find that, after the experiment is completed, some might not agree that it was a pointed test of the theory. The theorist may discount the test for one reason or another. Because of these possibilities, we might always view an experiment as being designed to make a substantial empirical contribution over and above the contribution it may make to theoretical decisions. This approach would recommend that the independent variable be manipulated at several levels—beyond the number required to test the theory. A second likely interacting variable might be included in the design. When the data are summarized we have empirical relationships of substance which may far outlive the theory that was also tested by the study.

Strictly empirical. To suggest that we should not undertake an experiment without a specific theoretical objective in mind would be nonsense. Many experimentalists seem quite happy in their work and we seldom find that their introductions to an experiment refer to intervening processes or a mathematical model. It is quite worthwhile to develop a body of knowledge about which others may want to theorize. Curiosity is still a good reason for doing research. We may choose a particular variable to manipulate simply because we have a hunch that it ought to influence the behavior of interest. Some may decide to elevate the status of their hunch to a hypothesis, but this does not make it one whit more theoretical. Sometimes we may proceed to manipulate a certain independent variable to fill a gap in our knowledge. All of this serves as a repetition of what we said in the first chapter: there are many reasons involved in deciding to do a particular experiment and many of them are not involved in specific tests of theory.

Even if the reasons behind the experiment include little if any theoretical thinking, however, it does not follow that we will not want to see if some theoretical perspective might be given the findings. We might look around to see if any theories include the influence of this particular variable in their predictions. A theory might be declared relevant to a given domain of research in which a particular experiment was conducted, and yet the assumptions of the theory in no way touch on the independent variable manipulated. If this is the case, at the very minimum the theory could be said to be incomplete. We may then decide to make some suggestions as to how the theory may be made more complete. If no available theory purports to handle the results, our decision may be to record certain notions which could form the start of a theory.

Puzzle worrying.   An experiment may be designed in an attempt to resolve an empirical contradiction which exists in a given domain of research. As was discussed in conjunction with another matter, a firm or reliable empirical contradiction implicates an interacting variable. The two experiments which produced the contradiction must have differed on one or more static variables, and the particular experiment we do is aimed at the discovery of this variable. We make an educated guess as to what the variable might be. To reach a clear decision on the validity of our guess requires the manipulation of two variables, the one for which the contradiction exists and the one we believe is the one which interacts with it. It might require several experiments before the puzzle is solved. Once it is solved we are ready, if we so choose, to propose some theoretical ideas or evaluate the available theories to see if they can accommodate the interaction.

New Phenomena.   Experiments may be undertaken in areas in which an empirical background is missing or in which available previous work is only tangentially related to that indexed by the experiment of the moment. Whether there is or is not a background of research, the first finding that an independent variable is sharply related to behavior can be said to be a discovery in the sense that a new phenomenon is defined.

Careful observations of behavior, our own as well as others, make it fairly obvious that not all important aspects of behavior have been brought under experimental scrutiny. One of the domains of behavior that is difficult to study experimentally is the domain dealing with the more profound emotional responses such as sorrow and hate and anger. In this, and in other domains, certain behaviors have not been studied because no one has figured out a way to make them operational. By this is meant that no one has perceived a way to apply the necessary treatment conditions in order to produce the phenomenon in the laboratory. To make them operational requires a given hypothesis about the critical defining variable, although sometimes the observations made essentially dictate what this variable is likely to be. Someone may have initially noticed that a light showing through a small hole into a dark room appeared to move, but when the light was turned on within the room, the light as viewed through the small hole no longer appeared to move. Such an observation may have suggested a phenomenon (apparent movement) for which the critical defining variable was the amount of light surrounding the small light source, or at least a sharp contrast between the point of light and the surround. Thereby the autokinetic illusion was given operational validity when brought into the laboratory.

Nearly all have had the experience of trying to retrieve a name or fact from memory, only to have it elude us. Then perhaps a few minutes later or several hours later the desired name or fact will "pop" into our mind even though we are no longer searching for it as we were initially. This can be observed in the laboratory, too, so the validity of the observation is not in doubt. The problem has been that of identifying the critical defining variable. What change in the internal or external environment occurred just prior to the "pop" and which, therefore, would be considered the necessary condition (independent variable) for it to occur? If we could form a reasonable hypothesis about this change we could try to give it a laboratory counterpart to see if the sudden retrieval could be produced as a consequence. No one has been successful on this matter thus far.

Any given domain of research requires the discovery of new phenomena to maintain its vitality. A good theory will frequently handle this by predicting new phenomena. But it also seems necessary that we be alert to the possibilities of giving operational meaning to phenomena which, from our observations, we think must exist. If we are successful in this attempt, the theoretical perspective will again follow the experiment, not precede it.

Sources of Theoretical Probes

We will certainly not be presumptuous to the point of telling how to go about theorizing for a given set of data. We have given a number of different kinds or levels of theorizing and in a sense any one of these might be taken as a starting point. The approach taken would certainly depend upon our tastes and skills, and because of this it is appropriate to point out that there is no one right approach. The best we can do, therefore, is to suggest some sources which may produce theory-like ideas, hence which might help initiate theoretical probes.

1. One source of ideas is the subject. In Chapter 2 we pointed out that to take the reports from the subject at their face value was not to be strongly recommended. This does not mean, however, that we should ignore this source of information. Subjects should be observed carefully as they "perform" in the experiment; they may be systematically questioned following

the experiment. It is a little difficult to question a white rat, but the observations of his behavior in the experimental situation may produce some ideas. Seeing that a rat sometimes paused at the junction of the T maze, looking back and forth between the two alternative goals, gave rise to the notion that some implicit or vicarious trial and error might be occurring. The college student who has served in an experiment is frequently quite articulate about the manner in which he went about the task. If a good majority of the subjects report essentially the same experiences, it is something that might be given a theoretical translation. Reports of the subjects represent an auxiliary response measure. The more formal case of auxiliary response measures is the next possibility to be discussed with regard to theoretical suggestions which may be derived.

2. If more than one response measure is used, any differences in their relationships with the independent variable may suggest a theoretical idea. Suppose, for example, that we have subjects learn lists of words by written free recall, using alternate study and test trials. Suppose further that the lists consist of several instances of each of several categories, e.g., several animal names, several flower names. Assume that the independent variable is X, and that the trials-to-learn is directly related to it. When categorized lists are used, to some degree subjects are likely to show clustering in recall by recalling together words belonging to the same category. Suppose that the amount or degree of clustering did not vary as X was varied. Clustering per se might be taken to indicate an organization process as a vital part of learning, but the failure of clustering to vary with X might indicate that something else is involved in the learning because X did influence the number of trials to learn.

Latency measures are taken in many discrimination experiments in addition to measures of correct responding. Again, if there were some disparity between the relationships for the two response measures and the independent variable, a lead might be offered for theoretical probes.

Secondary response measures, while sometimes useful for developing theoretical notions, may also be misleading theoretically. For example, it is not clear at the present time that clustering reflects a fundamental process which is intimately tied in a causal way to the learning process. Consider another illustration. It is known that associations develop between the members of the pairs in verbal-discrimination learning, but these associations may not be at all involved in establishing the discrimination. We might record the number of eye blinks which subjects produce in learning an easy and a difficult task, but if the number differs we must be careful in inferring that they reflect something fundamental to the learning. Automobiles have exhaust pipes in the rear which might lead to an inference that the exhaust was pushing the cars. Auxiliary response measures can be useful as sources of theoretical ideas, but there is always the possibility that they do not reflect processes fundamental to the performance of central interest. Such measures may be found to be irrelevant. These are sometimes called epiphenomena.

3. A third source of theoretical ideas is one's own introspections. There is nothing wrong in using this source, and probably, if we really knew, it would be found that most of the theoretical notions for the more complex psychological functions arise from this source. Of course such ideas must be given the same discipline as theoretical notions reached by other means.

4. Assume that, for whatever reason, we have conducted an experiment in which the independent variable was examined at, let us say, ten different levels. Assume further that when the results were plotted they showed a discontinuous function, e.g., the curve rose very slowly but linearly across the first five levels of the independent variable but then increased very sharply and linearly across the additional five levels. Such results do occasionally occur and they are almost inevitably taken to mean that two processes are involved, one being largely responsible for the first segment of the curve, the other being largely responsible for the second segment. The initial part of the explanatory process is to try to identify the two underlying processes or mechanisms. There may be relevant evidence in the background literature; others may have identified one of the processes and the nature of the experimental situation may readily suggest the other. One may even be led to postulate a process, or two processes, but perhaps other alternatives (such as suggested below) should be explored first. In any event, a discontinuous function for the independent variable literally demands theoretical thinking.

5. Earlier in the chapter we discussed how the paired-associate task could be analyzed as being constituted of subtasks. Many other tasks offer this same possibility. For example, in solving anagrams, at least two subtasks are evident. The subject must "think of" potential solution words. In addition he must also test them to see if they meet the requirements of containing the appropriate letters. We must not take it for granted that independent variables will influence these two stages in the same fashion. Reductionistic thinking of this type revolves largely around a careful examination of the stages or phases we think are reasonable. We then make judgments as to what degree of independence may exist among the stages. By independence, in this case, we mean the degree to which independent variables may produce different effects on the stages. For example, to use a subject variable to illustrate the point, if a subject is a very poor speller he may have difficulty in the second stage presumed above to be required in solving anagrams. Would spelling ability influence the first stage?

6. In instituting theoretical probes, a good policy is to examine the data with an eye toward determining whether individual differences interact with the independent variable. For the data from many diversified types of experi-

ments it is a simple matter to divide the results for each condition so as to represent a group of poor-performing subjects, and a group of good-performing subjects. We ask if the independent variable had the same influence on both groups. If it did not (if performance level and the independent variable produced an interaction), it may suggest the nature of the underlying mechanism associated with the independent variable. It can be seen that an interaction between performance level (good versus poor) and the independent variable should also be reflected in changes in the standard deviation of the scores across the different levels of the independent variable.

In general, any interaction occurring with any type of independent variable suggests the presence of at least two underlying processes. The theoretical task is to try to identify them in a meaningful way, or at least to characterize them in a way that will lead to further, more theoretically oriented experiments.

7. If we have used a within-subjects design, an examination of changes as a function of stage of practice may be useful in helping us obtain a theoretical foothold. If the influence of an independent variable becomes either less and less with practice, or greater and greater with practice, it would seem that the data are trying to tell us something about the nature of the processes responsible for the performance.

The presentation of these seven roads to theoretical immortality completes this book. If you have followed us carefully throughout the eight chapters we feel quite confident that you will be able to design an airtight experiment. By diligent work at the library you should be able to relate your findings to those obtained by other investigators. We are somewhat less confident, but hopeful, that you will be able to develop the first comprehensive theory of behavior.

APPENDIX A
STUDY PROBLEMS

Contents

Page

Introduction

The problems which follow were designed to enhance and broaden the learning which accompanies laboratory work in experimental psychology. It has been our experience that the most effective learning occurs when three conditions are met. First, the problems are used as a basis for class discussion so that appropriate elaborations can be provided by the instructor. Second, the student should try to arrive at the solutions prior to class discussion. Third, comparable problems are included on examinations.

The study problems are separated by chapters corresponding to those of the textual material. Generally speaking, the points at which particular issues are introduced in the sequence of study problems correspond to their introduction in the text.

Chapter 1 THE EXPERIMENT

1. a) Four statements, implying empirical relationships, are given below. Plot these relationships on the graphs, being careful to label the axes.

   (A) The more things a man is ashamed of the more respectable he is.
   (B) Many hands make light work.
   (C) Practice makes perfect.
   (D) How much people say behind your back indicates your standing in the community.

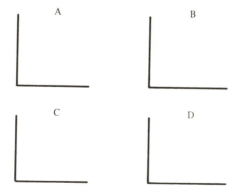

   b) Which two statements imply a causal relationship (as distinguished from a correlative relationship)?

2. The following experiment is performed. White rats receive a pellet of food each time a bar is pressed. The size of the pellets is exactly the same for

all groups, but the protein content differs. Let us say that increasing protein value is indicated by the numbers 2, 5, 11, and 20. There are four groups of rats, one for each protein value. All animals spend ten minutes in the cage and the number of bar presses made by each rat is automatically recorded.

a) What is the independent variable?

b) What is the likely response measure that the investigator will use?

c) The results, expressed as mean total responses in ten minutes, were as follows:

Protein Value:	2	5	11	20
Mean Number Responses:	70	56	42	28

Plot the results below, being sure to label the axes.

d) What hypothesis might you offer for the reduction in number of responses which occurred with increasing protein content?

3. A clerk sits at an information desk on the ground floor of a two-story building. Opposite his desk are an elevator and a stairway, both leading to the second floor. Some people use the elevator, some the stairway.

a) Name at least three characteristics of the people, which could be roughly assessed by the clerk, which might influence the choice between the elevator and the stairway.

b) Name at least one independent variable, not a characteristic of the person, which might influence the choice of one over the other.

c) Think of an independent variable that the clerk might in fact manipulate, and that might allow him to discover a condition in which the usual person might be in conflict as to whether to ride the elevator or climb the stairs.

4. In the late fall of 1973, certain states dropped the maximum speed limit on highways from 70–75 mph to 55 mph. This was done as a fuel-conservation step. Thus, in the natural course of events, a change in the level of an independent variable occurred. It was rather universally reported that the number of deaths due to highway accidents dropped sharply. Give at least three different reasons for the drop in number of fatal accidents.

5. A very experienced research worker used a one-trial training procedure for those people who came to work as his research assistants. The process was very simple. The experienced researcher took the novices into a room in which there was a gerbil in a glass tank. The novices were instructed to write a description of exactly what they observed. The researcher then placed an index card in the tank and eventually the gerbil took the card in its forepaws and brought the card to its mouth. The researcher then placed a pretzel in the tank and again the gerbil eventually picked it up and brought it to its mouth. Invariably, the novices described the two sequences in great detail, but there was one consistent difference apparent between the descriptions for the two sequences. The novices wrote that the animal *chewed* the card and that the animal *ate* the pretzel. The experienced researcher then used this "error" as a catalyst for a lecture on the need for rigor in observational studies. Why did the experienced researcher use this example?

6. A squirrel is seen feeding or searching for food on the ground near a tree. A dog barks nearby and the squirrel immediately runs up the tree. Soon he is back down on the ground. The dog barks again, and once more the squirrel runs up the tree. These events repeat themselves seven times.

a) What is the basic observation which seems to implicate a cause-effect relation between dog barking and squirrel running up the tree?

b) The statement above implies (or at least, let us assume it implies) that the squirrel always ran when the dog barked and never ran when the dog did not bark. Why would we be likely to conclude that the dog's bark is in some way responsible for the squirrel repeatedly scampering up the tree?

c) It is quite possible that the squirrel was not responding directly to the bark. Imagine a way in which this could have occurred.

7. It so happened that of 100 young people (ages 16-20) in a certain town, 50 were male and 50 were female. Half of the males and half of the females were smokers, and half of each were nonsmokers. An industrious investigator tracked these 100 people for 20 years, administering a physical-endurance test to all of them once every 5 years. The values tabled below represent the mean scores on the test as a function of age, sex, and whether the subjects were smokers or nonsmokers. For purposes of this exercise, assume that none of the subjects died or were lost for any other reasons, and assume further that all of the smokers remained smokers throughout the 20 years and that all nonsmokers remained nonsmokers throughout the period. In the table, the higher the score the greater the endurance. The maximum possible score on the test was 75, and a difference of 10 between means represents a statistically significant difference.

Males: Age

	16-20	21-25	26-30	31-35	36-40
Smokers	65	55	35	20	5
Nonsmokers	70	60	50	40	30

Females: Age

	16-20	21-25	26-30	31-35	36-40
Smokers	55	50	40	32	20
Nonsmokers	60	55	50	45	40

a) State verbally the influence of each of the three independent variables on endurance scores.

b) Determine if there is an interaction in the scores produced by age and sex. If so, state the nature of the interaction.

c) Determine whether there was a difference in the effect of the age variable depending upon whether the subjects were smokers or non-smokers. To do this, get a single score for each age for smokers and for nonsmokers by summing across sex. Plot the results on the graph below. Do these two variables interact?

d) Determine whether the differences between smokers and nonsmokers were greater for the males than for the females. State the nature of this effect verbally.

Chapter 2 INDEPENDENT AND DEPENDENT VARIABLES

1. An apparatus was constructed to measure the accuracy with which a subject could reproduce a given force. The apparatus included a vertical bar which could be pushed by the subject, and a spring tension set against the direction of push. Different forces could be imposed. The maximum force involved a change of about 30 degrees in the bar from its vertical position. On a given trial the subject was told to push the bar slowly forward until the experimenter's dials showed a given force was achieved. At this point the experimenter instructed the subject to release the bar, which, of course, returned to a vertical position. The subject then attempted to reproduce the force. Force is confounded with another independent variable. What is it?

2. a) Let X represent an independent variable, and Y another potential independent variable which might or might not change in magnitude as X changes. On the graph, draw a line representing a confounding between X and Y, and another which would indicate no confounding. Label each.

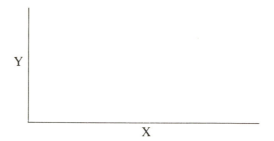

b) Let X represent height. What other continuous subject variable is naturally confounded?

c) Again, let X represent height. What noncontinuous variable is naturally confounded?

d) Let X represent time between successive trials on a task. What other variable is automatically confounded if number of trials is constant?

e) Let X represent the rated concreteness of a random group of common words. What other characteristics of words are confounded with concreteness?

f) Let X represent the size of a circular target on a rotating disc. The disc has a constant size. The subject is required to track the target with a stylus. What other variable is automatically confounded?

3. An investigator studied the perception of velocity. An apparatus allowed him to project a circular dot of light on a screen and the dot could be made to move at various speeds across the screen. The investigator's thinking led him to manipulate (as the independent variable) the distance of the subject from the screen. He found that velocity judgments were indeed influenced; the greater the distance from the screen the slower the apparent velocity. He interpreted this to be the result of the fact that the farther the distance the less intense the retinal stimulation.

The manipulation of distance is accompanied by changes in a correlated variable which may be responsible for the finding. What is this correlated variable?

4. Assume that you are responsible for the description of an object thought to be the remnants of an unidentified flying object from outer space. You are required to "measure" the object on each of the following dimensions: size, color, and beauty. Assume that you have available the facilities of a typical research laboratory, including the 25 people assigned to work in the laboratory as research assistants. Describe how you would go about measuring the object on each of the dimensions.

5. Psychological events (used broadly) frequently must be scaled in order to obtain some degree of quantification of how they differ on some characteristic or attribute. Probably the simplest of all scaling methods is the method of rank order, a method which will now be illustrated by a study carried out in the fall of 1973. The subjects were instructed as follows:

> Below are listed 21 problems which we face as a nation during the coming years. You are to make a judgment regarding the relative severity or seriousness of each of these problems. First look the list of problems over carefully. Then you are to rank order the 21 problems. To do this, you will assign the number 1 to the problem you consider most severe or serious, and so on, until the number 21 is assigned to the problem you consider least serious. You must assign a different number to each. Even if you think two problems are equally serious you must assign them different numbers (flip a coin, mentally). When you finish, check over your assignments to make sure you have not used the same number twice.

Thirty-five subjects carried out the rank-order instructions. Thus for each statement there were 35 ranks assigned. For each statement the mean of the ranks and the standard deviation were determined. These are shown below with 1 representing the most serious problem, 21 the least serious.

	Mean of Ranks	Standard Deviation	Rank Order
Prevention of war	4.29	4.43	1
Atmosphere pollution	4.89	3.20	2
Water pollution	5.60	3.54	3
Inadequate food supply	8.00	5.31	4
Care of poor	8.14	4.68	5
Shortage of minerals and oil	8.71	5.66	6
Integrity of public officials	8.89	5.07	7
Racial discrimination	9.14	4.72	8
Quality of education	9.71	4.91	9
Disease	11.11	5.40	10.5
Care of elderly	11.11	4.48	10.5
Control of atomic energy	11.20	5.48	12
Lack of interest in good government	11.69	5.20	13
Penal systems	11.80	4.03	14
Concentration of wealth in few hands	12.83	5.47	15
Sex discrimination	13.69	5.23	16
Urban transportation systems	14.74	6.94	17
Computer dehumanization	15.69	5.19	18
Deterioration of moral fiber	15.77	5.52	19
Labor-management relations	16.06	3.23	20
Revolutionary groups within the USA	17.94	4.32	21

a) Does this scaling study represent an experiment, i.e., are there different treatments?

b) If another group of subjects from the same population had also been tested at the same time, do you think the rank orders as shown in the right column would have remained precisely the same? Explain.

c) Which of the 21 statements might be expected to produce a bimodal distribution such that many subjects would rate it quite serious and many would rate it as being not very serious? Do you see any evidence that might "test" your idea?

d) A rank-order scale is commonly called an ordinal scale, as opposed to an interval scale. In an interval scale, the units reflect equal amounts of the given characteristic. The ranks, however, do not allow this interpretation; that is, observing only ranks we have no basis for saying that the psychological distance is equivalent between say, ranks 3 and 4, and ranks 8 and 9. However, given the mean ranks and the variabilities, it is possible to make some statements about "distance." Between what two ranks would you conclude that there exists the greatest psychological separation?

e) Supposing that a year after the above study was done, we get a rank order for the five statements holding ranks 1, 4, 9, 16, and 21. These are so widely separated that by any way of reckoning the differences on the first scaling were highly reliable statistically. However, in the rank-ordering of the five statements a year after the original study we find that the two statements holding ranks 4 and 9 are interchanged. How would you interpret this?

6. An investigator does a study on proofreading for typographical errors. There are three levels of the independent variable (three conditions), distinguished by the number of errors per line. In one case there is one error per every 5 lines, in another one error per every 10 lines, and in the third one error per every 20 lines. The three typescripts are exactly the same except for the typographical errors inserted. Random groups are used and the subjects are instructed to go through the script as rapidly as possible, identifying all errors with a slash. For his dependent variable (response measure), the investigator uses the mean number of failures to detect an error. For the three levels, these values are 5.0, 4.9, and 5.1. These do not differ reliably. The investigator concludes that the error rate is independent of the number of to-be-detected errors. This is probably an inappropriate conclusion. Why?

7. While 35 subjects provided rank orders for the 21 statements (as discussed above), another group of 35 subjects was asked to evaluate the statements by a method known as category scaling. The instructions were as follows:

Below are 21 problems which we face as a nation during the coming years. You are to judge these problems in terms of their severity or seriousness. To do this, you will assign a number from 1 through 7 to each according to the following scale:

Least Severe   Most Severe

Look through all of the statements first in order to get a "feel" for the range of seriousness involved; then start assigning the numbers. The problems you consider to be least serious will be assigned 1, those which you consider to be most serious, 7. Those in between should be given appropriate numbers. So use the full scale but do not be concerned about using each number equally often.

A mean scale value was determined for each of the 21 statements, along with the standard deviation for the 35 scores from which each mean was determined. A large mean scale value indicated the most serious end of the scale, a small value the least serious. It is a straightforward step, given the mean scale values, to determine a rank ordering of the statements. These are shown below. The statements are listed in order of the ranks determined by the rank-order method described in an earlier problem.

	Mean Scale Value	Standard Deviation	Rank Order
Prevention of war	6.11	1.26	1
Atmosphere pollution	5.74	1.19	3
Water pollution	5.77	1.23	2
Inadequate food supply	5.31	1.72	4.5
Care of poor	4.77	1.50	9
Shortage of minerals and oil	5.09	1.52	6.5
Integrity of public officials	5.09	1.39	6.5
Racial discrimination	4.51	1.49	10
Quality of education	4.94	1.48	8
Disease	4.14	1.56	13
Care of elderly	4.20	1.62	11
Control of atomic energy	5.31	1.58	4.5
Lack of interest in good government	3.89	1.44	15
Penal systems	4.17	1.77	12
Concentration of wealth in few hands	3.69	1.78	16
Sex discrimination	3.00	1.53	19

	Mean Scale Value	Standard Deviation	Rank Order
Urban transportation systems	4.06	1.54	14
Computer dehumanization	2.54	1.49	20
Deterioration of moral fiber	3.09	1.72	18
Labor-management relations	3.43	1.15	17
Revolutionary groups within the USA	2.40	1.29	21

a) The mean of the 21 means was 4.35. What does this tell you about the perceived seriousness of the 21 statements as a group?

b) Why should the standard deviations tend to be larger for statements in the middle of the scale than for those at the extremes?

c) Suppose a 21-point scale had been used with the subjects instructed to use each value only once. How would you characterize the method of category scaling under these circumstances?

d) In asking the subjects to provide scale values for each statement, we also specified that at least one statement must be classed as most serious, hence given a value of 7, and one as least serious, hence given a value of 1. This is said to provide a frame of reference for the scale. The subject is said to anchor the scale at the two ends. Suppose that we had included 23 statements, instead of 21, the two additional statements being "Mosquito control" and "Shortage of caviar." What do you think would have happened to the mean scale value of the statement ranked 21st? What is your assumption?

e) Suppose the instructions to the subjects had said: "Think of the most serious problem you can, and consider that to have a value of 7 on the scale. Then think of the least serious problem you can and consider that to have a value of 1. Then provide scale values for the 21 statements within this frame of reference." What would be the expectation for the scale values of the 21 statements had these instructions been used? What assumption or assumptions do you make in reaching your conclusion?

8. An experiment was performed in which the independent variable was level of frustration. All subjects were shown simple line drawings of people and were asked to write a brief description of the meaning of each picture, the notion being that the higher the frustration the more likely that the descriptions would have aggressive themes. How might these response protocols be quantified?

9. Another scaling method which is frequently used is known as paired comparisons. In this method, the subject is presented two stimuli at a time and is asked to choose the one having the greater amount of a specified characteristic. If used in the scaling of the 21 statements, he would be presented two of the statements and asked to decide which is the more serious problem. In carrying out the method of paired comparisons, each stimulus is paired with every other stimulus in the series and, of course, the subject must make a decision for each pairing.

a) Why would one probably not use the method of paired comparisons for the scaling of the 21 statements?

b) In terms of what is required of the subject, how would you describe the similarities between the method of rank order and the method of paired comparisons?

c) Assume that a scaling study using the method of paired comparisons had been completed. The raw data summed across subjects show the number of times each stimulus was chosen when paired with every other stimulus. How would you determine a rank order?

10. An employee at a certain cafeteria wanted to show his boss that the policy of serving "exotic" juices with breakfast (if the customer requested it) was a wasteful practice. He thought people just bought the exotic juices to impress their friends and that they did not really like the taste. In order to gather evidence, the man recorded the flavor of the juice contained in the glasses of those patrons who failed to finish their drinks. At the end of the morning he had counted a total of 50 less than completely empty glasses of juice. Of these, 40 were of the "exotic" variety and only 10 were of the non-exotic variety (e.g., good old orange juice). Because 80 percent of the unfinished juices were of the exotic variety, the employee concluded that his evidence was sure to convince his boss. Do you agree with him?

Chapter 3 INDEPENDENT-GROUPS DESIGNS

1. One procedure for attempting to understand territorial range of animals "in the wild" runs about as follows. First a certain number of a given species is trapped or captured in some manner and tagged with an ear clip, leg band, or some other device which does not interfere at all with normal behavior. Hunters and trappers are asked to return the tags giving the date, location, and circumstances under which the animal was captured, shot, or found. What are the "soft" points in this procedure if the interest is in generalizing to the species?

2. An investigator developed the idea that an excess of a certain chemical (X) in the brain during infancy produced permanent mental retardation. To gather evidence germane to this notion, he used two groups of 15 newborn monkeys each. The 30 babies were assigned to the groups by a block-randomized schedule. One group, the C Group, was nursed by the mother monkeys, and it is assumed that the investigator could control the amount of milk consumed. The other group, the E Group, was fed by bottle, but the milk was of exactly the same kind and of the same amount as that received by the naturally-fed monkeys. Of course, the baby monkeys in the E Group were kept separated from the mothers so that they would not nurse from the mother and thereby get more milk than those in the C Group. The independent variable X was given to the E Group by including the chemical in the nursing bottle. Tests of mental development were made on both groups at various points in time, even far beyond the nursing period. At every point of the testing the monkeys in the E Group were found to be inferior to those in the C Group. Such a finding would support the idea prompting the experiment.

a) The independent variable is confounded. How?

b) Should it be concluded that X is not responsible for the observed differences?

3. There was a thoroughly dedicated graduate student at X University who was, however, not very disciplined in his daily schedule. In fact he might be considered somewhat careless about many matters. The experiment for his dissertation consisted of four conditions using a random-groups design. He constructed a block-randomized schedule of these four conditions. The schedule consisted of 100 blocks, hence the plan was to place 100 subjects in each of the four conditions. The student occasionally tested subjects in the early morning, sometimes in the evening, and sometimes during the day. Several times during the testing his jerry-built apparatus broke down. When this happened he dismissed the subject and replaced him with the next subject arriving for the experiment. The temperature within the experimental room varied considerably. Several times the graduate student read instructions which were inappropriate for the particular condition but the error was always caught and again the subject was dismissed and replaced with the next subject. Several times the graduate student forgot to appear for an appointment with a subject. By the time 80 blocks were completed (80 subjects in each condition) the school year ended. He decided to "go" with the results for these 320 subjects and proceeded to analyze the data.

Another equally dedicated graduate student at Y University just happened to be doing exactly the same experiment. However this student was quite different from the one at X University. This student tested all of his subjects between 1:00 and 3:00 P.M. on weekdays in an air-conditioned room. There was never an equipment failure, never were the wrong instructions read, and no appointments were missed. The 100 blocks were completed.

a) Is there any evidence of bias in either experiment; that is, did the procedures result in one condition being favored over the other in terms of better subjects or differential effects of extraneous factors?

b) Which set of results has the greater generality?

c) For which student will the standard deviation around the means likely be smaller?

4. An investigator had a colony of rats, very heterogeneous with respect to age. He decided to test a pet notion that he had long held, namely, that implanting electrodes in the skull makes the animal behaviorally different. This would mean that studies in which such electrodes are used to introduce shock into the brain may be reaching false conclusions when a nonimplanted control group is used. He divided his animals into two groups randomly, 20 in each group. All of the animals in one group had electrodes implanted by the best techniques at the time, the other group did not have such implants. Following a recovery period, both groups were given training in learning a multiple-choice maze. Of course, the electrodes were never used to introduce shock. As is usually the case, the normal activities of the animals may dislodge the electrodes. This occurred for 6 animals during the course of the experiment and, of course, the records for these animals could not be used since they no longer carried the treatment. The response measure was the number of trials required to proceed through the maze without error (going into a blind alley) on ten successive trials. It was found that the mean for the implanted group was significantly higher than for the other group, indicating slower learning. This, it can be seen, might seem to support the investigator's pet notion.

a) Assume that had the 20 animals in each group been measured, the means would not have differed. How would one account for the obtained difference?

b) Of what value would pretest scores on maze learning have been?

5. A random sample of 100 three-letter words was chosen from the total population of three-letter words. These 100 words were paired randomly, thus producing 50 pairs. As the first step, this list was given to a large group of subjects for 20 trials as a free-recall task. A mean score was determined for each pair, summing across trials and subjects, with a high score indicating an easy pair, a low score indicating a difficult pair. The 25 easiest pairs and the 25 most difficult pairs were then selected, and these were randomized within a list and given to a new group of subjects (from the same population as the first) for 20 learning trials. Thus the two groups had learned exactly the same lists.

As a third step, the 25 easy pairs were re-paired, as were the 25 difficult pairs. These 50 pairs were then randomized within a single list and given for 20 trials to a third group of subjects from the same population as were the first two groups.

a) Let us assume that the mean scores for the first group were 15 and 5 for the easy and hard pairs, respectively. What do you estimate these values would be for the second group?

b) For the third group, the easy and hard pairs were re-paired separately. What should be the consequence of this for the scores on these pairs?

6. An investigator set about to get a definitive answer on progressive changes in learning as a function of practice (learning-to-learn) for free-recall lists. He decided to study learning-to-learn as a function of 2, 4, 6, 8, and 10 successive lists. Five different random groups were used, the subjects being assigned to the five conditions (2, 4, 6, 8, or 10 lists) by a block-randomized schedule. In terms of method, procedure, balancing of lists, and so on, the experiment was immaculate. However, we would have to say it was a very inefficient way to obtain the information he sought. Why?

7. An investigator has a particular hypothesis he wishes to test. He has available a population of subjects between the ages of 10 and 21. For the experiment, he needs only two groups, an experimental group and a control group. However, for reasons which need not be of concern here, he can test only 15 subjects for each group. In planning the experiment he faces the following decision: whether to draw his two groups randomly from the entire population or to choose a homogeneous population in terms of age, say, all 15-year-olds, and then select his two groups randomly from that group. Either alternative is quite feasible mechanically. There is no record of his decision, but if he was thoughtful about the matter, two points were foremost in his thinking. What are they?

8. In paired-associate learning, the subject must learn to give a particular word when another is shown to him. It is quite possible to measure the speed with which the word is given, thus latency measures may supplement measures of correct responding. In this particular experiment, an easy and a difficult list of pairs were used, being assigned randomly to 20 subjects in each of two groups. Both lists contained 12 pairs. Ten trials were given; on the tenth trial,

latency measures were taken of the correct responses, there being 5 correct responses on the average for the difficult list and 11 for the easy list. The mean latency was also greater for the difficult list than for the easy list. Why is it probable that the latency differences are much underestimated for the two lists?

9. Letters differ widely in the frequency with which they follow each other in words. The letters T and H, in that order, follow each other very frequently, while the order TK is very rare. An investigator formed a paired-associate list of eight pairs of letters in which sequence frequency was very low. The first letter, e.g., T, was the stimulus term, the second, e.g., K, the response term. Four randomly formed groups practiced the list until all response letters could be given to the appropriate stimulus letters. The independent variable was the length of the retention interval, being five minutes, one day, one week, and one month.

a) Why is this a difficult experiment to complete without possible subject selection?

b) Forgetting occurred as expected over the month as indexed by an increase in the number of omissions and by a decrease in the number of correct responses. The interest of the investigator was primarily in the overt errors made on the recall test. These errors consisted of giving the wrong response letter to a stimulus letter, or giving a letter which was not in the list. He found that the number of such errors increased as the retention interval increased. It is probable that this measure of raw number of errors is not the best for theoretical or analytical purposes. What error measure would be better?

c) The investigator noted that erroneous responses almost always completed two-letter sequences which were more frequent in words than were the correct two-letter sequences. Why is this not very meaningful?

10. An investigator studied free-recall learning as a function of the length of the list, namely, 10, 20, 30, and 40 words. The lists were formed by drawing randomly from a pool, with each subject getting a different list. Four groups were assigned to the list lengths through the use of a block-randomized schedule. A single study trial was given followed by recall immediately after the last word in the list was presented. Length of list is confounded with another variable. What is it?

11. For reasons which need not be of concern here, an investigator wanted to test the effectiveness of two different interview formats. On the average, one form required three minutes to complete, the other required five minutes. A large group of subjects was available. They were requested to appear between 10:00 A.M. and 12:00 noon on a given day, but they were told that they could come anytime within that two-hour period. As the subjects appeared they were sent to one of the two interview booths on a random basis. Thus, a line formed outside of each booth where the interviews were being conducted. All subjects were asked to wait in line, and all complied (none left after having arrived). At noon, 33 subjects had completed the short interview, 19 the long. All subjects remaining in the two lines were dismissed.

  a) The investigator worked up the data on all subjects, 33 who had taken the short form, 19 who had taken the long. This was inappropriate. Why?

  b) How should the data have been handled?

  c) A still further objection might be raised. What is it?

12. A long paired-associate list was constructed in which the pairs differed widely in known difficulty of learning. A heterogeneous group of 100 subjects was given ten acquisition trials on the list. Then, each stimulus term was presented, and the subject was requested to give the correct response as

quickly as possible. The latency of responding was determined. No subject produced all of the response terms correctly, but errors (giving an incorrect response) constituted less than 1 percent of the total responses produced. Of course, in many cases the subject did not respond at all. The investigator had fully expected that the easier pairs would show the shorter latencies. However, when he plotted the results, with pair difficulty along the baseline, the latencies were seen to decrease as pair difficulty increased.

a) How could this finding be accounted for by a combined item- and subject-selection process?

b) How would you derive a response measure from the data which might indeed show, as the investigator had anticipated, that the latency would increase as pair difficulty increased?

13. A teacher developed a technique which she thought would be guaranteed to improve the reading skill of her students. In order to make what she believed to be the most stringent test of her new method, she decided to try using it with the ten poorest readers in her class of 50 students. She selected these ten worst readers on the basis of their performance on the most recent reading test given in class. For a comparison group she selected the ten best readers in her class (the selection again being made on the basis of the most recent reading test). After two weeks of intensive application of her technique with the ten poorest readers, the teacher administered an equivalent form of the previously given reading test. She found that her ten poorest readers had a mean score of 55 while her ten best readers had a mean score of 80. The mean scores for these same poorest and best readers on the first reading test were 40 and 90, respectively. The teacher argued that it would be unreasonable to expect any technique to eliminate the differences between her poorest and her best readers after only two weeks. In that she had cut the difference between the two groups in half from the first to the second test, the teacher concluded that her method had been demonstrated to be effective.

a) Do you agree with the teacher's conclusion?

b) How might the teacher have made a better test of her new method?

14. Fifty factories, which were subsidiaries of a large national industrial firm, were required by the national office to participate in a program designed to compare the effectiveness of two supervisory methods. The critical issue was which of these two methods provided the higher level of employee morale among those working under the supervisor.

Each factory was required to send (to the national office) two people who were scheduled to be promoted to supervisor but who had not yet had any actual experience in a supervisory role. One member of each pair was randomly assigned to training in one of the two supervisory techniques, with the other member obviously receiving training in the second method. At the end of the training period, each of the new supervisors returned to the factory from which he or she came. The director of personnel at each factory agreed to assign 25 workers to each new supervisor with this assignment being done randomly from the pool of available workers. Each supervisor obviously agreed to use the supervisory technique which he or she had learned during the training period.

After ten weeks on the job with their new supervisors, all employees were given a test designed to assess their morale (the test was known to be reliable and valid). The 1000 workers from all the factories who had been supervised by people trained in supervisory technique A had a mean morale score of 89.72. The 1200 workers who had been supervised by people trained in supervisory technique B had a mean morale score of 89.48. The difference was not statistically significant, and the national office decided to abandon the supervisory-training program. Can you find evidence to suggest that this may have been a hasty (and incorrect) decision?

Chapter 4 WITHIN-SUBJECTS DESIGNS

1. Earlier, problems were built around the scaling of 21 statements dealing with national problems. For the method of rank order, the subjects had all 21 statements in front of them. If we study this situation, it will be seen that as far as design is concerned, we could use 21 random groups, with the subjects in each group assigning a rank to a single item, with, of course, all other 20 items available for inspection.

a) Why is it unlikely that such a method would ever be used?

b) Suppose we gave each of the 21 groups a single item without the other 20 available and asked the subjects in each group to assign the item a rank. Why is this a bit ludicrous?

c) Could category scaling be used with the situation described in (b)?

2. An investigation was directed toward determining the signal intensity required in order for a subject to hear it over a noisy channel. Various intensities were used. On each trial a ready signal was given, followed immediately by the signal presented in the noisy channel. The subject responded YES if he heard the signal, NO if he did not believe he heard it. The experimenter occasionally gave the ready signal but did not follow it with a signal. If the subject said YES under these circumstances it was classed as a false alarm. As noted above, several different intensities were used but for the present problem the results for only one intensity will be given. The entries below represent the percent of signals which were missed (the subject said NO when a signal was presented) and the percent of false alarms (the subject said YES when no signal was present). The results for two subjects are shown:

	Misses	False Alarms
Subject #1	2	20
Subject #2	20	2

a) It may be said that the two subjects were equally good or sensitive in detecting the signal. What is the reasoning?

b) The subjects did differ in some way, however, as is obvious. How may this be described?

c) What quantitative measure can you devise to give a score to each subject that would express the difference asked about in part (b)?

3. Assume there is a situation using a within-subjects design (complete) in which the anticipation of the nature of the next stimulus to be presented will influence the subject's judgment of that stimulus. There are only two different stimuli in the experiment. Under these circumstances, neither counter-balancing of the stimuli (abbaabbaabba etc.) nor block-randomization (ababbaabbabaabbaabbaab etc.) should be used if many trials are to be given on each stimulus.

a) Why not?

b) How can progressive error be balanced while avoiding the anticipation problem?

4. For reasons known only to him, an investigator held a hypothesis about length discrimination as a function of age. More particularly, he believed that there were rapid changes in discrimination during the period of adolescence. He chose five small groups of subjects, ages 11, 12, 13, 14, and 15. The task for the blindfolded subject was to estimate the length of a stick held between the thumb and index finger. He manufactured ten sticks which were all exactly the same except that they differed in length by steps of one-fourth inch. He decided to use the method of absolute judgment wherein the subject gave the estimate of length in inches and fractions of inches. He did this only after first determining that the subjects at all five age levels understood the length scale and could give reliable judgments in absolute terms. Since he had only a small number of subjects in each group, he wanted to give each subject many trials on each length in order to produce stable results. The decision of moment was whether he should use block-randomization to balance changes with practice or *abba* counterbalancing. What would you advise him, and why?

5. An investigator wanted to study the effect of imagery instructions on free-recall learning. This independent variable called for him to instruct the subject concerning how images should be used to relate the words in the list. In fact, he wanted to use three different conditions, one in which instructions emphasized bizzare imagery, one that emphasized nonbizzare imagery, and a control with no instructions given. In conducting such an experiment, the same subject should not be tested under all three conditions.

a) Explain why this is true for this particular experiment.

b) What general principle can be stated to cover all such cases?

6. Assume that there is a perceptual-motor task requiring precise control of several movements. Learning proceeds at a slow rate but is linearly related to trials over many periods of practice. An investigator wishes to determine the influence of time of day on the performance on this task, there being four different times. The subjects will receive a constant number of trials under each condition. He has to decide whether to use an incomplete within-subjects design (in which a subject will serve in all four conditions, with the orders being counterbalanced across subjects), or a random-groups design. He plans on 96 subjects.

a) Is the incomplete within-subjects design an appropriate one? Why?

b) In which of the two designs would the variability of the scores for a given condition be greater?

c) With four conditions, there are four stages of practice. Show how, with the incomplete within-subjects design, he can determine whether or not there is an interaction between time of day and stage of practice. Assume there was no differential transfer.

d) Show how, with the within-subjects design, the investigator really has included the random-groups design as he originally contemplated it.

e) In most cases when an environmental variable (such as time of day) is manipulated in a learning experiment, it is not possible to determine changes in performance from stage to stage because a different task is used for each condition, e.g., four different lists of words. Unless the order of the four tasks is counterbalanced, task difficulty and changes from stage to stage are confounded. In the present experiment, however, one can determine stage effects directly using scores on the single task. Why is this possible here and not in the usual experiment?

7. Two distinctly different modes of dress, A and B, were used by an experimenter in an effort to determine if mode of dress influenced the behavior of others. Specifically, the experimenter accosted people on the street of a large city and asked directions for reaching a museum that was located a few blocks away. In making half the inquiries the experimenter was in A attire; in making the other half, the experimenter was in B attire. The response measure was the number of respondents who were willing to give directions.

This is a random-groups design in that those people asked for directions under A should be "equivalent" to those asked for directions under B.

a) One possibility for achieving random groups would be to alternate between conditions A and B. There is a mechanical problem which would advise against this. What is it?

b) Another possibility would be to test under Condition A on one day and Condition B on the next. This will not do. Why?

c) How could this problem of randomization be handled and still avoid mechanical problems or problems in inconvenience?

d) This situation would seem to be particularly vulnerable to experimenter bias. That is, if the experimenter has a hypothesis about the outcome it might influence choice of people in a subtle way. How could this be avoided?

e) Should the language in which the question is asked of the subjects be in "tune" with the attire?

f) Assume that the study was carried out properly. How might it be argued that the results may have little generality?

8. An experiment was done to determine if performance on an arithmetic calculation test could be influenced through the provision of monetary incentives. A total of 100 subjects was randomly assigned to one of four treatment conditions. All subjects were given one practice trial on the arithmetic test under standard instructions. The control subjects were then given three equivalent forms of the same test with the same instructions. The subjects in the first experimental group were told that they would receive three additional arithmetic tests and that they would receive one dollar if their performance on the second test was better than that on the first test and one dollar more if their performance on the final test was better than that on the second test. The subjects in the other two experimental groups were similarly instructed except that they were offered incentives of five dollars and ten dollars respectively.

Performance on the practice trial was essentially the same for all four groups. On the three subsequent test trials the performances of the three incentive groups did not differ, and all three were poorer than the performance of the control group. The investigator concluded that a monetary incentive serves to depress performance on an arithmetic test.

a) Why is the investigator's conclusion inappropriate?

b) How might the data be analyzed to see if the subjects in the experimental groups were approaching the test trials differently from those subjects in the control group?

9. In an earlier problem, the following saying was presented: "The more things a man is ashamed of, the more respectable he is." This statement is probably intended to mean that respectable and nonrespectable men differ in their propensities for showing shame (for admitting mistakes). Assume, however, that these propensities are equal for the respectable and nonrespectable man. How might the saying still be valid?

Chapter 5 MIXED DESIGNS, INTERACTION, AND SUBJECT VARIABLES

1. A psychologist was interested in the ability to assemble a certain puzzle she had designed. It was her contention that once a person had attained a certain insight, this person would be able to construct the puzzle very rapidly. Fearing that there would be a large variation in puzzle-solving ability, and knowing that there were only a few subjects available for testing, she decided to use a matched-groups design.

Twenty subjects were given the puzzle to solve. The times to solution varied between 2 minutes and 55 minutes, with a mean of 35 minutes. The experimenter matched subjects by pairs, being able to get close matches on nine pairs. The subjects in each pair were assigned randomly to a C Group or to an E Group. The members of the C Group spent 30 minutes reading magazines. During this same period the members of the E Group read prepared material on puzzle solving which, it was thought, would provide them with the critical insight to solve the puzzle in question. At the end of the 30-minute period the subjects in both groups solved the puzzle again.

The subjects in the C Group finished the puzzle in an average time of 3 minutes; the corresponding value for the subjects in the E Group was 4 minutes. These means did not differ statistically. The investigator concluded that either the printed material had not conveyed the proper insight or this was just not important for this puzzle.

a) This is probably an inappropriate conclusion. Why?

b) In retrospect, how should the experiment have been done?

2. An investigator wanted to do some experiments to test various implications of a hypothesis he had developed about the cause of the horizontal-vertical illusion. Knowing that this illusion is not of great magnitude for the average subject, he decided on a scheme which he believed would maximize the possibilities of showing that certain variables were indeed relevant ones.

His first step was to set up a standard situation for measuring the magnitude of the illusion. He then gave 500 subjects a single trial on the illusion in this standard situation. From the 500 scores he chose the 50 people showing the greatest magnitude of the illusion and these 50 subjects were recalled for further experimentation. In this further work he included several independent variables, and many trials for each subject by a complete within-subjects design. However, included among the many conditions was another measurement of the illusion under the standard situation he had used originally.

a) In working up his data he found that the mean magnitude of the illusion for the 50 subjects under the standard situation was significantly less than it had been in the original measurements. There are at least two possible causes for this finding. What are they?

b) His use of subjects who showed a large illusory effect might be questioned on the grounds that the effect of the independent variables could not be generalized to anyone except those showing large illusory effects. However, this criticism has a hidden assumption. What is it?

3. A group of Norwegian college students was given many, many trials on a memory-span test for digits. Half the time the digits were presented aurally, half the time visually. The same procedures were administered to American college students. There were 100 students in each group. The mean spans for each of the two groups were found to be as follows:

	Aural	Visual
Norwegian	9.2	9.0
Americans	6.2	8.0

It is clear that the span length for the Norwegian students was greater than that for the American students. However, the critical data for the investigator concerned the interaction between the two variables. After the fact, the investigator speculated about the cultural differences that could lead to the American students being more proficient in handling visual stimuli than in handling aural stimuli, and why this would not be expected with students raised in the Norwegian culture.

It may be that cultural differences have nothing to do with the interaction. What alternative hypothesis could be offered and how could this be tested by analyzing the data in a particular way?

4. A theory about how the individual relates to groups was based on notions about introversion and extroversion of the individual. The theory (by steps that need not be of concern here) led to the prediction that an extrovert would underestimate the size of a crowd of people and an introvert would overestimate the number of people in the crowd. An investigator selected 100 introverts and 100 extroverts by a test which was valid for this purpose. To each group he displayed a series of pictures showing situations in which varying numbers of people were gathered. Each picture was shown for a brief period of time and the subject was required to make an absolute judgment of the number of people shown in each picture.

The results showed that the extroverts as a group did consistently under-estimate the number of people pictured and the introverts overestimated the number just as predicted. Even as a first step in theory testing this experiment leaves much to be desired. In fact, it can be stated that at least one other set of judgments should have been obtained from a group before the investigator could even think about pushing the theory. What should this other set of judgments have been?

5. An experiment was performed to determine whether simple addition of five digits could be done more rapidly when the digits were presented in columns or when the digits were presented in rows. The response measure was the time taken to complete each of four trials. Each trial consisted of a set of 20 different problems, i.e., 20 problems requiring the addition of five digits each. A total of 48 college-student subjects was assigned randomly to two groups, one receiving all problems with digits presented in rows and one receiving the same problems with digits presented in columns. For purposes of balancing, the four different problem sets were presented in a different order to each of the 24 subjects in each group, with all possible orders of the four sets being used once. The results showed that the mean solution time decreased across trials (sets) for both the row and column groups, but the mean solution time was consistently lower on each trial for the column group.

a) This experiment can be viewed as containing two independent variables, namely, columns versus rows, and problem-set difficulty. What design was used for each?

b) There could have been an interaction between successive problem sets (trials) and the row-column variable. Draw the most likely interaction and tell why you think it most likely.

c) What secondary response variable would be readily available from this experiment? Why might it be of little value?

6. A teacher was interested in the effectiveness of two different learning strategies (A and B) on two different types of material (X and Y). In order to save subject-testing time, the teacher constructed a single task with an equal number of instances of Material X and Material Y. This single long task was divided into four parts with an equal number of X and Y instances in each part. Pretesting had shown that these four parts were equivalent in difficulty when summed across X and Y. The teacher gave the task to 20 subjects, with Strategy A instructions given for the first and fourth quarters, Strategy B for the second and third quarters. The subjects were given three minutes to study each part. The results of a recall test showed that Strategy A was clearly superior to Strategy B for learning for X and Y, but that the recall was better for Material X than for Material Y under both strategies.

a) What design was used for the two independent variables?

b) The design was inappropriate for two reasons. What are they?

c) How should the experiment have been done?

7. Attitudes, it is believed by some, may influence perception. The following represents a test of such a notion. There was a hotly contested election in which citizens took very strong positions on the two candidates, A and B. In some way the experimenter was able to find a group of people who were very pro-A, another group that was very pro-B, and a third group that was neutral. He showed all three groups a five-minute filmed speech given by Candidate A. The subjects were told that they would be tested following the speech but the nature of the test was not specified. After the speech was finished, all subjects were asked to estimate its temporal length.

The experimenter had the notion that when a speaker expressed ideas consonant with already established attitudes, the duration of the speech would appear relatively short compared with the case where the speaker's ideas were antagonistic to already established ideas. Thus the expectation was that the pro-A subjects would estimate the time of the speech to be less than the pro-B subjects, and the neutral subjects would fall in between. This is precisely what the results showed.

  a) Why can these results not be taken as supportive of the notion that attitudes influence temporal perception?

  b) What additional condition or conditions should have been included to make the test a "tighter" one?

8. An investigator believed that the perceived attractiveness of a stimulus would be a direct function of the number of times the subject had seen the stimulus before. In order to use stimuli with which college students would be relatively unfamiliar, nonsense shapes were used. An artist prepared 32 distinct nonsense shapes, and the investigator more or less arbitrarily sorted these into eight sets of four shapes each. He then assigned each of the eight sets to one of the eight frequencies of exposure, namely, 0, 1, 2, ...7. Because there were only four stimuli in each set, there was no reason to believe that the sets contained stimuli which were, on the average, equally attractive for all eight sets. In order to avoid confounding frequency and set, therefore, the investigator made seven additional assignments of sets to frequencies such that each set was assigned to each frequency once and only once. Each of the assignments can be spoken of as a form. A matrix may help in understanding the procedure. Each set was identified by letters A, B, C, ...H. Remembering that the induced frequencies varied from 0 through 7, the matrix could be constructed as follows:

Induced Frequency

	0	1	2	3	4	5	6	7
Form 1	E	G	C	H	D	F	A	B
Form 2	G	C	H	D	F	A	B	E
Form 3	C	H	D	F	A	B	E	G
Form 4	H	D	F	A	B	E	G	C
Form 5	D	F	A	B	E	G	C	H
Form 6	F	A	B	E	G	C	H	D
Form 7	A	B	E	G	C	H	D	F
Form 8	B	E	G	C	H	D	F	A

Lists were constructed for each form in order to present the shapes to the subjects. Each shape was shown to the subject for five seconds, with the number of exposures for a given shape being determined by the particular form being used. For example, a subject assigned to Form 4 would have the four shapes in Set D presented once each, those in Set F twice each, and so on. Ten subjects were assigned randomly to each form for a total of 80 subjects. Following the presentation of the lists, all subjects were given the task of rating each of the 32 shapes on a seven-point scale of perceived attractiveness. The investigator's hypothesis was supported in that the mean scale value increased directly with increasing exposure frequency, where the higher the mean the greater the attractiveness.

a) In presenting the shapes to the subjects, each shape was shown on a card for five seconds. When a shape was shown more than once, a different card was used for each occurrence. How many cards would the investigator need for a given subject?

b) In constructing the order of the cards within a pack to be presented to the subject, the investigator divided the total number of cards into four quarters. Within each quarter one shape from each set was assigned to a given frequency and all cards for those seven shapes occurred with the appropriate frequency within the quarter. The other three shapes in each set were assigned to successive quarters under the same plan. The assignment of cards to position within a quarter was done randomly. Another investigator might have assigned the cards on a random basis throughout the entire list, disregarding quarters. In either case, however, there is a negative correlation between induced frequency and another potential independent variable. What is it?

c) Although forms as an independent variable was of no particular interest to the investigator, what design was used to manipulate this variable?

d) For any given subject, the procedure could be viewed as a complete within-subjects design. Under this view, the four shapes used at each frequency level would be considered as four repetitions of the same condition. However, because of possible unknown differences in attractiveness among the eight sets, a single subject's rating data for a given frequency could be the result of either frequency, initial attractiveness of the four shapes within a set, or both. Therefore, the investigator wisely decided to balance possible set differences by using the eight forms. As a consequence of this balancing, the matrix became much like that of a matrix for a basic design method. What is this basic design method?

e) It would be possible to determine from the data whether the eight sets differed on attractiveness without them having been exposed in the list. How?

f) This experiment might have been done using a random-groups design for manipulating frequency of exposure. All 32 shapes would be used. One group would receive one exposure of each shape, another group two exposures of each, a third group three exposures, and so on. What might argue strongly against the use of such a design for this experiment?

Chapter 6 HERE-AND-THERE DESIGN PROBLEMS

1. A difference threshold is the magnitude of the difference between two stimuli on some characteristic (pitch, brightness) which can be detected 50 percent of the time. Several different methods may be used to determine difference thresholds but all are most frequently inserted in a complete

within-subjects design. Under these methods the subject is given many, many trials. The investigator believed that the subjects often became bored with this tedious task and as a consequence often responded somewhat haphazardly, thereby producing difference thresholds that were larger than the subject could in fact discriminate under ideal conditions. He set about to see if he could manipulate the size of the difference threshold by offering monetary incentives for correct responding. He used a mixed design, with two independent groups differentiated in terms of the amount of money given for each correct response (twenty-five cents and one dollar). The threshold measurements were taken by a complete within-subjects design. The results of his experiment showed that the difference threshold was smaller (statistically) for the group given twenty-five cents for each correct response than for the group given one dollar for each correct response. State carefully the conclusion that can be made concerning the empirical finding.

2. A study was designed to examine the effect of intertrial interval on a reversal task. The rats all first learned a left turn in a T maze. They were then divided into four groups and given ten trials on the reverse habit, i.e., making a right turn to receive food. The variable was the length of the intertrial interval between the ten trials on the reversal task, the durations being 0, 1, 3, and 5 minutes. It was found that the performance on the reversal task was directly related to the intertrial interval.

a) Why can it be said that the results associated with the independent variable may not at all be a function of reversal learning?

b) What is the necessary design to answer the question as to whether the effect of intertrial interval is tied wholly or in part to reversal learning?

3. The task for the subject in an experiment was that of turning cubes. Each cube was two inches on a side. Each of the six sides had a symbol on it, each symbol being distinctly different from the others. Each cube fit into an insert on a tray. Only the symbol on the top side was visible when the cube was in the insert. The subject lifted out each cube from its insert, found the specified symbol and replaced the cube in its insert with the specified symbol

on the top side. Before any given trial, the experimenter randomized the placement of the cubes in their inserts with the only restriction being that the symbol appropriate for a given trial never appeared on the top side. The response measure was the time required to complete the turning of the 100 blocks.

In one study the investigator gave the subjects ten massed trials, each trial consisting of the turning of the 100 cubes. In this procedure, as soon as a subject completed one tray, another tray replaced it and the subject continued turning the blocks as rapidly as possible. After completing the ten trays, a five-minute rest was given. The subject was then given one additional trial. The question asked of the experiment was whether or not the rest interval would result in an increase in performance. A single group of subjects was used, all subjects being given the five-minute rest. The investigator's idea was that he could infer a value for an eleventh-trial performance had an eleventh massed trial been given. By so doing, he could avoid running a separate group of control subjects.

The mean performance scores for the ten trials in order were: 3.4, 2.6, 3.2, 3.0, 3.6, 2.8, 2.6, 3.4, 3.6, and 2.8 minutes.

a) Suppose he drew the best-fitting straight line through a plot of these ten points. Extrapolating this line to the eleventh trial yielded a value of 3.1 minutes. He decided, therefore, that if performance on the eleventh trial was any value less than 3.1, it would be concluded that the rest interval improved performance. This decision is not appropriate. Why?

b) Suppose he said that if time to complete the eleventh trial was less than 2.6 minutes he would conclude that the rest interval had enhanced performance. Would you accept this? Why?

c) What simple statistical procedure could one use to set a performance score below which we would be quite willing to conclude that the rest interval enhanced performance?

d) Suppose the ten performance scores, in order of the ten trials, had been as follows: 3.6, 3.4, 3.2, 3.0, 2.8, 2.6, 2.4, 2.2, 2.0, 1.8. What could be said now about the level of performance that could be used to infer with confidence that the rest interval enhanced performance?

4. Each of the 56 students in a senior highschool class was given one trial or test on the Müeller-Lyer illusion:

In this illusion the horizontal lines are the same length but they do not appear to be equal. There are several ways to determine the magnitude or amount of the illusion. One of the ways is called the method of average error. In this method (which has several variants) we would consider one of the segments of the illusion a standard stimulus and hold its length constant. The other segment is varied; that is, we would have several samples of it differing only in the length of the horizontal line. These lengths would be varied in small steps. The subject is asked to choose from among the series of samples the one which he perceives as being equal to the standard. For the present study, the left figure above (>——<) was the standard, the other (<——>) the variable stimulus. For each subject the length of the variable chosen as being equivalent to the standard was determined. The standard was always six inches in length. The mean of the 56 variable stimuli chosen (one by each subject) was 4.25 inches. The mean magnitude of the illusion for the class, therefore, was 1.75 inches.

a) All subjects were treated alike, hence there was only one condition. How can this procedure be classified as an experiment when two conditions are required to define an experiment?

b) What is the critical property of the Müeller-Lyer illusion which is responsible for the illusion; that is, if we had to specify one characteristic which, if absent, would destroy the illusion, what would it be? Of course if there were no wings at all there would be no illusion. But given that all lines are present, what is the critical feature?

c) Using only the data as gathered, how might the scores be classified so as to result in an experiment in which a natural-groups design was ostensibly involved?

d) The difference between the length of a standard stimulus and the length judged equal to the standard is called the constant error. When a visual display results in most subjects showing the same direction (positive or negative) to the constant error, it is spoken of as an illusion. Let us assume that in the study described above, each subject was shown the two figures with the horizontal lines being equal in length. The subject is forced to "choose the figure with the longer horizontal line." How do we determine whether or not the illusion was present under these circumstances?

e) The Müeller-Lyer illusion is a very potent one for human subjects. Briefly describe the gross procedures which might be used to determine if a chimpanzee is subject to the illusion.

5. In a reaction-time study, an investigator measured the speed of discrimination between two letters as a function of the frequency with which the letters occur in words. The letters X and K were used to represent low-frequency letters, O and E the high-frequency letters. Two random groups were used, one given trials on the low-frequency letters, the other trials on the high-frequency letters. In the former group, the subject was to respond as quickly as possible by saying the letter whenever K appeared, but never to respond when X appeared. For the second group (high frequency) the subject was to respond as quickly as possible when O appeared, but never to respond when E appeared.

a) There is a confounding. What is it?

b) If the confounding is removed, and if the desire is to establish the difference in speed of discrimination between two low-frequency letters as compared with two high-frequency letters, two control groups are required. What are they and why?

6. The intensity of a noxious stimulus was manipulated in order to determine the effect it would have on extinction rate. Animals learned to escape from a compartment of a test chamber in which they received electrical shock. Escape was accomplished by turning a wheel which raised a door leading to a safe compartment. Three randomly formed groups were given different intensities of shock. All animals were given five trials, and all escaped successfully on all trials. Immediately after the five acquisition trials, extinction was begun. Each animal was placed in the test chamber (with no shock, of course), and the time required to escape measured. Each animal was given ten such extinction trials. Each trial was two minutes in length. If the animal had not left the chamber during that period on a given trial the time was recorded as two minutes and the animal was removed. Five minutes separated each extinction trial.

The results showed that the mean time across the ten trials was inversely related to the intensity of shock during the five training trials. That is, the animals with the strongest intensity of shock escaped (on extinction) more quickly on the average than did the animals with the weaker shocks during acquisition.

a) Although the conclusion about the relationship between intensity of shock during the training and rate of extinction seems straightforward, why is there an interpretative problem?

b) Supposing the animals with the most intense shock extinguished more rapidly than those with the lowest intensity. Would this make the interpretation "cleaner?"

c) What other data would be useful in helping to understand the extinction scores regardless of the outcome (faster or slower extinction as a function of shock intensity)?

7. An applied psychologist reached a tentative conclusion that waitresses must be fairly good judges of people's temperaments. To test this idea he arranged the following procedures. In a given large restaurant, each waitress was directed to assess a customer before moving to the table. The waitress recorded her assessment on a five-point category scale labelled "will enjoy this meal a great deal" at one end, and "will thoroughly dislike this meal" at the other end. After the rating was made, the waitress went to the table and served the customer.

As a measure of the degree to which the customer enjoyed the meal, the size of the tip left for the waitress was used. This was expressed as a percent of the total bill. The experiment continued over a period of time so that the many different waitresses made many different ratings. The results were handled as correlations between the ratings and tip size for each waitress. These were all high, and averaged .85. The psychologist concluded that the evidence indicated that waitresses were indeed good judges of temperament, at least insofar as who will and who will not enjoy a meal reflects temperament.

a) Why might the test of the hypothesis have been inadequate?

b) How might the problem have been avoided?

c) Another approach was tried. The investigator simply required five waitresses (drawn randomly from those available) to rate each customer. What must be true of these ratings before any further steps need to be taken to test the hypothesis?

Chapter 7 STEPS TOWARD THEORY

1. When an initially neutral event becomes associated with a food reward in animal learning, the neutral event may itself take on some of the properties of the food reward. Such an event is spoken of as a secondary reinforcer. In the present study, the experimenter used two groups of white rats, 50 per group. The treatment for the animals in the E Group consisted of a light which continuously flashed on and off everytime the animals were fed in their home cages. This treatment was carried out for 30 days. The animals in the C Group had exposure to the same flashing light for the same period of time as had the animals in the E Group, but never during the feeding period.

On a test, the animals in each group were placed in a small open pen. The flashing light was presented on one side of the pen, the animals were placed singly on the other side, and the response measure was the number of rats in each group that approached the light source. When the animal approached within three inches of the light the experimenter designated this as a positive response; if two minutes elapsed without the animal approaching within three inches of the light, it was recorded as a negative response.

a) Assume that of each of the groups of 50 animals, 45 showed positive responses. This should lead to the conclusion that the flashing light had not become a secondary reinforcer. However, a further response measure, had it been used, might have shown a difference for the two groups. What is this additional measure?

b) Assume that a second C Group (C2) had been used for which the flashing light had never been experienced prior to the test. Assume further that the animals in this group showed more positive responses than did those in Group C1, but fewer than the animals in the E Group. From such results it might seem reasonable to conclude that the light had taken on secondary reinforcing properties for the E Group. But what alternatives are there for accounting for the differences in the two C Groups?

c) For a further question, we will concentrate on the E Group. Two assumptions about intervening processes will be made, processes which are assumed to accompany the procedures administered during the 30-day training period. First, assume that the flashing light does have an intrinsic attraction, but that this extinguishes very rapidly with trials. Second, assume that the light does become a secondary reinforcer but that with trials the association between the light and eating grows slowly but linearly. Using these assumptions, a very clear prediction emerges which relates number of training days prior to being given the test to positive responses on the test. What is this prediction?

d) How would it be possible to get an independent measure of each of the two assumed processes described in the immediately preceding question?

2. Learning theories may include a positive process and a negative process, both of which increase with trials. In these theories, performance is assumed to reflect the positive process minus the negative process. What set of relationships between trials and the two processes would be necessary for performance to first increase and then decrease?

3. In a verbal-discrimination task the subject is presented a series of pairs of words or pairs of other verbal units or items. For each pair, the experimenter randomly designates one of the words to be the correct one. The subject's task is to learn which word in each pair is the correct word. When the anticipation procedure is used to study the learning, the technique is as follows. A pair (A-B) is presented for perhaps two seconds; then the correct word (let us say A) is shown alone for two seconds. Of course, the subject is instructed that the word shown alone is the correct word in the pair. After A is shown alone, another pair is presented, then the correct word from that pair, and so on, for all of the pairs in the list. During the first trial the subject merely observes the pairs and the correct words. On the second trial, he is instructed to say aloud the word in each pair he thinks is correct. He must do this during the two-second period in which the pair is presented, hence before the correct word is shown. The pairs are shown in different orders from trial to trial, and the spatial positions of the right and wrong words in the pairs are randomized across trials. The theoretical question is how the subject learns to discriminate between the right and wrong words in each pair.

One theoretical proposal for handling the learning of the verbal-discrimination task is known as frequency theory. The basic assumption is that the subject learns to discriminate the frequency difference between the right and wrong words in a pair and responds by choosing the word with the higher situational frequency. As may be seen, when the pairs are presented by the anticipation method, the correct word in a pair is shown twice on each trial, the incorrect word only once. Further, the subject may rehearse the correct word so that the frequencies after a single trial may be greater than two-to-one. Therefore if the subject applies a rule applicable to all pairs ("choose the more frequent word"), and if he can discriminate the frequency differences of the right and wrong words in a pair, he will choose the correct word.

a) In the anticipation procedure as described above, only the correct item (A) was shown following the presentation of the pair (A-B). Suppose that instead of showing only A, A-B was shown with A underlined to indicate that it is the correct word. What would the theory predict about the learning in the two cases (A shown alone, or A-B shown with A underlined)?

b) What does the theory predict about learning as a function of the length of the list, i.e., number of pairs constituting the list?

c) Assume that the subject learns a verbal-discrimination list until he can give all of the correct words. The experimenter then informs him that he will be given further trials but that on these further trials the role of the two words in each pair will be reversed in that the word formerly correct will be incorrect and vice versa. To be successful on the reversal task the subject must now apply a new rule, namely, to choose the less frequent word in each pair. Most subjects can do this without difficulty. However, as trials on the reversal task increase in number, the subjects run into trouble. Why should this trouble arise according to the theory?

d) In the study-test procedure, as contrasted with the anticipation procedure, the subject is given alternate study and test trials. On the study trials the subject is shown the pairs with the correct word in each pair underlined. On the test trials, A-B is shown without the correct word being underlined and the subject must choose the word in each pair he thinks was underlined (correct) on the study trial. Suppose that in using the study-test procedure we require the subject to pronounce aloud both words in each pair during the study trial. According to the theory, how would the rate of learning when the subject is required to pronounce both words compare to that when he is not required to pronounce both words?

e) Suppose the right and wrong words are re-paired from trial to trial. That is, rather than A-B being paired on all trials, A is paired with B on the first trial, D on the second, F on the third, and so on, with B, D, and F always being wrong words in the list. Of course, all correct words remain correct on all trials and all incorrect words remain incorrect. What effect on learning would this have according to frequency theory?

f) Assume that we present a list of pairs of homonyms, such as *bear-bare, rain-reign, minor-miner,* and so on. Assume further that we find that such a list is much more difficult to learn than a list of pairs of nonhomonyms. What might this tell us about the "carrier" of frequency?

g) Assume that we give the subject a verbal-discrimination list in which all of the correct words are presented in red ink, all of the incorrect words in black ink. It would be expected that the subject would apply the rule of choosing the word printed in red. After five trials on the list, we tell the subject that on further trials all words will be printed in black ink. According to frequency theory, what should be the consequence of this change?

h) What alternative interpretation might be given if the results are as expected from frequency theory?

4. An investigation was conducted to study the changes in the affective reactions to geometrical designs. Eleven quite distinctly different designs were used. The designs were rated along a 7-point category scale in which 1 was most unpleasant, 7 most pleasant, and 4 neutral. The investigator's hypothesis

was that extreme affective reactions (whether pleasant or unpleasant) become less and less so with continued exposure of the stimuli which elicit them. Or to say this another way, extreme reactions tend to move toward the neutral point with continued exposure to the stimuli. A complete within-subjects design was used wherein each subject was given all conditions. Pilot work had shown him that there were wide differences in the initial affective reactions to the stimuli; some were judged very unpleasant, some very pleasant, some in between. In the main experiment he presented the 11 stimuli 20 times each. Each time the ordering was random, and on each of the 20 trials the subject assigned a scale value for each of the stimuli.

The investigator examined the results for each subject independently. The results to be discussed refer to a single subject, although all subjects showed essentially the same outcome. He determined a mean scale value for each of the 11 stimuli for trials 1-5, and separately for trials 16-20.

a) Would it be correct to say that his hypothesis predicts that the standard deviation for the 11 mean scale values for trials 1-5, would be greater than for the corresponding measure on trials 16-20?

b) Would it also be correct to say that the hypothesis would predict that the mean of the mean scale values of the 11 stimuli would be equal (statistically) for trials 1-5 and trials 16-20? Why?

c) He correlated the mean scale values for the 11 stimuli on trials 1-5 with their mean scale values on trials 16-20. He found this correlation to be very high. Would this be sufficient grounds to reject his hypothesis? Why or why not?

d) In fact, when he examined his data he found that the scale values for trials 1-5 and 16-20 for the 11 stimuli to be almost identical, i.e., there had been no movement toward the neutral part of the scale. At first he was going to report that his hypothesis was not tenable, but then decided that he had not made an appropriate test. Why was the test not appropriate?

5. In many tasks given to both animal and human subjects, one of the central problems is to determine the stimuli or events to which the responses are made. Often this requires a series of analytical experiments. The experimenter may perceive that there are a number of possibilities and he may set about to test them. In effect, he has to discover the events which are intimately linked with the behavior of interest in order to proceed with a theoretical formulation. His experiments attempt to answer questions like the following: "If that is the critical stimulus event, then if I do this, such and such should happen."

The problem being used to illustrate such analytical experiments is somewhat fanciful, although it has some ties with experiments that have been performed. Dogs are used as subjects, and they are taught to run down a 60-foot straight alley for a reward. The problem for the dog is made difficult by requiring it to run at a particular speed. In teaching the animal to run at a particular speed, the food is given only if the speed in traversing the alley is within a required rate zone (calculated as the time required to go down the alley at a constant rate of speed). To speak of a zone is merely to indicate that some tolerance is allowed. We will assume that this discrimination can be learned by the animal.

The question is what constitutes the basis for the learning (particular speed). Initially, we will say that the experimenter offers two alternatives. One, the learning or discrimination is based on interoceptive stimuli which differ in some unspecified way as a function of speed of running. Second, the discrimination is based on elapsed time (duration of time in alley), and it will be assumed that a duration discrimination can be made on the basis of stimuli quite independent from those used in making the speed-of-running discrimination. The following problems, then, relate to evidence which might favor one alternative over the other.

a) It is observed that as learning progresses the dogs will speed up as they approach the goal box on some trials and on other trials they will slow down as they approach the goal box. Which of the two alternatives would be favored by such observations?

b) After the discrimination is learned, the length of the maze is doubled. What should the animal do over the initial trials on the lengthened maze if the temporal-discrimination alternative is to be supported?

c) In this experiment, as the first task the dog is loosely strapped in a cart and is pulled through the maze at various speeds (speed is constant on a given trial), but reward is received only when the speed is in the specified zone. Of course, many trials are given. After the experiences with the cart, the animal is given a number of trials under self locomotion. Why would these procedures be given?

d) By this time the investigator had developed a third alternative. He repeated the procedures used in (c) but the dogs were blindfolded on all cart trips. What do you think the third alternative might be?

e) As a further step, dogs first learned the discrimination by the usual self locomotion, although the level of learning was considerably less than perfect. Then, many cart trials were given. Finally, the dogs were once more given trials under self locomotion. What was all of this aimed at?

Chapter 8 DIMENSIONS OF THEORY

1. A theorist held that knowledge of performance (or knowledge of results) is a very powerful factor in human learning of all kinds. The theory, as developed in detail, had feedback loops and other mechanisms, but these need not be of concern for the present problem. Of concern is the expectation that learning (according to the theory) would be markedly enhanced when the subject was allowed to determine periodically how his efforts to learn were reflected in his performance. Another investigator doubted that this expectation would be supported by an experiment. He used free-recall learning to make the test. The list consisted of 100 words and all subjects were given ten alternate study and test trials. On test trials the subjects wrote their responses on a large sheet of paper. Two groups of subjects, randomly formed, were used. Both groups were given five minutes to write all of the words they could remember on each test trial. Following the five-minute recall period, the subjects in the E Group were asked to count the number of words they had recalled, and this information allowed the subjects to have knowledge of their performance from trial to trial. The subjects were allowed two minutes to make the count. The subjects in the C Group, on the other hand, were given their next study trial immediately after the five-minute recall period.

a) The study was presented at a meeting attended by the theorist who had proposed the importance of knowledge of results. After hearing the details of the procedure, he said (to himself): "Knowledge of results has been ineffectively manipulated in this experiment." To what do you think he was referring?

b) Furthermore, it was pointed out that two other independent variables that might influence performance were confounded with the procedures for giving knowledge of results to the subjects in the E Group. What are they?

2.   Two observations led to a model dealing with spelling errors. One observation was that good spellers generally know when a word is spelled incorrectly as indicated by such comments as "it doesn't look right." It is as if there is a picture of the word in the mind which can be used to assess the correctness of the spelling. Poor spellers, according to this notion, cannot monitor the spelling by the "looks" of a word.

The second observation is that if the index finger is used as a "pencil," a person can print letters on our backs and we have some degree of accuracy in telling what these letters are. Again, it is as if we have an internalized picture of letters and in some way we can match the stimulation on the skin of the back with the internalized picture.

The theoretical approach simply assumed that the laws of discrimination based on "back writing" could serve as a model for understanding spelling errors. Before such a model can "get off the ground," what empirical relationship must be demonstrated?

3.   A theory led to two predictions concerning the relationship between frustration and aggression: (1) as frustration increases, aggression increases; (2) the greater the initial aggression, the more rapid the reduction in aggression as a consequence of aggression. Five random groups were used. By methods which need not be of concern here, five different levels of frustration were induced. Immediately after the procedures used to induce frustration were terminated, tests of aggression were introduced. The subject was shown 10 slides, one at a time. On each slide were stick figures which could be viewed as people. For each slide the subject was asked to write a sentence or two describing what the stick figure was doing. These sentences were scaled by neutral judges in terms of aggressiveness of the themes. The results did indeed

show that across the combined slides the average degree of aggressiveness of themes increased as frustration increased.

a) In the discussion section, the investigator indicated that if the results of the subsequent research he was planning proved compatible with the second prediction he would consider the theory to be viable. In fact, from this experiment as reported, he has at least two different tests he can make of the second prediction that would give data relevant to the hypothesis. What are they?

b) A critic indicates that these tests could only disconfirm the hypothesis, but that it will take a new experiment to get data which could be viewed as positive toward the theory. What did he mean?

4. A theory about the functioning of anxiety was being formulated. Initially, two assumptions were made: (1) a person is able to perceive his own changes in anxiety; (2) the perception of an increase in anxiety further increases anxiety. At least two further matters must be handled in formulating the theory. What are they?

5. In a two-category classification task, the subject is presented a list of items, e.g., words, one at a time. He must learn to give one response, YES, to half of the items and to give a second response, NO, to the other half. The experimenter informs the subject as to which class each item belongs. This is done for all items on a study trial. Then on a test trial the subject tries to classify each item appropriately, being required to give a response to each item. Another study trial is given, followed by a test trial, and so on. When the items consist of unrelated words there is no obvious way for the subject to discriminate between the two classes. Nonetheless, if a list consisting of 24 such items is presented for several trials, there is a steady decrease in errors. It might be argued that the decrease in errors reflects the fact that some subjects "catch on" by finding some way to discriminate the two classes, whereas other subjects make no progress at all across trials. With a 24-item list, of course, the failure to learn by a subject would be reflected in rather consistent

scores around chance (which would be 12 errors). There are probably several ways to determine if the argument (about there being a group of learners and a group of nonlearners among the subjects tested) has any basis in fact. Indicate at least one.

6. Theories of problem solving often start with the notion that subjects generate and test hypotheses about the solutions to problems. For example, when a four-letter anagram is given to the subject, there are only 24 possible hypotheses because there are only 24 different orders in which the four letters can be arranged. If only one word can be constructed from the letters, there are obviously 23 incorrect hypotheses which may be generated and tested.

In trying to formulate a mathematical or statistical theory for such problem solving, a theorist may make an initial assumption that the choice of a particular hypothesis for testing is completely uninfluenced by previous choices. In effect, this assumes that the subject has no memory for the previous hypotheses he has generated and tested. Such an assumption is probably incorrect.

a) If this assumption is incorrect, why would a theorist use it?

b) Another alternative would be to assume that there is no forgetting of any hypothesis tested and found wrong. This assumption, too, would probably be wrong in fact. However, assuming that the subject generates hypotheses randomly, which assumption (complete forgetting versus no forgetting of previously tested hypotheses) predicts the more rapid solution when number of hypotheses tested before solution is the response measure?

c) A computer could be programmed to solve the four-letter anagrams using either of the two assumptions. Why is it likely that number of hypotheses tested before solution is reached would be greater for the computer than for the usual college student when the solution words are common words?

7. In the procedures used in the present study, any given trial had three steps. First, the subject was shown a letter of the alphabet which, for the trial, was the target letter. This was shown for a time sufficient for the subject to identify it without error. On the second step the subject was shown a second letter. For the third step, the subject had to respond "same" or

"different" to indicate whether the target letter and the following letter were the same or different. The critical measure was the reaction time required to make the decision. Of particular interest for the present problem were the results when "same" was the appropriate answer. The subject was instructed that the two letters were to be considered the same regardless of the case in which they were printed. Thus, if the target letter was A, "same" was the appropriate response if the test letter was either A or a. For simplicity, the data presented here are for the letter A (a). The values are milliseconds.

		Target	
		A	a
Test	A	200	300
	a	300	200

As noted above, the response for all four cells was "same," but it is apparent that decision time was faster when the target and test letters were perceptually identical. The investigator believed that this difference was due to the fact that the A-A and a-a combinations had identical perceptual configurations and that a match (leading to "same" response) was based on this identity. For the other two combinations (A-a, a-A) he believed that the identity decision had to be mediated through a common semantic response ("Ay"). The investigator decided to undertake some further studies to test his thinking before attempting to construct a more formal theory.

Below are indicated the critical procedures carried out by the investigator, again with reference only to "same" responses. You are to indicate how the results of each would be critical or at least pertinent to his theoretical thinking. Of course, in all cases he had conditions in which both same and different responses were required, many trials, and so on. Only the critical procedures are given here.

a) He used the letters O and o, C and c, K and k as critical letters.

b) With the subject appropriately instructed, he presented five different letters in succession but with the first letter of the five being the target letter.

c) Both an upper and lower case letter were presented as the target, e.g., A and a, with the test being on one or the other.

d) A word was presented as the target with the subject instructed to response "same" if the test word was the same as the target word or if it represented an instance of the same class as did the target word. For example, if the target word was *cow* and the test word either *horse* or *cow*, the response was "same."

8. Ten men comprising a government task force were assigned to solve an important problem. The material with which they were working was quite complex, and the group members had widely different levels of understanding of it. Recognizing that these differences could result in a communication problem, it was decided to try to equalize the men's abilities by having all of them participate in the same crash instructional program. All ten men took all of the sessions of the special course.

The investigator had prepared two equivalent test forms, one being given to all men before the course and the other being given to all after the course. These tests were reliable and valid. The findings showed that across the ten men the pretest scores averaged 47 percent correct, and the posttest scores averaged 69 percent. Clearly, the average level of understanding of the group had been increased substantially by the course.

As an index of his success in equalizing the abilities of the men, the investigator decided to use the standard deviation. The standard deviation on the pretest was 15, while on the posttest it was 27. How could it have been that the investigator's attempt to reduce the differences in ability had actually served to increase these differences?

9. One theoretical approach sometimes used is that of trying to comprehend performance on a relatively complex task by conceiving of this performance as being produced by simple processes underlying two or more relatively simple subtasks. Frequently, much is known about these simple processes. In this final problem, which will be elaborated in detail, this is the theoretical approach taken. In the act of considering the details of the experiment, we will review a number of the issues.

The purpose of the experiment was to see if some understanding could be reached of the processes or mechanisms involved in a rather complex paired-associate task. More specifically, the independent variable was the number of different response terms in the list, with the number of pairs and number of stimulus terms constant. There were four levels of the independent variable, and it will be necessary to examine the lists representing these four levels before turning to the theoretical problem. These lists are shown below. The stimuli, or left-hand terms, are the numbers 1 through 16, and these same 16 numbers are used for all four lists. The words used as response terms are all five-letter nouns. The independent variable, number of different response words, is indicated by the list label. List 16 can be seen to be a typical paired-associate list in which each of the 16 words is used once as a response term. For List 12, four response terms are used twice, and eight are used once each. For List 8, eight response terms are used twice each, and for List 4, each of four response terms is used four times. To sum up, the number of different response terms increases from List 4 through List 16. The strict empirical question is: how does this variable influence paired-associate learning?

List 4	List 8	List 12	List 16
7-globe	7-globe	7-globe	7-globe
13-globe	13-globe	13-globe	13-ulcer
9-globe	9-ulcer	9-ulcer	9-banjo
12-globe	12-ulcer	12-ulcer	12-pearl
14-ulcer	14-banjo	14-banjo	14-lilac
5-ulcer	5-banjo	5-banjo	5-ranch
6-ulcer	6-pearl	6-pearl	6-attic
2-ulcer	2-pearl	2-pearl	2-olive
15-banjo	15-lilac	15-lilac	15-dairy
11-banjo	11-lilac	11-ranch	11-scarf
1-banjo	1-ranch	1-attic	1-hotel
8-banjo	8-ranch	8-olive	8-cloud
10-pearl	10-attic	10-dairy	10-valve
3-pearl	3-attic	3-scarf	3-flask
16-pearl	16-olive	16-hotel	16-thorn
4-pearl	4-olive	4-cloud	4-moose

The four lists as presented here have the identical response terms blocked. In presenting the lists for learning, of course the order of the pairs from trial to trial will be random so that the subject will not see, for example, the word *globe* in List 4 in four successive pairs. The task for the subject is to learn to say each response term to its appropriate stimulus term.

a) To what class of independent variables does the present variable belong?

b) If we used the above lists only, there is a confounding associated with the response terms. What is it and how should it be corrected?

c) What design for executing the experiment did the investigator have in mind?

Theoretically, the overall learning of the lists can be broken down into two subtasks, namely, acquiring the response terms as such, and associating the stimulus terms with the response terms. Considering only the response learning, it can be seen that it is really a length-of-list variable, hence time to acquire the response terms should be directly related to the number of response terms. That is, this subtask should be more and more difficult as we move from List 4 through List 16. In the case of associative learning, there is evidence from other situations (between-lists A-B, C-B transfer paradigm) that interference may occur when the same response term must be associated with two or more different stimulus terms across lists. Let us assume, as a tentative theoretical position, that the amount of interference, hence difficulty in associative learning within a list, is inversely related to number of different response terms. Finally, let us assume that these two processes are linearly related to the independent variable.

To summarize: we assume two intervening processes, one (response learning) which increases the difficulty of overall paired-associate learning as the number of response terms increases, and one (associative interference) which influences overall paired-associate learning in the opposite direction. In other words, as the independent variable increases from List 4 through List 16, an interaction between the two intervening processes is assumed to occur. A problem for the theory at this point is the lack of knowledge concerning the relative magnitude of the influence of each process on overall paired-associate learning. Nevertheless, we will proceed with the experiment. The subjects are given trial after trial until the response terms are produced to the appropriate stimulus terms on three consecutive trials. No subject reached this criterion in seven trials or fewer. Of course, we have the correct pairings given by each subject on every trial.

    d) The number of correct pairings on any trial may differ across lists even though the associations have not been truly learned. Why or how?

    e) We will assume that the problem referred to in (d) was not present, or was solved. Assume that in terms of the mean number of trials to reach the criterion (three successive perfect trials), we find a linear decrease from List 4 through List 16. In terms of the theoretical thinking, what would be concluded given this result?

    f) Assume that the results showed there was no difference among the the four means. What would this lead us to conclude about the two processes?

    g) How might we analyze the data to see if we could detect differences in response learning, remembering that logically, response learning must precede associative learning?

    h) There is no independent evidence that interference occurs when two or more stimulus terms share the same response term within a list. However, a careful inspection of the lists will show that such a test is available in one of the lists. Which one is it? Why should we be cautious about the outcome of this test?

    i) Assume that the results show that the mean numbers of trials to learn were 22, 28, 22, and 16, for Lists 4 through 16. It is apparent that our two-process theory with linear functions cannot handle this outcome, particularly the increase from List 4 to List 8. A third factor must be involved even if we are correct basically in the assumption of our other two processes. What might this other process be? As a hint, several different subjects who had learned List 4 told us that they learned only 12 associations.

j) Suppose again that the results were as described in (e) above. Using precisely the same four list structures, how could we, in a further experiment, reduce and perhaps even reverse the slope of the line (defined by mean trials to reach the criterion) by manipulating another task variable?

k) For studying the response-learning function alone, unencumbered by paired-associate learning, what task might we use?

l) How might we study the role of associative interference in these lists, unencumbered by response learning?

m) Assume we are successful in (k) and (l); that is, that we can successfully measure directly the two presumed subtasks. We can now proceed to include an individual-difference prediction in our theory. How will we do this, and what are the implications of this step?

APPENDIX B
RANDOM PERMUTATIONS
OF SIXTEEN NUMBERS

1000 Random Permutations of the Numbers 1-16 (Computer Generated)
Courtesy of Richard C. Galbraith and Charles S. Reichardt

```
16  12  15   9   1   4  11   4   2   1  11   1   7  16   4   1   2   6  14   7
11  14  14  12  15  10   1   7  14   8   1   6  15  10   5  15   4  13  11   8
 2  13   9  16   4   3  13  15  11   3  14   7  11   2   9  14   3   4   9  15
 9   9   7   7   2  16  10  16  10   5   8   3   2   8  14   5  12   7   1   6
 6   2   6   4   5   9   6   1   4   2   6  10   9  13  12   4   8  14  16  16
 7  15   5  11   7   8   7   3  15   7  13  16   4   3   2  10  14   5  13   3
 1   3   3  15  15  12   8   6   8  13   9  14  16   1  15   6  15   9  12   4
15  10   2   1   3   5   3   5   1  16   5   2   1   5  11   7   5  12   8   1
14   6  12   2   6  11   4   9   7  15  10   5  14   4   7  16   6   2   3   5
 4   1  16  10  12  13  15   8  13   4  15   8   8  15   3  11   1  15   6  13
 5   7   8   5  14  16  13   3   3  14   3  15  13  11   1   8   9  10   7  14
10   5   1   6  13   2   5  10  12   9  16  13   3   9  16  12  11   8  10  11
 3   8  11   8  10   6  12  14   5  10   4   9  12   6  10   3  13  11  15  10
13   4  13   3   8   7   2  12   9  11   7  11   5   7   8   2  10   1   5  12
 8  16  10  14  11  15   9  11  16  12  12   4  10  14  13   9   7  16   2   9
12  11   4  13   9   1  14   2   6   6   2  12   6  12   6  13  16   3   4   2


 7   6   7  16  15   1  15   3  15  13  14  14  15   8   6   2  12  13  16   6
 4   2  11  15  16  16   5  14   5  16  10  15   1  12  10   8   1   1   3   1
14  12  12   8   1   5   8   2   6   8   5   8   3  16  11  11   3  16   7   3
 9   7  16  11  11  15   4  12   1   3   1   1   5   3   7  14  14   9  11  12
 5   3   6   9   7   2   3   6  13  12  15  12  16   5  16   5   2   2  12   4
 1   9   5  10   9   3   7  16   7  14  11  10  13  13   7   5   3   2  15
16   8   3   7  13  14   6  11   2   2   8   7   2   2   1  10  13  15   5   2
11  10   2   3   5   9   1  10  12  15  12  11  14  14  15   3   6   7  13   7
10  11  14  14  12  12  10   8   8   9   3   2   4   4   5   1   9   5  10  16
13  14   4   1   8  13  13  13  11  10   9   3   7   6   3  16   8   4  14  13
 8   4   9   4  10   4  16   4  14   4   4   6  11  11  12  13   7  10   4   8
12   5   1   2   3   7   9   5  16   6  13   5  10   9   8   6   4   6   6   5
 3  15   8   6   4  11  11   1  10  11   6  13  12   7   2  15  16  12   1  11
 2  13  15  12   6   8  14   9   4   7   7  16   6   1   4  12  15   8   9  14
15  16  10   5  14   6  12   7   9   5   2   4   9  10   9   9  11  14  15  10
 6   1  13  13   2  10   2  15   3   1  16   9   8  15  14   4  10  11   8   9


 7   7   8   9  12   3   7   4  14  13  14  16   4  12  15  14  14   9  15  11
 1  15   2  15   1   2   4  16  16  15   6   4   3  14   5  10  16   2  12   5
10   3   7  14   6   9   6   6  10   7  10   8   6   1  11  15  15  13   8   3
11  10  15  13   2  12   8  11   9  16  12   7   9   5  12  11   7   6   9   1
15   9   6  10  15   1  13   2  12   9   1   2   2   8   9   7   8   8   6   9
 5   4  10   2  10   4  11  13  15   1   8   3   7   3  14  16  11  16   5   2
13  13  14   6  15  16  10   9   5   8  16   9  15  15   7   8   1   7   3  12
 6   2   1  12   5  10   1   8   1  11   3  12  13  11   3   6   3   3  14   7
12  14  13   5  14  13  12   3   4   3  12  13   6   8  13  10   5  10  14
 8   6  12   4   7  14   3  12   3   2   7  15  12  13  10   1   9   4  13  10
 9   8   9  16   9   7  16   5  11  14  15   5   1   2   1   2   4  11   7  16
16   1  11   8   3  15   2  14   6   6  11  14   5  16   2   9   5  10  16  15
14  16  16   3   4   6   5   7   2   4   2   1  10   4  13  12  13  12   4   4
 2  11   4  11  11   5  15   1   8   5  13  10  16   7  16   5   2  14   2   8
 3  12   3   1  13   8  14  10  13  12   9   6  14   9   6   3   6  15   1  13
 4   5   5   7   8  11   9  15   7  10   5  11  11  10   4   4  12   1  11   6


 9  12  12   9  15   6  15   8   9   1   2   3   6   1  13   7  11   4   7   8
14  16   1  13  11   8   7   3   4   9   6  11   4   3  16   4  10   2   4  13
 5  14   9  12   5   2  14  10  13   3   4  12   5   7  14  15   8  16   3   7
12   1  14   1  14   3   5   1   3   2   5   7   7  15   3  14   7   6  14   4
 8  13  10   4   8  14  11   7   8  13  11   6  16  10   4   5   9   3   9  10
 7  15  15   3  12   1  12   5   6   6  13  14   3   2   6   6  14  13   2  16
 2  10   6   5   4   7  16   9  11  14   9  16   2  11  10   2   1  15  13   2
13   5  13   2   3  16   9  15  16   4   8  13  15   9   8  11  16  12  11   1
 1   4   4  15   1  12   6  11   1   5  12   1   9   8   1   1   2   5  15  15
 4   6   7   7   9  15   4  16   2  15  16  10  13  12  12  16   3  11   1  12
11   3  11  10   6   5   8   2  12  12   1   2   8   6  11   9  15   1  16  11
16   8   3   8  13   9   2   6  14   7   7   8   1   4   7  12   5  10   8   9
 3  11   2  16  16  13  10  13  10  10   3   9  12  14   9   3  12   7  10   5
10   7   8   6   2  11   1  12  15   8  15   5  11  13   2  10   4   8   6  14
 6   9   5  11  10  10   3  14   5  16  14   4  14  16   5  13  13   9   5   6
15   2  16  14   7   4  13   4   7  11  10  15  10   5  15   8   6  14  12   3
```

```
 4  10   5   5   4  15  13   7   1   5  11  11  12   5   8   5  16   5  11   1
 2   5   8  14  16   2   4   1   2   1   7  15  14  13  10   1   1   8   3   8
13   7   2  10  13   1   3  11  10  14   3   8   3   9   3  13   4  13  13   2
 9  16   4  12   6   3   9   4   4  16   8  10   7  15  14  10   8   9  15   6
 7  12   3   1   2   4  12  16   3   2   1  12  16   4  13   2  13  11  14  13
 3   3  12   2   9  10   8   5   6  15   9   9   2  12  16  11   9  12   5   7
 5   4  16  13  11  12   1  15  13  11   2   7   9  10  15  15   7   2   2  15
11   6   9  11   7  16  10  14   5  10  15  16  10  14   7  16  14   4   4  12
 8  14  13  15  10   6  15  10  12  13   6   3   5   3   6   3  11  14   7  14
15   1   6   8   3   7   7   6  11   3   5   1   8   1  12   7   3  10   6   3
 6   8  14   6  12   8  16   9   8  12  10   6  11  16   9   8   5   1  16   9
12  13  11  16  14  11   2   3  16   9   6   4  13  11   4   9  10   3   9   4
14  11   1   4   9  14  14  12   7   4  12  14   4   8   2   4   2  16   1   5
16  15  15   9   1   9  11   8  14   8  16   2   1   6  11  14   6   7   8  16
10   9   7   7   5   5   5   2  15   6   4   5   6   2   5   6  12  15  10  10
 1   2  10   3  15  13   6  13   9   7  13  13  15   7   1  12  15   6  12  11


15   4   6  15  11   4   7  13   8   9   9  13  13   6   1   4  13  11   8   8
 9  16   2   3  15   1   2   2   1  16   3   7  12   4  10   1   9  13  10  11
 1   5   4   8   9  12  12   7  15  12  14  11  15  16   6   3   3   1   1   3
 8  10  13   7  14  11  13   6   9   6   4  15   7   5   5   9   7   8   9  15
 6   3   8   6   4   3   3  11  11   2  13   2   3   9   8   2  14   5  12   5
11  12  15  11  12   6  16   9  10   5   2  14   1  12  15   7   5  14   3   1
10   8   3  16   3   8   9  10  14  10   7  10   8  15  11   6  12  16   6  16
16   2   5   1   6  16   8   4  13   3  11   8   2   8  13  11   4  12   2   2
 4  14   1  12   2   2   1   5   7   1   5   6   6   3   3  12  15   3   4   9
 7  13  11   4   8   5  10  16  16   7   6   1  11  10  16   8  16  10  13  12
13   1  10   2  13   7  11  15   5  13   8   9  15   1   9  14   1   2   5  13
 3  15  16  13   5   9  14   8   4   8  16   3   4  13  12  10  11   4   7  10
 5   7   7   9   1  15   6   3   3  14   1  16   5  14   7  15   8   6  15  14
14   6   9  14  16  14   4   1   2  15  10  12   9   2   2  16   6   7  11   6
 2  11  14   5   7  13  15  14   6   4  12   4  14   7  14   5  10  15  16   7
12   9  12  10  10  10   5  12  12  11  15   5  10  11   4  13   2   9  14   4


15  11  15   2   1  14   6  14   7  10   8  10  13   6  13   3  16  11   4  13
 8   8  12   6  14   5  10   6   4   4   5   5  11   2  12  14  13   2  12   5
11  12   3  16   9   6   9   8   3   5   6   6  15   1   7  15   6   3  11   6
14   2   7  10  10  12   2  11  12   2  13   8  16   7  11  16  11   4  15   4
 9  16   1   9   3   1  15  13  11  13   9  15   9   4   5   6  15   6  16  11
 4  10   9   1  13   4   3  16  10  12   1   3  10   3   2  13   5  14  10  12
12  14   6   3   2  11  14   9  15   8  15  14  14   8   8  11   7  15   9   7
10   3  14   7  12  16   8  12   6   1  16  13   2  14   1   8   9   1   2   3
13  15  13   5   5  13   5   3  16  11   7  14   6  15  10   4  12  12   7   8
 7   7   8   4  11   8   7   5   9  16   4   7   5   5   3   9   4   9   8  16
16   4  16  14  15  15   4   1   8   3  12   9  12  12  15   1  10   8   1   2
 1   6   2  11   7  10  11   2  14   6   2   1   1  13   6   5   3  16  14   9
 3   5   4  15   6   3  16   7   2  15   3  11   3   9   7   2   5  13   3  14
 2   1  11  12   4   7  13  10   1  14  14  12   4  10  16  12   1   7   5  10
 5  13  10  13   8   2   1  15  13   9  11   2   7  16  14   2  14  13   3   1
 6   9   5   8  16   9  12   4   5   7  10  16   9   9   4  10   8  10   6  15


10  11   9   6   4   9   1  12   8   6   2  11   4  12   2   4   9  11   3   2
 3   9   3   8  14  11   9   1  14  14  15   9   8   6   1   2   7   6   5  10
 4  14  12   5  12   7  13  14  16  15   9   3  14  16   6   5   6  16  11   1
16  15   6   4  15   3  11   6   1  13  11  13   7  14  14  14   4   1   2  11
 7  16   7   7   5   6   5   4  13  16  14   7  12   4  11  16  12   3  13   4
 8   4   8  11   3   2  10  15   3  12   7   8   9   8   4  15   2   2  15  13
 9   3   5  10  11   1   3   8   2   3  10   1   6   3   8  13   8   7   9   3
13   8   2   3   6  10   8   7  15   4   1   6   5  13  16   1  11   8   7   9
 2   5   4  13   7   5  16  16  10   7   3   5   3  15  15   3  14   4   4  14
 1  13  10  15   8  15  14   3   5   8  12   2  13   9   7   7   1  10  10   8
 6   2  11   1   9   4   4  10   4   1  16  16   2   2   9  11  13  12   8  12
12   6  15  12  13  16  15   9   7  11   5  14  10   5  13   8  16  13  16  16
 5  10  16   9   2   8  12  11  11   2   6  15  16   1  10  12   5   9   6  15
11   7  13   2   1  14   6  13   6   9   8  12   1  10   3   6  10  14  12   6
15  12  14  14  10  13   7   2  12   5  13  10  11  11  12  10   3   5   1   7
14   1   1  16  16  12   2   5   9  10   4   4  15   7   5   9  15  15  14   5
```

```
7    3    2    4    4    4    13   10   15   13   16   1    6    2    16   10   1    13   3    9
5    6    7    13   12   3    5    14   8    14   14   11   1    5    9    5    13   7    4    5
3    9    15   3    7    13   3    15   12   6    5    16   14   14   11   8    3    1    14   13
15   13   9    1    15   10   2    4    11   16   7    4    12   10   2    15   9    16   12   12
9    14   1    6    16   7    9    5    16   3    15   14   9    8    1    11   4    6    7    16
2    16   3    12   1    16   10   3    1    8    9    2    13   3    12   9    6    5    16   10
8    11   6    16   3    1    11   13   2    15   13   12   16   12   8    6    7    9    10   14
13   5    4    7    9    6    4    9    4    7    10   13   3    13   5    12   5    12   8    4
10   12   8    8    10   14   7    6    10   5    2    3    5    9    14   3    16   3    5    15
11   10   5    5    6    9    16   8    9    9    12   6    10   6    4    13   12   11   9    8
12   15   12   14   5    12   15   1    7    11   3    7    15   15   7    2    14   2    1    2
1    8    16   9    8    11   12   11   3    1    8    5    11   1    6    16   10   8    6    11
14   1    11   11   11   8    14   2    5    2    4    10   7    4    3    14   2    15   2    6
16   2    13   10   14   15   6    16   14   10   1    9    2    7    13   1    15   14   15   3
4    4    14   15   13   5    1    7    13   12   6    8    4    16   15   4    8    10   13   7
6    7    10   2    2    2    8    12   6    4    11   15   8    11   10   7    11   4    11   1


5    11   11   8    8    7    16   13   14   12   8    1    10   6    8    9    3    5    7    3
8    3    1    7    5    1    12   6    1    6    15   7    7    10   4    10   12   12   6    13
6    12   7    13   9    12   9    12   9    5    5    2    14   11   2    5    7    2    14   14
11   4    3    6    14   5    6    9    15   9    11   3    16   1    13   4    9    14   2    16
4    5    8    11   12   8    10   10   2    3    1    12   3    9    12   2    14   4    5    12
2    8    2    12   11   3    15   2    5    13   9    10   4    15   5    6    16   1    13   11
16   15   15   5    2    6    1    7    11   16   4    16   2    2    16   3    5    13   8    2
14   13   13   4    3    11   3    3    12   8    2    9    9    14   9    8    1    16   11   9
13   7    5    9    6    13   4    11   10   2    10   13   5    8    3    14   4    10   9    8
15   2    12   1    16   14   7    8    4    4    7    15   11   3    15   16   11   3    16   15
12   9    6    15   7    4    5    5    7    10   3    4    13   7    7    7    15   11   12   7
10   14   14   14   1    16   11   1    8    11   13   11   1    12   6    11   10   6    10   5
7    1    10   10   10   9    2    4    6    14   14   14   12   5    1    12   6    7    15   1
3    10   16   16   4    2    8    15   3    7    16   8    6    16   10   15   13   8    3    4
1    16   4    3    15   15   14   14   16   15   6    6    15   13   14   13   2    15   4    6
9    6    9    2    13   10   13   16   13   1    12   5    8    4    11   1    8    9    1    10


5    10   3    8    16   9    2    7    5    14   11   11   9    3    16   16   8    13   10   15
3    5    2    5    3    5    15   14   11   9    8    14   14   9    13   2    6    10   9    14
1    13   10   2    5    2    5    5    8    5    14   6    13   13   6    3    7    7    6    8
16   6    13   10   6    6    1    6    7    8    2    16   15   4    15   8    9    16   14   12
12   14   7    9    12   12   12   4    9    12   9    12   12   14   1    13   3    4    13   6
13   9    8    12   11   3    6    13   16   1    13   9    5    10   14   6    5    5    4    4
10   11   5    15   14   8    16   9    12   16   6    15   6    11   9    12   16   3    8    11
15   1    4    3    15   14   7    3    10   7    10   2    3    8    4    10   2    1    1    16
2    16   14   1    10   11   4    11   14   6    4    4    4    16   10   15   1    6    12   9
9    12   6    16   4    16   10   16   1    15   16   10   16   12   12   9    12   15   3    10
11   4    11   14   8    1    8    10   6    5    4    5    7    2    5    5    14   11   11   2
14   7    15   11   7    7    3    12   3    2    3    13   11   1    2    14   15   12   15   3
4    8    9    7    1    4    13   8    13   3    12   3    10   6    7    7    4    9    16   7
8    15   12   13   9    13   11   2    15   13   7    7    1    15   3    1    13   14   2    5
7    3    1    6    2    10   14   1    4    10   15   1    2    7    11   4    10   8    5    13
6    2    16   4    13   15   9    15   2    11   1    8    8    5    8    11   11   2    7    1


15   5    3    14   7    6    16   16   13   2    1    9    10   11   11   7    14   12   4    9
2    6    1    12   11   5    14   7    8    9    15   16   9    10   12   10   2    16   11   2
14   3    9    16   4    16   5    9    3    14   14   15   2    4    7    2    5    11   5    7
5    2    11   6    14   2    10   12   1    13   4    8    11   3    4    14   4    10   1    5
6    7    2    8    10   12   15   2    16   1    8    13   8    14   6    12   3    5    14   10
12   16   8    11   5    7    7    15   11   5    10   12   15   12   3    9    13   15   8    16
16   8    13   2    8    10   12   11   7    10   7    5    3    9    9    13   9    4    10   6
7    4    7    15   6    11   1    14   15   15   11   2    6    1    15   3    16   14   6    15
3    13   5    10   9    13   13   1    5    4    2    3    1    2    14   4    7    3    15   3
13   11   6    3    16   14   2    5    6    11   12   10   14   6    10   11   10   13   16   8
10   10   16   7    13   3    9    3    12   3    6    7    4    16   2    15   11   2    2    1
1    15   4    4    1    1    4    4    9    6    13   4    5    5    1    16   15   9    12   11
9    14   15   13   12   15   3    13   10   7    5    11   12   15   8    1    12   7    7    13
4    9    10   9    3    4    8    10   14   12   16   14   16   13   16   6    6    6    3    14
8    12   12   5    15   9    6    6    2    16   3    6    13   8    13   5    8    8    9    4
11   1    14   1    2    8    11   8    4    8    9    1    7    7    5    8    1    1    13   12
```

```
12   1   4  11  12   6   8   1   2   3  13  15   6  14   3  11   8   8   6  16
 2   3   1  10  16   1  16   2   8   2   5   5  11  13  10   8  14  14  12   9
 4   5   9   7  13  14   4   3   1  16   3   7   8  16   4  12   9  16   5  11
 5  15  14   6   9   2  11  10  14   9   6  10  12   4  16   1   6  13   4  13
 7   7  12  15  11   5  15  12  12   4   7   1   7   5   9  14   3   5  10  10
 6  13  13  13   7  11  10  16   7  13   2   2  13  15   8   5  11  10   3   2
13  11   6   8   8  15   3   8   3   6  16   4  10   9   6  13  10   4   9   6
11  14   8   1   5   3  14  11   6  11   4  14   5  10  14  15  12  11  11   4
15   4   5   3   3  13   1   7  13   5  15   6   4  11  12   3  16   2  14  15
 9  10  10  12   2   4  12  14   4   8  11   3   9   8   7  10   4   1   1  12
 8   2   7  14   4   9   2   6  15   1  12  11  16   3  15   9   5   9  15   5
10  16  15  16  15   8   6  13  11   7  14   8   2   7   5   6   1   6   2   8
 1   6  16   4   6  10   9  15  16  15   9  16  14   1  11   4   2   3  13   3
16   9   3   5  14  12   5   9   5  10   1  13  15  12  13   7   7  15  16   7
 3   8  11   9  10   7   7   5  10  12  10   9   1   2   1   2  13   7   8   1
14  12   2   2   1  16  13   4   9  14   8  12   3   6   2  16  15  12   7  14


15  12   3   3   9   7   8  12   5   7  11  12  16   9   4  14   7  13   8  13
 4   7  13   7   6   5   7   7   6   3   2  16   1  16  14  10  16   9   2   7
14   9  16  16  13  16   3   2   8  15  14  11   3   2   7  16   6   5   7   6
13  16   8   4  12   4   5  11   2   4   7   1   5   1   6  11  15  11  12   4
11   6   6   1  14  11  14  14   4  12  13   2   7  11  10  12  12   3  10   9
 7  15  11   2   8  13   6  16   1  11  15  13   9  10   8   1   5  12  13  14
16   8   2  12   5  14  16  13   7  14  16   7   6  14  13   2   1   7   9   3
 1  13  15  14   2  12  11   8   9   5   3   6  12   4   1  15  14  14  16  11
 6   5   1   9  10   3   2   1  10  10   9   4  14  12   9  13   4  16   4   5
 3  10   5   5  15   8   1   4  12  13   6  15  10   3  15   9  13   1   6   8
 8  14   4   8   3   2  10  10  14   1   4   9  11   8  11   4   8  15   1   2
12   2  12  10   1   1  13   3  11   2   1   5   2   6   5   8  11   6  11  10
 5   3  14  11   4  15  15   9  16   6  10  10  13  15  16   6   2  10   3   1
 2   4   7   6  16   9   9   5   3  16   5   3   4  13  12   5   9   4  14  16
10  11  10  13   7   6   4  15  15   9  12  14  15   5   3   7   3   2  15  12
 9   1   9  15  11  10  12   6  13   8   8   8   8   7   2   3  10   8   5  15


 5   2   2  14   9  14   3   3  14   4  16  14   6   5   1   3   5   3  15  11
 1  16   7   7  15   9   7   6   7   1   2  15  11   7  14   4   4  16  11   2
10   9  13   2   7  10  15   9  16  16  10   4   3   8   6   7   3  10   6   4
 7  14   6   9  14  11   2   8   5  13   5  10   2   1  16  12  13  14   5   7
11   8   8   6  12   6   8   4  10   2   9   9  10  14   3  13  14   5  12   3
 2  15   5   5   8   8  16   1   8  11  13  12   9  11   9  16   6  12   4  16
 4   7   3  15   5   4   9   7  12   7  12   8  16   2  15  14   9  11   8  12
12   6   4   8  10  15   4  12   1   8   4   1   7   9  10  15  11   4  10   1
13   3  14   1   2   7  12   5   3   9   6   6  13  10  11   1   2   7   1   9
14  13  11  11  13   5  11  13   9   6   8  11   4   6   2  11  16  14   9  14
 8   5  15   3   1  13   1   2  13  12   1  13   8  12   4   9  15  15  16  13
 6  10   1  12  16  16  10  10   6  15   7  16  15  13  13   5   7   9   7   8
15   1   9  13   6  12   5  15   4  10  14   7   1   3  12   6  10   6  13  10
16  12  12   4   4   2   6  11  11  14   3   5   5  15   7   8  12   2  14   5
 3   4  10  16  11   1  13  16   2   5  15   2  12  16   5   2   1  13   3  15
 9  11  16  10   3   3  14  14  15   3  11   3  14   4   8  10   8   8   2   6


 6   4  11   9   4  11  10  15  14  15  13   4  16   5  12  14   3   7   8   7
16   7   6   1   1   8  15   4   9   8   6  10   4   8   7   1  13  16   3   8
14  13   2   6   6  12  11  12   3   7  10  13   8  16  10  11   1  11  16   6
 5   1   9   8   7  16  14  13  11   6  12  15   2   7   5  12  11   3  11  14
 2  14  12  10   8   5   3  16   4   3   8   1  10   2  13  15   7   8  14  10
11   2  16   2   2   2  16   9  15  12  15  16  12  11   6   3  14  12   6  16
 8  15  14   5   9  14   9  11  16  13   7   3  13  10   2  13  12   4  15  12
 4  12   8  14   3  15   7   7   5  10   5   5   7  14   3   7   6  14  10   9
12  16   3  16  15   7  13   8  13   1   9   2   6  12   8  10   8  10   4   1
 1   3   5   3  13   4   2   6  10  16   4  11  11   1  16   5  16   6   1   3
10   5   4  13  16   3   4   2   7   4   1   6   5   6  15  16  15  13   9  15
13   6   7  15  11   9  12   3  12   5   2   7  15   4   9   8   2   2   7   2
15   8   1   4  14  10   8   1   6   9  16  12   3   9   4   6  10   9  13  13
 9   9  13  11   5   1   1  10   2   2   3   8   1  15  14   9   5  15   5   4
 3  11  15  12  10   6   6   5   8  14  14   9  14   3   1   2   4   1   2  11
 7  10  10   7  12   3   5  14   1  11  11  14   9  13  11   4   9   5  12   5
```

```
 2   2   3  14   7  11   3  13  13   2   2   6   4  15  14  11   8   5   8   6
11  13   5   9   6  16  16   8   2   3   9   8   7   2  15   9  10   2  12   5
 9  11   1   7  13   4  12  16   1   9   5  11  15   7  16   2  16  10   7   7
 4   4   7  12   8   3   4   2  16   6   8  14   3   5   8   5   6  15   2  12
15   3  16   6   1   5   5   4  14  16   4  12  16   3   5  14  15   3   3  16
 3   7  11  10  10   9   7   6   5   8  12   7   6  13   3   3   9   9  15  13
10  12  15   3  16  12  11  12   9  14  15   4   5   4   9   1   3  16   6   2
16   1  12   5   2  10   8   9   7   1  14  16   8   8  11   8   5   7   9  15
12  16   4   8   4   1   6  15  11   4   3   5  10   6   6   6  13   6  11   1
 5  14  14   4  12   7  14   1   6  10   7  15   9  16  12  10  14  11  13  11
 6   9   2   2  14   8   9  14   4   7   1   9  12   9   1   4   7   8  10   3
 1   5   9  13  15  15   1   3  15  13  11   2  11  14  13  15   1  12  16   8
 7  15  10   1   3  13  13   7  12  11  16   1   2  12   4   7   4   1  14  14
 8   8   6  16   5   2   2   5  10  15  10   3   1  11   2  13   2  13   5  10
14  10   8  11  11   6  10  10   8   5  13  13  14  10  10  12  12   4   1   4
13   6  13  15   9  14  15  11   3  12   6  10  13   1   7  16  11  14   4   9
```

```
 9   1   4  14  12   6  16   2   6  15  16  14   6  15  16   5  15  11  11   4
15  16  15   2   8   8  15  12  12   4  12   3  15  13  15   2  12   3  14  16
 3   3   5  11  16   5   5   6   9   1   9  12   2   1   9  13   3   8  16  12
 2   8   6  12  13  14   4   1   1   3   5  10   7   2   8   9   5  13   5   5
 7   9   7   6   7   9   2   5   5   6   3   9   9   9  13  11  13  16  13   2
 6   4  16   4  15  16  12   8   7  12  13  15   3   5   3  12  11   9   6  10
16  13  14   7  11   2  10  13  13  11   1   1  10  10   7   8   4   1  12   7
14  10  10   8   4  11  11   4   3   5  15   5   8  12  11  16   1  10   7   3
 5  12  11   1   2  12   8   7  16  16   2  11  16   4   1   4  10   2   2   9
12   6   2  10  14   3  14  16  14   9   8   4  14  11  12   1   9  12   1  15
13  11   1   5  10  10   1  14   4  13   4   6   1  14  10  15   8   5   9   8
 1   7   3  16   9   4   3   3  15  10   7   8   4   6  14  14  14  14  10  13
 8  14  13  15   1  13   7  11   2   2  14  13   5  16   5   7   6   4   4   6
 4   5   8  13   6  15   9  10  10  14   6   7  11   7   2   6   7   6   8  14
10  15  12   9   5   7   6   9  11   7  10  16  13   8   4  10  16   7  15   1
11   2   9   3   3   1  13  15   8   8  11   2  12   3   5   3   2  15   3  11
```

```
15  12   1  10  14  12   9   4   3  16  12  15   8   1  15  10   6  16   7   4
10   6   2  11   8  16  10   3   2  12   2   1   6   6   6   9  11   9   3   7
 1  15   7   4   5  15   7  11  16   3  10  13  10  10   1   7   8  14   9  15
16   5  13   7   7   8  13  13   9  14  14   8  14   8  12   8   2   2  12  10
 7   8  14   5   4   4   1   8  14   2  13  16   1  15   3  14  15   3  15  12
11  14   6   2   6   5  15   4  11   9   7   7   2  12   5  15   4   5  14   5
13  10   9  13  16   9   8   6   5   1  11  16   5  15  14  11   1  13  10  13   3
14   4   5  16  15   2   6  16   4  15  15   9   9   7   4  12  14  13  16   1
 2   9   8   1  10   6  12   5  12   6   9  11   5   2   9   6   1   7   8   2
 5  16  12  14  12   3   2  12  15   5   3   6  11  13   7   3  12   4   1   6
 4   1  16   3  13  13   5  14   6  13   6   3  12   9  13   5   3  11   6   9
 3  11  10   8   1  10  16   2  13  10  11   4  13   4  14   4  10   6   2   8
 6   7   3   9   3  14   7   5   1   5   2  16   3  16  13   9   1   5  16
 9   3  15  12  11   1  14  15  10   4   1  10   7  16  10   2   5  12   4  13
12  13   4   6   2  11   4  10   7   7   8  14   3  11   8  16   7   8  10  14
 8   2  11  15   9   7  11   1   8   8   4  12   4   5   2  11  16  15  11  11
```

```
 7   8  11   1  10  11   5   9  16   8  15  13  16  13  16   7   6   8   9   3
13  10  10  15  14  12  15  11   8   3   1  16  14   4   2   4  16  12   1   6
 1  16  13   5   5   5   2   5   6   1   4   3  11   6   4  12  15  15  10  10
 8   7   4   7   2   7   6  12  12   2   9  14   6  11  10   5  12  11  16  13
16  13   1  12   3  13   9  13  13   7  11   1  15   1   1  13   5  13   6  12
11   9  14   2   1  14   1  15   5  13  12   2  13  10  13  10   7   9   4   7
15  15  12  10   9   9   7  14   3   9   8  10   4   9   9  11   4   6  13   9
 9  11   9  13  12   3   8   4   7   6   5  15   9   7   8   9   1  14  12   2
 2   2   7  14   6   1   4  10  15   5   2   6   1  15   5   1   9  10   7   1
12   6   8   3   4  15  11   6   2  10  14   7   3   8  12  16   2   3  14  16
 5   3   6   6  16   9  14   8  10   4   7   8   8   2   7   6  11   4   2   4
 4  14  16   4  15   4  16   7  11  16   6  12  10  14  15  15   8   7   8  11
14   4   5  16  11  16  12  16   9  12   3  11  12   6  14  13   2   3   3   8
 6   5   2   9   7  10  13   3   1  11  10   9   7   3  14   3  14   1   5  14
 3  12   3  11   8   2   3   1   4  14  16   4   2  16  11   2   3  16  15  15
10   1  15   8  13   6  10   2  14  15  13   5   5   5   3   8  10   5  11   5
```

```
 9   6   2  12   5  12   4  15   4   3   1  13  14  14  10   6   3   1  10   7
13   1   6   2  11  11   7   8  11   6  15  14   4   7  12  10  14   5  13  10
12  13  11   6  13  15  15  11   8  11   6   4   5   9   4   5   2  16   8  13
 1   5  13  15  14   6  14   5  15  16  12   5   9   5  16  12   5   3   7  14
11  12  14  10   2  13  11  16  10  14  11   1  16  11   7  13  16  14   4  11
10  14   7  13   3   2   5  14  12  12   4   7  10  15  14   4   6  11  15  15
 4   4   1   8   6   1   9   1   6   9   5  16   2  12   9  11   4  15   6   2
 5   9   4   7   4  14  10   7   3   2   7  12   3   6   8   8   8   9  16   6
 8   7  10   5  10   8   3   4   9   8  16  15  12  16  13  15   7   7   2   8
 2   8   5   1  12   7  16   2   5   7  13   6  13   8   2  16  10  10  14   3
 7  10   3   9   9  16   2   6  13  15  10  10   7  10  15   9  13   6  11  16
 3  11  12  16  15  10  12  10   7   5   3   3  15   4   3  14   9  13   5   1
 6  15   8  11   7   5  13   3   2  10   9   9   1   2   1   1  12   4  12   9
14   3  15   4   8   3   6  12   1   4  14   8  11   1   5   7  11   8   3   5
16   2  16   3  16   4   8  13  16  13   8   2   6   3  11   2   1  12   9  12
15  16   9  14   1   9   1   9  14   1   2  11   8  13   6   3  15   2   1   4
```

```
 3  14   5   3   3  16   2  12  10  16   6  16  10   2   9   6  12  13   6   8
13   4  15   6   4   1   9  11   8   5  11   1  12   5   2   7   4   4  12   3
 2   8  10  11   9   3   5   7   7  15   5   4  16   8   5   5   1   9   8   1
 7  11   7   8  14  10  15   9  13   9   4   2   7   7  11  16   8  16  14  15
16  15   3  16  11   4  12   1  14  14   1   3   5  10  10   4   9   2  16   5
 9   6   8   5   5   9  16   5   5   3   2   7   6   6   8   6   7  10   6   6
 1  13   6   4  10  11  13  ·3  15   4  10   5  15  12  16  15  13   1  15   9
 5   3  14  12  13   5   3   2   3  11  16  12  11  15  13   9  15   3   7  14
 4   7   1  13  16   8  10  15   1   6   3  11   8  11   4  11   2  15   1  10
15  16  16   7   6   2   1   4   6  10  13   8   9   4  12  13  10   5   9   7
11   1   9   9   2  13  14   8  12  12  12  14   4  13  15  12  11  10  13  11
 6   2  12  10  15  12  11  14  16   2  14   9   1  16   1   3   5  14  11   2
 8   9  11   2   8   7   8   6   4   7   7  15   2   9  14  14  14  11   3  13
10   5   2  15  12   6   4  16  11   8   9   6  14   3   3   2   3  12   2   4
12  10   4   1   7  14   7  10   2  13   8  10   3   1   6  10  16   6  14  16
14  12  13  14   1  15   6  13   9   1  15  13  13  14   7   1   7   8   5  12
```

```
 5   1   3   8   1   6   8  13  13  14  12   7   8  14  15  14   5  15  14  10
 3  15   6  11  12  12   9   6  10   7  14   8  12   6  16  15  16   1  16  14
 4   7  10   9   6   8   3  12   9   8   8   3  14   8   8  12   7  12  15  15
 1  16   1  16   5   2   6   1  14   9   3   1  16   9  14   8   4   2   8   9
 9   3  14   5  15  13  11   7  16  10   4   4   2   7   2   7   3  14   5   4
10   9  16   1   4   9  16  16   1  13  11  12   1  15  10  13  12   6   7  12
15   4   8   4  16  16   4   9  11  11  15  13  10  16   5  10   6   8   2   3
16  11   2   2  13  15  10  15  12   6  16   5  11   4  12   9   9  16   9   6
11  14  12   7   2   7  14   3   6   4   2  14   4   2   4   3   8   4  12  13
 7   6   5  14   7   3   1  11  15  15   9  10  15   1   3   1  10  10   3   2
 8  10  13  12   9   1  12   2   8   2  10  11   9  12   6   5   2   3  11   8
 6  13   4  13  14   5   7   4   3   3   6   6   3  13   1   6  14   9   1   7
13   2   9   6  11  11   5   5   4   1   5   2   5  10  11   4   1   5  13   1
12   5  11   3   3   4  15  10   7  16   7  16   6   3   9   2  13  13  10  16
 2  12   7  15  10  14   2  14   5  12   1  15   7   5   7  16  11  11   4  11
14   8  15  10   8  10  13   8   2   5  13   9  13  11  13  11  15   7   6   5
```

```
12  11   7   7   2   4   1  11   1   3   9  14  10  13   4   4  15  16   3  13
 2  13  12   9  14  11  16   8   7   9  10   6   8  12   3   2  12   2  14   9
 3   4  13  16   7  10   2   4  14   8   2  12  15  10  15   8  11   5   7   6
16   5   2  15   1  15   6  16  16   4  12   4   6   2   2   1   5  11  15  15
10   9   3   2   9   5  10  13  12   5  13  16   1  15  14  13  13   3   4  12
 6   8   9  10   8   8   3  10  15   6  15   9  16   3  13  15   4  14   8   1
 4  16   1   8  12  13   7   5   5  13  16  11   3   8   9   9   7  15   2   5
 1  15   5  11   6   2   9   2   4  12   7   8  12   9   5  10   3   8  12   7
 7  10   6  14  10   9   5  15  10   2  14  13   9   4   7   7  14  10  10  10
 8   6  10  13  11   6  13   6  13   7   6   7  13   1  12  14  10   6   6  11
15   3  15   5   3  14  11   7  11  11  11   5  11  14  11   6   1  12  16  14
14   7  11   6  15  12   4   9   9  14   8  10  14   6   8  11  16   4   1   3
 9   1  14  12   4   7  14  14   6  10   5   3   5  16   1   5   9   1  11   8
13   2  16   1   5  16  12  12   2  15   1   1   4   5  16   3   8   7  13  16
 5  14   4   4  13   1  15   1   8   1   4  15   7  11   6  16   2   9   9   4
11  12   8   3  16   3   8   3   3  16   3   2   2   7  10  12   6  13   5   2
```

```
16  11  10   1  15   2  14   1  12   9   9  12  10  11   4   8   1  13  11  13
 6   3   1   2  13  10   3  10   1   3   6   3  16  13   8   2  12  15  10  12
 4  13  16   6   3   9   7  16  14   6  10  13   ~   3  15  14   4  14   8  16
12  10  11  12   5  12   1   3  15  13   1  11  12   4   7  13  10  11   7   2
 8  12   4  16   6   3  16  15  13  11  13   7   3  10   5   3  13  10  15  14
 9  15   8   8  12  11  13   7   2  12  12   1  11   1   9   1  16   6   3   4
10   1   5   4   2   8   2  12   4  16  11   9  13  15   1  10   9   7   4  15
 1   2  15   9   9   5  10   4   8   2   7  14   4   9   3   6   6   3   9   9
 7   5   9   7   4  15   4   8  11  10   5  16   9   6  11  11  15   1   1  11
 5   4  12  14   1   1  15   6   6   4  16   5   1   8  12  16   2   4  12   3
11  14  13  11   7  13   9  14   7   1   2  15  14  14  14   7   8   9   2  10
14   6   7   5  11   4   5  11   5   8   8   6   2   2  10   5  11  16  16   5
15  16  14   3  16   6   8  13  16  14  15   2   6  16  16   4   3   5  13   6
 3   9   2  15   8  16   6   5  10   5   4   4  15  12   6   9   7   8   6   1
13   7   6  13  14  14  11   2   9   7   3  10   5   7  13  15  14  12   5   7
 2   8   3  10  10   7  12   9   3  15  14   8   8   5   2  12   5   2  14   8
```

```
 2   5   3   5   7   4  10   6  15  16  15   7  12   8  14   4  10  13   1   4
 1  16   1  10  16   1   3  16   8  12  12  12   2   7   8  11   3   9  16   7
13   9   7  13  13   5   8   4   3   1   2   5  16   4   1  14   5   7  11  10
 5  15  14   4  12  14   2  14   9  11   5   1   8   1   7  15   2   1   8  12
10   4   2   9   4  13   9   7   4  14   6   9  13   3  10   2   1  15   9   9
16   1  10   7  10  10  12   9   2   2   1   3   6  13   3   3   8   3  12  13
12   6  12   3  15  11   6  10  12   7  10   4   3  15  13  12  12   2   7   2
14  14  16   2   5   7   5   2  10   4   4  15   9  10   2   6  14  16  10   6
 6   7  13   8   8   9   1  15   5  13   3   6  15  10   6   5  10  15   5   1
 7   3  11  12   3  16   4  12  13   9  11  10  10  11   4   8   4   6   6  16
 3   8   6  14   2   8  15  11   1  10   7  16   1  14  16   5   9  10   5   8
15   2   8   1   9  15  14   5  11   3  14  14   5   5   9  13  11   4  15  11
 9  13  15  15   1  12  13   8  14  15   9   2  11  12  15   7  13  11  14   3
 8  12   5  16   6   3  11  13   6   5  13   8  14  16   6   1   7   8   2   5
11  10   4   6  14   2  16   3  16   8   8  11   7   2  12   9   6  14   4  14
 4  11   9  11  11   6   7   1   7   6  16  13   4   9  11  16  16  12  13  15
```

```
 9  10   4  10   7   2  10  13  16  14   2  12  13   7  12  11  14  15  14   4
 3   4   1   2  16   8   4   7   9  11  14  13   7   4   1   6   5   7   6  14
14   6  12   5   2   1   9   8  13   8  11   8   4  16  13   4  11  16   9   9
 1   5  16  15   1   6  13   4  10  13   1   9  16   6   6  10  16  10   1  10
12   3   2  16   5   5   7   3   7  10  13   2  15   9  16   7  12   5   5   1
16  15   3   6   3  10  16  12   1  15  15  10  11  15   5   8  13   4  15  13
 5  12   8   8  15  15   5   5   5  12   5  10   8  12   9   3  10   6  12   8
15  14  14   4  13  13   8  14   8   2  10   6   5   2   3  13   7   9   7   3
11   2   7  13   8   4  14   6   4   3  16   5   3   5   8  12   1  13  16   5
10  16  11  14  11  12   3   9  15   6   4  16   1   1   2   2   3   1   2  16
13   7   9  11   4  14   6  11  12   5   3   1  12  11  11   5   2  12   4   7
 6  11  13  12  12   7   1  10  11   9   9   4   6   3   4  14  15   3  10  15
 2  13  15   9   9   3  11  15   6  16   6   7  14  10  14  16   4   2  11  12
 7   9   6   3  14  11  15   1   2   7   7  14   9   8  10   9   8  11   3   2
 8   1  10   7   6  16   2   2  14   1   8   3  10  13  15   1   6  14  13  11
 4   8   5   1  10   9  12  16   3   4  12  11   2  14   7  15   9   8   8   6
```

```
11   2  13  11   4  11  11  11   2  11  10  10   6   6  11   8   6   2   3   6
16  14   7   1   9  10   5   2  15  15   5   2   5   3  16  16   5  15  13   5
14  11   9   5   1   1  15   6  12   8  12  13   8   1   4   6   8   1   1   7
 1  10   8   6   2  15   8   5   8   6   4   7  14  12   3   9  12   6   8  11
 3   9  12  12   7   4   4  16   7   1   7  14  11   4   2   2  10   9   9  12
 8   1  11  10   8   7   9  13   1   7  15  15   3  13   1  14  16   3  15  13
10   4   5   2  12   9   1  15  13   3  14  16   1  14  13   7   9  10  16  10
 7   7   4  14  13  14   7   1  10  14   8   6   4   7  12   5   1   8  12  15
 6  13  16   9  11  16  13   9   6   9   2   3  16   2  10   3  14  14  10   3
12  15   2   8   6   6  10  10   4  10   3   4   9  11   9  15   2  11  11  16
 4   6   6   7  10   3   3  14   5   5  13   8   7   9   5   1  11  12  14   8
 9  16  15   3  14   8  16   7  16   2   1   1  12  15   6  10  15   4   2   4
13   5   1  16   5   2   6   4   3   4  16  12  15   5  15  11  13   7   7   2
 5   8  10  13  15  13  12  12  14  13  11   9  10   8   8  13   3   5   4   9
 2  12   3  15   3   5   2   8  11  12   9  11  13  16  14  12   4  16   5  14
15   3  14   4  16  12  14   3   9  16   6   5   2  10   7   4   7  13   6   1
```

```
 2   6  13   5   1  16   6   5  14   6  14   1   4   8   1   2  11   7   2  16
16  11  16  16   3   2  12   2   4   8  13  11  10   5  13   6   3  12   3   9
 3   3   9   2  12  15   3   8   3  10  12   3  12   4  15  16   4   6  14  12
10   4  10   1   9  12   1   4   1  12   5  14  15   2   8   8   5  14  16   8
 4  13  11  14   2  10   8   9  11   3   8   4  13   7  16   7  13   2   7  11
 9   9   5  11  11   3   7  15  10   1  16  10  11  12  10  10   7  13  12   2
12   2   8   9   7   7  16   6   2  15   4  16  16  15  11  13   6  15   4  15
14  16  15   7  10   8  14  12  13  16  10   7   1   3   3   1  15  16   9   5
 6  12  12   6   8  14  15   3  15   4   6   9   8   6   2   9  12  11   1   6
 5  15   7   8   4  11   5  13  16   9   7  13   6  13  12  14   1  10  11   1
 1   1   1  10  14   5  10   7   6  14   2   6   2   9  14   4  14   9  15  10
11   7   2  15  15   4  11  16   7   2   3  12   7  11   9   5  10   3   6   3
13  10   4  13   5  13   9  14   9  13   9   8   9  16   4  15  16   4   8   4
 8  14   6   4   6   1  13  11   8  11   1   5   5  10   5   3   8   1   5   7
 7   8   3  12  16   6   2   1  12   5  11  15   3   1   7  11   2   5  13  14
15   5  14   3  13   9   4  10   5   7  15   2  14  14   6  12   9   8  10  13
```

```
14  15   5  15  13  14  16   4  15   1   5   9   9   5  15  10   9   3  13  10
 3  14   1  12   7   4   5  13  14  13  11  10   3   4   9  15   5  13  14  12
 2  13  10  13  12   9  10  10  16   9   2  15   2  16   3   4   1  15   8   3
 1  12   2   3  10   2   3   3   4   5   6   5  14   2   5   2  13   5   4   2
 7   8   6   5   5   3   8   1   1  11  14  11  13  12   7   5   4  12   9   4
 4   1  13   4   8   6  13  12   9   4  13  12   7  12   6  14  16  13   3  13
12   9   8   9   6   5  15   9   6  15  10  16  15  10  13   1   8  14   7   5
 6   5   9   7  11  13   1   2   2   6   3   7   6   1   8  14  16   8  10  14
 8   3  11   2   9  16   6  14  12  14  12  13   4  15  11   7   2   1   6  16
 9  11   7   1  14  10  11  11  13   2   8   8  16  11  10  12  10   9   1   6
16   6  12  11   1   8   2  15  10   8   7   2   5   3  16  11  12  10  11   9
 5  10  15   8   3  12  14   6   8   3   1   3  11   8   6   9   3   6   5  11
10   2  16   6  16  15  12   5  11  12  16   6  10   4  16   6   4   2   8
11   7   4  16  15   1   4   8   5   7  15   1   8   9   1   3   7  11  16   1
15  16   3  10   4  11   7   7   7  16   4   4   1  13   2   8  15   2  15   7
13   4  14  14   2   7   9  16   3  10   9  14   7  14  14  13  11   7  12  15
```

```
 4   7  13  13  16  14   3   3   9   9  15  12   7   2  13  15  12   1   7   7
 5  12   5   4   4   6   1   4   7  10   2  10   4   3  16  11  10  14   6  15
 2  15   2  10   9   7   6   5   3  15  11   1  14   7   7   5   7   3   2  11
 6   1  14   7  11  16  11  12  14  12   6   5  10   8  10   1   4   8   9   1
 9  11  15  14  12   4  14  15  12   5   8  16   9  16  14   8  15   7   4   3
10   4   8  16  13   2  15   7   5   6  10   4   3   9  12  14   1   4   1  10
16   5  12   3   2  13   8  13  13   4   3   2   8  11   6  12   2  10  12   8
11   3   9   2  14  15   5  10  11   3  12   8  12  10   4  13   5  12   8   2
12   9   3   8  10  10  16  16   8   8  13  14   2   5   9   7   3   9  13  16
 3  13   4  12   1  11  10   2  10   1   4  13  16  15   5   2   9   2   5   5
 8   6   1   1   3   5   7   1   4  13   5   9  13  14   2   6  13  15  10   6
 1  16  10   6  15   8   2   9   2  14   9  11  11   6   1  15  11  16  14  14
 7  10  11  15   6   3   9  14  16   2  14   7   1  12  11   3  16  11  15  13
14   2   7   5   5  12   4   6   6   7   7   3  15  13  15   4   3   5  15  13
15  14  16   9   8   9  12   8  15  11  16  15   5   1   3   9   6  13  11  12
13   8   6  11   7   1  13  11   1  16   1   6   6   4   8  10  14   6   3   4
```

```
16   7  15   5   8   4   8  14   3   6  11   7  16  10   7   3   8  13   5  10
 6   9  16   9   1   6  10   4   8  13   1   2  12   5  15  16  10   4  10  13
 5  16   8  14   4  15  16   1   4   3  12  14   9   6   3   7   3   8  12   2
 2   5   3   3  13   2   4  10   6  16  10  10   3  12  12   8   1   6   7  14
 4   1  10   1   5   1  11  16  12   7   9   8   4  16   9   6  14   5   4   9
 9   4   1   6  15   8  14   9  13  14  13   3  14   2   1  12   7  10  14   5
14   2   4   8  10   7   5   3   5   5   7   4  15   7   8   9  16   7  16   3
 8  14  13  15   6   3  12   7  11   8   3  13   7   8   8   5  11  12  15  15
 7  12  11   4  16  14   2  15  10   2  15  12  11   1   1  11   4   9   6  16
11  10   7  13   3  11  15  11   7  15  16  11   8   4   4  13  13  15   1  12
 1  15  14   7  11  13   1   8  16  10   6   6   2  15   6   1   9   1  13  11
12   3   9  11   9  16   6   5   9  11   8  15  10   3   2   4   6  16  11   7
 3   6  12   2   9  13   2   2   9   4   1   6  14  10  10  15   5  14   9   6
13  11   2  12  12  10   7  13  14   1   2   5   1  11  16  15   5   2   8   8
15  13   6  10  14   5   3  12   1  12   5   9  13   9   5   2  12   3   2   4
10   8   5   2   7  12   9   6  15   4  14  16   5  13  11  14   2  11   3   1
```

```
13  13  14   6   4  13   6  12   3  14   2  13   9  11   6  13  10   1  11   6
11  11   2   9   6   2  13  15   6   4   1   2   8  13   7   2  12  11   5  13
12  10   5   5  15   4   8   6   2  15   5  15   1   3  15  10   9  10   3  10
10   9  16  10  14   1   3  13   4   8   8   5  14   8   4   9   3  12   1   5
 8   6   1  15   3  16  12  10  11   3   7  12  15  14   3  14  14  14  14  11
16  15  12   1   1   8  11   9   1  11  13  10  12  12   8  11   1   5   2  16
 9  14   4  14   9  15  15   3  12   7  16   6   6   7  10  12   6   6  12  15
 5   7   6  12   8  10   5  16   9  12  14   9  10  16   1   4   4   8  10   8
15  12   9   8  11   7  16   2   7   9  10  11   7   4  14   3  11  13  15   1
 4   3   3  11  10  11   4   5  16  10  12   1  13  10  13  15   2  16  13  14
 3   1  13   2  12   3   2   8   5   6   3  14  11   9  11   7  13   4  16   2
 7   4  11  13  13  14  14   1   8   2   9   8   5   5   5   5  15  15   7   9
 1   8   8   3  16   9  10  14  13  13  11   4  16  15   2   8   8   3   9   4
 6   2  10   4   2  12   1   4  14   5   6   3   2   2  12  16  16   9   8   7
14   5  15   7   7   5   4   7  15  16  15   7   4   1  16   1   5   7   4  12
 2  16   7  16   5   6   7  11  10   1   4  16   3   6   9   6   7   2   6   3


16   7   7  15  16   2   5   5   5  13  10  12   5  14  10   1  15   6  10  16
 2  16  16   9   4  11   7  10  13   8   4   2  12   3  12  13   2  16   5  13
 8   9   2   7  10   1  14   3  15  12   7   6   4  10  14  15  10   5   3  12
14  13   9   4  15  13   3  14  11   4  16   9   8  16   4   8   8  13   7   8
 4  14  14  10  12   3  12   4   3   5   5  11   3   9   6   2  14   2   2  10
11  11  10   1   1  15   4   9   8  10  15   5   6  15   9   6   5  10   1  15
 1  15  12   8  11  14   9  16   9  14   8   8  11  11   3  10   9  14  14   5
 5  12   8  13  14   9   1   6   6   7  12   3   9   8   7   4   1   7   4   2
10   5  13  12   8  12  11   1   1   1   1  10  13   2   5   5  16   9   9  14
 3   3  15   5   6  10  10   8   2   3  14   7  15  13   2  11  11   1  12   7
13   8   1  11   7   4  15  12   4  15   9  15   2   1   8  12  13   3   8   6
15  10   5   2   2   8   6  15   7   2   2   4   7   6  15  14  12  11  16   4
 9   4   3  16  13   7  13  11  14   9  11  16  10  12   1   3   3   8  15   9
 7   6   4  14   5   6   2  13  12   6   3   1   1   5  16  16   7  12  13  11
12   2  11   6   3   5   8   7  16  11   6  13  14   4  13   9   4   4   6   1
 6   1   6   3   9  16  16   2  10  16  13  14  16   7  11   7   6  15  11   3


 6   3   1  11   3   9   7  11  14   6   7   8  11  11   7   7  10   6   9   6
13  12  12   5  14  12   5   7   6  14   8  10   7   2   5   8   9  13   6   5
 9   5  11   1   9   4   3  12  13  10  14   2  13  14   8  15   3   4  12  13
 2  11   6   3   2  16   8  14  10   5   5   4   1  15   3  10  14  15  13   7
12   8   8  13  16  11  13   6  16   9   9  11  14   1   4  16   7   9  10   2
 5  13   2  15   1  15   1  13   5  16  11  12  16   7  15  12  16   3  16  15
14  15  10   2  15   5  12   4  11   8  15  15   8   6  12  13   4   8   1  12
 8  10  15  14  10   3  10   5   8   7   3   6  15   5  13   5  13  11   2   4
16   7  14   8   6   2  15  10  12   4  10   9   3  10   9   9   5  14   8   8
10   2   5   7   4   1   4   2   3  15   6  14   5  13  11  14   8   1   4   3
11  14  13  12  11  10   6   8  15   3   4   7   4   3  14   2   1  10  14   9
 1   9   4  16   3   6  16  15   4  11  16  13   6  12  16   6  11  16   7   1
 4   6   9   4   7   8   9  16   2   2  12   3  12   9  10   1   6  12  11  10
15   1   7   6   5  13  11   3   7   1  13   1  10   8   2  11  15   5   5  14
 3  16  16   9  12   7  14   9   9  13   1   5   2  16   6   4   2   2   3  11
 7   4   3  10  13  14   2   1   1  12   2  16   9   4   1   3  12   7  15  16


 4   3   8   2  10  16   4  12   9   8  13  10   9  10  16   7  10  14  11   5
 5  15   3   7   4  12  15  16   4   6  15   2   4   4   3   5   3  11   4   2
 1   4  14   4   6  13  14   8   5  14  12   3  14   5   7   4   6   1   2  14
16   5   9   8  12  11  10  14   3   1   5  15   6  14   4  16  11   2  16   8
12  14   6   1   7   2   2   9   8   9   1   5  13   7  15   8  16  15   7   4
15   8   2  15  13   5   1   4  15   5   2   4  11   8   9  14   4   3   5  16
 3  11  15   9   1  14   9  10  12  15   8  13   2   6  12  10   9   6  15   1
13  16  13  13   2  10  13  13  14   7  14   6  15  15   8   1   1  12   1   7
 7   9  10   3   8   7   7  13  10  10  14  12   1  13   2  12  16  14  15   5
11  13   4  12   3   8   3   5  10  13   6  16  16   3  11  11  15   8  12   9
10   5  11   5   5   4   5   7   3   7  11   7  11  14  15  14   4  10  11
 2   2  12  14  11   9  12   1   6  12   4   1  10  12   5   3   7  10   9   6
 8  12  16  11  16   1  11  11   1   2  11   9   8   2   1   6   5   7  13  10
14   1   1   6  14   6   5   3  16  11   3   8   5   9   2   9   2   9   8  12
 9   7   7  16  15   3  16  15   2   4   9  12   3  16  10  13  13   5   6  13
 6  10   5  10   9  15   8   2  11  16  16   7   1  13   6  12   8  13   3   3
```

```
 8  11   1  12   9  16  14   7   6  16   4   6  13  13  13  12  12  12  16   5
 1  15  13   2  11  14  11  14  16   7   2  15   9   3  11   3   8  14  12   7
 7  12  15   7   2  10   6   4  14  14  15   7  14   6   3  15  13   7   5  15
11   6   5   6  16   1  13  15   7   1  11   8   8   1   6  14   1   2   2   6
 2   1   4  16   4   5   8   8  12   5   9  10   4   7   5  11   3   1  15   9
 3  14  11   1  15   9   7  10  15  13   1   9   7  10   9   7  15  16  14  10
13   8  12   4  14   4   1   3   4  12   8   2  16   8   4   8   5  10   1  16
 9   9  14   3   3   8  15   6  10  11   6   5   5   4   2  13  10   4   8   1
 6  13  10   9  10   2  16   5   9   8  13   3  11  11  12  16   4   6   4  14
10  16   2  11   7   6   9   1   5   4   7  11  10   5   7   5   2  11  11  12
14  10  16  10   8   7  12  13   2   9  10   4   6   2  15   9  11   5   3  13
16   3   9  13  13  15   3  12   3   6  14  13   2  15  14   2  14  13  10   4
 5   2   7   8   6  11   5  16   8  10   5  14   1  12  16   4   6   3   7  11
 4   5   3  15   1   3  10  11  13   2  16  12  15   9  10  10   9  15   9   2
12   7   8   5   5  12   4   9  11   3   3   1   3  16   1   6  16   8  13   3
15   4   5  14  12  13   2   2   1  15  12  15  12  14   8   1   7   9   6   8


 9   9   2  16   1  14  11   1   3  16   3   6  14  16  10   2   5   6   7  16
15  16   9   4   6   6  14  15   7  13   5   2   1   7   8   3   7  15  16   7
 1   5  14  14   5   7   4   5   5  10   7  16  11   2  13  10  10  13   9   4
 7  12  16   7  13   4   2   9   6   8  12   9  15  10   7  16  16   1   6  11
 3   7   1   2   9  13   9   3   9   2   4  14   3   3  12  14   2   8   5   2
 8   2  15  12   3   8   6   6  10  11   1  11   2   9   5   8   9   5   2  10
16   4  11   3  14   5   8  10  15   3   9   7   4  14   1   5   6   4  12   1
 4   3   3   6   4  15  13   2  12  14   8  10  10  15  16  13   4   2   4  13
10   1  12  11   2  11   5   7   8  12   6  12   8  13   2   4   1   9   3   6
13  10   5   5  11  16  15  13  16  15  13  15   9   6  11   6   8  10  11  15
11   6   6  10  15   2   3   8   4   6  16  13  12  12   4  12  14  14  13   8
14  14   7   8   3  12  11  14   1   2   4  13   1   3   9  12   7   8   3
 5   8  13  15  10   1   1  14  13   4  14   3  16   8   9   1  15  16  10   5
 2  15   4   1  12  10  16   4   2   5  15   1   6  11  14  11   3   3   1  14
12  11  10   9  16  12  10  16  11   7  11   5   5  15  15  11  11  14   9
 6  13   8  13   7   9   7  12   1   9  10   8   7   4   6   7  13  12  15  12


 6   5  11   8   9   6  14   5   1  16   8  13  12   4   9  11   4  16  14  16
10   7   8   1  15   9   4  13  10   7   9   8   5   3  15   6   2   3  11   8
 4   4   3  12   4  15   8   2   5   1  16   9   8  14  12  13   9  13  15   7
 9   9   7  10  11  16   6  14  14   8  13  16  11  10  13   4  13   8  10  10
 7  15  14   4  16  11  12  16   6  15  14   7  13  13   7   8   7  10   1   4
11  16   1   6  14   1   1  10   4  13   3   4   2  12   1   7   1  15  13  11
12   8  13   5   3   2  16   8  15  11  12  11  10   7   2   1  16   9   4  15
 3   3   6  14   5  13  10  15  16  10  10  14  16  15  16  12  11   2   9   5
14  11  10   2   1   7   9   4  13  14   2   3   7   1  11  16  12   6   2  13
13  12   2   9   7  12  15   7   2   4   4   6   4  16   3  14  14  11   5  12
 8  10  16  13  13   8  11   9  11   6   1   1   9   5   8  15   6   5   8   9
 2   2   4   3  12   5   5   6   9  12  15  12  14   8   5   3  10   1  12   1
15   6  12   7   2   3   2   3   3   2   5   5  15   1   2  14   9   8   4   6
 1  13   9  16   8  10   3  12  12   5   7   5   3   9   4   2   5  12   3   3
 5  14   5  11  10  14   7   1   7   9   6  10  15  11   6   5  15  14   7   6
16   1  15  15   6   4  13  11   8   3  11   2   6   6  10  10   3   7  16  14


 4  11  11   7   3  12  13   4  15   8   5  10   5  14   5  14   6  15   9  12
12  10  13  14   5   7   7   1  13   2   4   3   2   3  11  15  11   3  15   1
 2   9  12  11  13  10   4  12   1   4  16  12   1   2   7   1   1  12  13   6
 1   4   8  13   6  14   8  10  14   5  14  11  15  13   3   6  15   8   7   3
13   1   9  15  12  11   9  14   8  11  10   1  11  10  10   7   4   1   3  10
 9  15   3   3   8  13  12   2  10  14   3  15  16   7  16   2  14   2  10  14
16   8  10   5  11   3   2  16   4  13   1   2   9  16   2  10  12   5  14   2
 7   5   2   9   2   2  10   8   7   3  13  14  13   8   8   4  10   9   8   4
11  14   5   8  10   9   3  15  12   1  12  13  14  11  15  12  13   7  16   9
10   2   7   4   7   1   6  13   5  16   6   4   7   9  14   3   9  10   5   5
 3   3  15  12  10  15  14   7  16  13   7   9   3   6   1  13  16  13   1  11
 8  12   1  16  16   4  16  11   6   6  15  16  10  12  12   8   8  11   6  15
 6   6   6   8  15   6   5   6   2   9   2   8  12   5   9   9   3   4  12  13
14  16  16   6   4   5  15   5   3  15   8   5   8  15   6   5   2   6   2   7
 5   7   4   1   1   8  11   9  11   7   9   7   6   4   4  16   7  14  11   8
15  13  14   2  14  16   1   3   9  12  11   6   4   1  13  11   5  16   4  16
```

```
15  11  14   9   3   7   3   1   9   9  11   3   4   6   6  14  12   5   2   3
 3   7  16   2   1   5  10   4  15   5   4  12   5   9  10  11   3  16   9  16
 4   4   5  16  10   1   1   2   7   2   5   4  12   7  16   7   2   7   6   5
 6  15   6   6   4  10   7  15   2   4   3   9  11   3  11  10  15   6  15  12
 7   2  10   4  12   6   2   8   6   7  10  16  14  15  13   5  14  13   1   7
14   8  15  15  13  15   6  12   3  16   8  10  10  11  12   9   1   4   3   6
13  14   1   8   7  13  11   6  12  15  15   7   6   8   7   4   9   9  16  11
11  10   8   1   6  16  13   7  11   6  16  11  15   5  14  12  10  15  11   8
 1  13  11   5  15   9  15  14  14   8   1  15   8  16   8   2   7  12   8   9
 9   1  13  14  16  14  14  10  10  10  13   6   1  14   3  13  16  10  12   2
 8   5  12   3  11   4  16   3  16  12   2  13  16  10   2  15   4   1   5   1
 5   6   7   7   9  12   5  11   5   3   7   5   7   2   5  16   8   8  13  14
16   3   4  11   2   3   8   5   8  14   9   1   9   4   9   3  11   3  10  15
 2   9   9  10   5   8  12  13   4   1   6   8   3  12   1   1  13   2   4   4
12  12   3  12   8   2   4   9   1  13  12  14   2   1   4   8   5  14   7  10
10  16   2  13  14  11   9  16  13  11  14   2  13  13  15   6   6  11  14  13


 8   6   4  15  16   6  10   6   9   9  14   2   2   9  15   4   2  12   7   6
14   2  15  10   9   9  14   8   3  10   5  11   3   5  10  11   1   2   9   1
 7   3   2   4  14  15  12  13  14   1  15   3  16  16   9   9  11  16   5   4
 4   9   3  13   4  12   8   5  15  11  16   9  12  12   5  13   5  15  15   3
 1   5  12   8  11   4   9  10  12   5  12  13   6   7   3   8   9   9  12   9
 6   4  13  16   1   2   3   9   1  12   4   6   4  11   7   7  13  14  10   7
 5  14  14   6   3  13  15  16   8   6  13  14  10   8   6  10  15  13   1  11
15  13   8   9  12   3   7   3  11   2   1  15   5  14   1  12  16   8  14  13
11  12   7   5   6   1   5  12   5   3   6   1  11   2   2  14  14   5   4  10
 9   8   9   2   2  10   2   2   7  13   8   8   1  15  13  16  10   6  11   2
12   1   5   7   7  14   6   1   4   8  10   5  13  10   4   3   8  11  16   8
16  10  16   3   3   7   4  11  13   7  11   7   9   1  12   5   3   3   2  12
13  11  10  12   5   5   1  14   2   4   2   4   8   6  14   2  12   4   3   5
10  16   5  14  13  16  16   7   6  15   3  12  14   4  11   1   4   7   6  16
 2  15  11  11  15   8  11   4  10  14   7  10   7   3   8  15   6   1  13  14
 3   7   1   1  10  11  13  15  16  16   9  16  15  13  16   6   7  10   8  15


13  16   3   3   5   2  10  16   1  15  16   8   2  16   1   9  10   1   9   2
 6   9   8  14   6   8   2   7  16   7   5  12   7   2   6  11   9   2   4   7
 8   7  10  15  10  15   6   5  14   6   6   3   9  12  13  15  15   9  11   3
 5   8  14   7   2   5  12   1  15   4   9   7  11   3   4  14   3  15   7   6
15  13  16  16  16   4   7   8   2   5   1   1  13  15   9  13  13   5   1   4
 3   2  11  10  11   1  11  12   3  10  15   4  16   7  11   8   6  14  16  16
 1   5   2   5  12  10   4   9   8   1  14   2   3   5   3   3   2  16   8  13
10   4   4   9   9   9   5  13   6  13   4  16  15   1  16  12   8   3   2  12
 7   6   1  13  14  13  13  14  12  12  10   9  12   4  15   4   4  10   5   1
14  14  13   8   7   3   8   2   9   8  11  11  14   6   5  16  14  11  15   5
 2   3  12   6   3  14   1  11  10   9  13   5   4  10  14   5  11   4  14  10
 4  10   9   1  15   6   9  15   7  14   7   6  10   9   8   2   7   6   6   9
11  15  15  11   4   7  14   6  11   2   2  10   8  14   2   1  12  12  12   8
12   1   5  12  13  16  15  10  13  11   3  14   6  13  10   7  16   7  10  14
16  12   6   2   8  12   3   3   4  16  12  13   1  11  12   6   1   8  13  11
 9  11   7   4   1  11  16   4   5   3   8  15   5   8   7  10   5  13   3  15


 7   4   6   6   8   8  10   8   5  16   6   7  16  16   5  15   9   4  15  14
10   9   8  13  16  11   6   4   9   4   2   9   8   5   2   1   8  13   5  12
11  11   4   8   3   9  16  10  15  13  15   8  14  13  12  11  11  14  16   6
16   8  14   9   4   2  11  15  14  11   4  12   6  15   8  14   1  10   4   8
 9  13   5  11   9   7   8   5   2  14   5  15  12   1   1   6   3   1  13   7
 3  12   1   1  10  13  12   1  10   2   8  10  13   4  11   7  13   6  12   2
12   3   7   4  13   1   1   3   1  15   1  14   4  14  16  12   4   7   8   3
14  14  12   5   5   6  13  12  16   8  10  13   5  11   9  10  12   8  14  10
 5   6  13  16   6   5   2   7  12   3  16   2   1  10  13  16  14  12   9   1
15  10  16  10  15  14  15   2   7   7  13  16   9   2   4   8  15   9   6   5
 4   5   2  14   1   3  14  16  13  10   7   4   7   7   4  10  16   7  16   6
13   1   9  12   7  10   9   9  11   6   9   1  10   3  15   9   7   2   3   9
 8   7   3   7  11  15   7  14   8  12   3  11  11  12   3   5   5  11  13  15
 6   2  15   3  14   4   4   6   4   5  11   5  15   6   6  13   2   5  10  13
 2  15  10   2  12  16   5  11   6   1  14   3   2   8  14   3  16  15   1  11
 1  16  11  15   2  12   3  13   3   9  12   6   3   9  10   2   6   3   2   4
```

```
13  15   9  16   4   7   8   6   7  15   1  15  11   2   7  14   7   1  11  12
 8   8  13  12   7   5   6  15   4   4   6  10   8  10   4  15  10  12   2   3
12   2   1   8   9  12  11  16   3   5  13   1   5   1  11  12   8  14   7  13
 6   3   6   9  15  15   9  11   1   7   7   4   2  16  10   1  11   5  16  16
 2  16   5   3   6  14  13  14  10  13   8  11  13  15   9  10   2  15   6   6
 9   5   8   1  14   6  15  10  14   8  11  12   9   3   5   3  15   4   4   9
15   1  12  11  11   4   4   3  13  10   9   6   6  14  12   5   9  13  15  15
 4   6  14  10  12  13  14   1   9   3  16   3   7  11  13  11   4   3   5   8
 5  13  15  13  13   3  12   7   8  14  14   5   3   5  14  16   3  10   1   5
16   4   7  14   3   8  16   9  15   9   3  16  14   8   8   8   6  11  10   1
 3  10   2   5   5  16   5  13   5  12  12   2  15  13  16   7  16   8   8   2
 1  14   3   7   8  11   1   2  16   1  10   9   4   9   2   6   5   6   9   7
 7   9  10   4   1   2   7   4   6  11   4   7  12  12   3  13  13   9  14  11
11  12   4   2   2   9  10  12  12  16   5  13  16   4   6   4  14  16   3  10
10   7  11   6  16  10   3   5  11   6  15  14   1   7  15   9   1   7  13  14
14  11  16  15  10   1   2   8   2   2   2   8  10   6   1   2  12   2  12   4
```

```
10  10   9   8   5   1  10  16  12   9   5  10  16  11  14  12   4   6   8  13
 9   8  14   4  14   6   8   7   5  14   8   3   4   4   1   4   2  13   7   1
15   1   8   2   7  12  11   4   2  10   3   8   5   8  10   9  14  10   5   3
14  15  11  12  12  10  15  13   1  15  12   7  13  12   5   8   3   2  11   8
 4   4   4  16  16   9   4   3  14   4   7   5  10  13   8   6  15   1  14   9
 3   6   7  10  10  13  13   8  10  13  15   6   3  16   3  10   5  16  16   4
 6  16   5  13  13  11   3   2  13   8   1   9  15   9  11   1   3   1  16
 5   3   6  14   1  16   1   9   9   1   6  14  11  10   7   5  10  12   4  14
11   2  16   3   4   3  12  10   3  11  14  13   1   7  15  14   9  11   3  10
16  12  15   1   8  15  16  11  11   5   2  15  15  14  12  15   8   8   6   2
 1  11   3   6   6   8   2   5   7  16  10   9   2   6   2   7   7  15  12  11
13  14  10   5  15   5   7   6  15   2   9   1  14   1  13  13  12   7   2   7
12   9  12  11   3  14   6  12   4   6  16   2   6   5  16   2  11   4  13  15
 8  13   2  15   9   4   9  15  16  12  11  12   8   3   4   1   6  14  15  12
 2   7  13   9   2   7  14  14   5   3   4  16   7   9  11   3  13   5   9   6
 7   5   1   7  11   2   5   1   8   7  13   4  12   2   6  16  16   9  10   5
```

```
16   4   2  11  16   4  12  12   6  10   5  15  14  16  10   9  11  12   1   5
 6  12   8  12  11  10   6  15   7   4  10  14   3   1  11  15   2   4   5  13
 2   3   3   4   6   2   1  16  15   7   3  11  12  12  15   8   1  11  13   9
10   7   7  13   8  12  14   9   5   8   2   7   2  13  16  16   5  10   4  14
15  13   6   7   1  11   3   1   1  13   7   8   4  11  14   4   8  13   2  11
 9  11  15   3   9  16   7   7  13  16   6  13   7   4   3  14   9   2  10   2
 4  16  10  15   4  14  15  10   9   2   9   9  11   6   7   3  12   8  12  12
 8  10  13   5   5   5  13   8   4  12  13  12  10   7  12  10  14   9   8  16
14   8  12  10  15  13   4  13  14   5   4  16  15   9   6  12  15  14   6  10
 7   9  11   1  12   6   5   2   2  11   8   4   9   8  13  11  13   6   3   1
13   6  16   6  14   7   8   5  10   6  15   2   6  10   9   5   4   7  14   8
11   1   9  14   2   3  11   4  16   9  12   3  13   2   8   7  16   1  15   3
12  15  14   8   3   1  10   3  12  15  11   5  16   3   4   1   3  16  11   4
 5  14   4   9  10  15   2  11   8  14   1  10   8  15   1  13   6  15  16   7
 1   5   1  16  13   8   9  14  11   3  16   1   1   5   2   2   7   3   9   6
 3   2   5   2   7   9  16   6   3   1  14   6   5  14   5   6  10   5   7  15
```

```
10  12  12   8   5   4  15   2   4   2  15   7   2  15  15  15   6  13  16  10
 3   8   7  13  14   6   8   9  15  13   8  14   9  11   7   4  11   1  10   6
 1  13   3   5  16   5  13   1   7  14   4   8  15   4   6   9  16  15  15  12
13  11   5  11   2   8  12  15  14  12  13  13   6   9   3   2   3  10   3  13
 6  15  16   9  10  14   7  14  13   6   6  12   7  14  14  11   5  12   1  16
 5   2   8   4   6   3  16  13   8   3   2   9   4  12  10  10  15   9   5   4
 4   3   2  10  13  13   1   6   9   4  14   2   5   6  12   3  13   2   7  11
15   9   6  14   7  10  10  10   3  10   5  11   8  16   8  14  12   4   9  14
11   5  13   7   8   9   9   3  12   5  11   6  11   7   4   6   7   5  11   7
 7  10   9   2  12  11   3   8   2  11   7   1  12   8  16  16   8   6   6   2
 2  14  10  15   9  16  14  11  16   9   1   5  13  10   5   1  10  16   8  15
14   1   1   3   4   2   6  16   5  15   3  16  10   1   2  13   4   8  14   9
 8   6   6   1   3  15   4  12   6   7  10  15  16  13   1  12   2  14  13   1
16  16  11   6  15   1   2   7  10   8  16   3  14   2  13   7   9  11  12   3
 9   7  15  12  11  12   5   4  11  16   9  10   1   3   9   8   1   7   2   8
12   4   4  16   1   7  11   5   1   1  12   4   3   5  11   5  14   3   4   5
```

```
13  16   3   3   5   2  10  16   1  15  16   8   2  16   1   9  10   1   9   2
 6   9   8  14   5   8   2   7  16   7   5  12   7   2   6  11   9   2   4   7
 8   7  10  15  10  15   6   5  14   6   6   3   9  12  13  15  15   9  11   3
 5   8  14   7   2   5  12   1  15   4   9   7  11   3   4  14   3  15   7   6
15  13  16  16  16   4   7   8   2   5   1   1  13  15   9  13  13   5   1   4
 3   2  11  10  11   1  11  12   3  10  15   4  16   7  11   8   6  14  16  16
 1   5   2   5  12  10   4   9   8   1  14   2   3   5   3   3   2  16   8  13
10   4   4   9   9   9   5  13   6  13   4  16  15   1  16  12   8   3   2  12
 7   6   1  13  14  13  13  14  12  12  10   9  12   4  15   4   4  10   5   1
14  14  13   8   7   3   8   2   9   8  11  11  14   6   5  16  14  11  15   5
 2   3  12   6   3  14   1  11  10   9  13   5   4  10  14   5  11   4  14  10
 4  10   9   1  15   6   9  15   7  14   7   6  10   9   8   2   7   6   6   9
11  15  15  11   4   7  14   6  11   2   2  10   8  14   2   1  12  12  12   8
12   1   5  12  13  16  15  10  13  11   3  14   6  13  10   7  16   7  10  14
16  12   6   2   8  12   3   3   4  16  12  13   1  11  12   6   1   8  13  11
 9  11   7   4   1  11  16   4   5   3   8  15   5   8   7  10   5  13   3  15


 7   4   6   6   8   8  10   8   5  16   6   7  16  16   5  15   9   4  15  14
10   9   8  13  16  11   6   4   9   4   2   9   8   5   2   1   8  13   5  12
11  11   4   8   3   9  16  10  15  13  15   8  14  13  12  11  11  14  16   6
16   8  14   9   4   2  11  15  14  11   4  12   6  15   8  14   1  10   4   8
 9  13   5  11   9   7   8   5   2  14   5  15  12   1   1   6   3   1  13   7
 3  12   1   1  10  13  12   1  10   2   8  10  13   4  11   7  13   6  12   2
12   3   7   4  13   1   1   3   1  15   1  14   4  14  16  12   4   7   8   3
14  14  12   5   5   6  13  12  16   8  10  13   5  11   9  10  12   8  14  10
 5   6  13  16   6   5   2   7  12   3  16   2   1  10  13  16  14  12   9   1
15  10  16  10  15  14  15   2   7   7  13  16   9   2   4   8  15   9   6   5
 4   5   2  14   1   3  14  16  13  10   7   4   7   7   4  10  16   7  16  16
13   1   9  12   7  10   9   9  11   6   9   1  10   3  15   9   7   2   3   9
 8   7   3   7  11  15   7  14   8  12   3  11  11  12   3   5   5  11  11  15
 6   2  15   3  14   4   4   6   4   5  11   5  15   6   6  13   2   5  10  13
 2  15  10   2  12  16   5  11   6   1  14   3   2   8  14   3  16  15   1  11
 1  16  11  15   2  12   3  13   3   9  12   6   3   9  10   2   6   3   2   4


13  15   9  16   4   7   8   6   7  15   1  15  11   2   7  14   7   1  11  12
 8   8  13  12   7   5   6  15   4   6  10   8  10   4  15  10  12   2   3
12   2   1   8   9  12  11  16   3   5  13   1   5   1  11  12   8  14   7  13
 6   3   6   9  15  15   9  11   1   7   7   4   2  16  10   1  11   5  16  16
 2  16   5   3   6  14  13  14  10  13   8  11  13  15   9  10   2  15   6   6
 9   5   8   1  14   6  15  10  14   8  11  12   9   3   5   3  15   4   4   9
15   1  12  11  11   4   5   4   3  13  10   9   6   6  14  12   5   9  13  15
 4   6  14  10  12  13  14   1   9   3  16   3   7  11  13  11   4   3   5   8
 5  13  15  13  13   3  12   7   7   8  14  14   5   3   5  14  16   3  10   5
16   4   7  14   3   8  16   9  15   9   3  16  14   8   8   6  11  10   1   1
 3  10   2   5   5  16   5  13   5  12  12   2  15  13  16   7  16   8   8   2
 1  14   3   7   8  11   1   2  16   1  10   9   4   9   2   6   5   6   9   7
 7   9  10   4   1   2   7   4   6  11   4   7  12  12   3  13  13   9  14  11
11  12   4   2   2   9  10  12  12  16   5  13  16   4   6   4  14  16   3  10
10   7  11   6  16  10   3   5  11   6  15  14   1   7  15   9   1   7  13  14
14  11  16  15  10   1   2   8   2   2   7   8  10   6   1   2  12   2  12   4


10  10   9   8   5   1  10  16  12   9   5  10  16  11  14  12   4   6   8  13
 9   8  14   4  14   6   8   7   5  14   8   3   4   4   1   4   2  13   7   1
15   1   8   2   7  12  11   4   2  10   3   8   5   8  10   9  14  10   5   3
14  15  11  12  12  10  15  13   1  15  12   7  13  12   5   8   3   2  11   8
 4   4   4  16  16   9   4   3  14   4   7   5  10  13   8   6  15   1  14   9
 3   6   7  10  10  13  13   8  10  13  15   6   3  16   3  10   5  16  16   4
 6  16   5  13  13  11   3   2  13   8   1  11   9  15   9  11   1   3   1  16
 5   3   6  14   1  16   1   9   9   1   6  14  11  10   7   5  10  12   4  14
11   2  16   3   4   3  12  10   3  11  14  13   1   7  15  14   9  11   3  10
16  12  15   1   8  15  16  11  11   5   2  15  15  14  12  15   8   8   6   2
 1  11   3   6   6   8   2   5   7  16  10   9   2   6   2   7   7  15  12  11
13  14  10   5  15   5   7   6  15   2   9   1  14   1  13  13  12   7   2   7
12   9  12  11   3  14   6  12   4   6  16   2   6   5  16   2  11   4  13  15
 8  13   2  15   9   4   9  15  16  12  11  12   8   3   4   1   6  14  15  12
 2   7  13   9   2   7  14  14   5   3   4  16   7   9  11   3  13   5   9   6
 7   5   1   7  11   2   5   1   8   7  13   4  12   2   6  16  16   9  10   5
```

```
16   4   2  11  16   4  12  12   6  10   5  15  14  16  10   9  11  12   1   5
 6  12   8  12  11  10   6  15   7   4  10  14   3   1  11  15   2   4   5  13
 2   3   3   4   6   2   1  16  15   7   3  11  12  12  15   8   1  11  13   9
10   7   7  13   8  12  14   9   5   8   2   7   2  13  16  16   5  10   4  14
15  13   6   7   1  11   3   1   1  13   7   8   4  11  14   4   8  13   2  11
 9  11  15   3   9  16   7   7  13  16   6  13   7   4   3  14   9   2  10   2
 4  16  10  15   4  14  15  10   9   2   9  11   6   7   7   3  12   8  12  12
 8  10  13   5   5   5  13   8   4  12  13  12  10   7  12  10  14   9   8  16
14   8  12  10  15  13   4  13  14   5   4  16  15   9   6  12  15  14   6  10
 7   9  11   1  12   6   5   2   2  11   8   4   9   8  13  11  13   6   3   1
13   6  16   6  14   7   8   5  10   6  15   2   6  10   9   5   4   7  14   8
11   1   9  14   2   3  11   4  16   9  12   3  13   2   8   7  16   1  15   3
12  15  14   8   3   1  10   3  12  15  11   5  16   3   4   1   3  16  11   4
 5  14   4   9  10  15   2  11   8  14   1  10   8  15   1  13   6  15  16   7
 1   5   1  16  13   8   9  14  11   3  16   1   1   5   2   2   7   3   9   6
 3   2   5   2   7   9  16   6   3   1  14   6   5  14   5   6  10   5   7  15
```

```
10  12  12   8   5   4  15   2   4   2  15   7   2  15  15  15   6  13  16  10
 3   8   7  13  14   6   8   9  15  13   8  14   9  11   7   4  11   1  10   6
 1  13   3   5  16   5  13   1   7  14   4   8  15   4   6   9  16  15  15  12
13  11   5  11   2   8  12  15  14  12  13  13   6   9   3   2   3  10   3  13
 6  15  16   9  10  14   7  14  13   6   6  12   7  14  14  11   5  12   1  16
 5   2   8   4   6   3  16  13   8   3   2   9   4  12  10  10  15   9   5   4
 4   3   2  10  13  13   1   5   9   4  14   2   5   6  12   3  13   2   7  11
15   9   5  14   7  10  10  10   3  10   5  11   8  16   8  14  12   4   9  14
11   5  13   7   8   9   9   3  12   5  11   6  11   7   4   6   7   5  11   7
 7  10   9   2  11   3   8   2  11   7   1  12   8  16  16   8   6   6   2  15
 2  14  10  15   9  16  14  11  16   9   1   5  13  10   5   1  10  16   8  15
14   1   1   3   4   2   6  16   5  15   3  16  10   1   2  13   4   8  14   9
 8   6  14   1   3  15   4  12   6   7  10  15  16  13   1  12   2  14  13   1
16  16  11   6  15   1   2   7  10   8  16   3  14   2  13   7   9  11  12   3
 9   7  15  12  11  12   5   4  11  16   9  10   1   3   9   8   1   7   2   8
12   4   4  16   1   7  11   5   1   1  12   4   3   5  11   5  14   3   4   5
```

```
14  13  12  11   1   4  11  14  11  14  11   6   7   5   4  14   2  12   9   1
 1   3   1  15   8  14  15   4   6   7  14  13  12   3  14  13   6   2   6  15
10   1   7   1   4  15   1   2  10  16  10  16  11  16  15   9   9  14  15   5
 5   8   5   4   7   6  16  13  14  11   4   2   3  13  10   7   1  10   5  11
 4  11  11  14  12   7   4   7   2   3   7  15  14   1   7  12   3   8  10   2
 6   5   4  16  11  16  14   1  13   8  12   9   8   9  11   6   4  11   8  16
13   7  13   9  10   1   8   6  12   9   1  11   6  12   8  15   7   7  13   9
 3  10  16   7  13  10   3   5   5   5   2   5   9   7   4  10  14   1  14   7
 2   6  14   6   6  13  10   3   7  12   8   4  10  11  13  11   5   6   2   4
16  14   9   3   3   2  12  11  16   6   6  12  13  10  12   1  15  13  11  13
15   4   2  10  14   8   5  12   3   4  16  10   1   8   1   3  10   5   7  12
 7   2  10   8  16   3   9  16   8  13   5   1  15   4  16   8  12  16   4  14
11  12   8  12   2   5   2   9   9  10   9  14   5   6   6   2  11   3  12   3
 9  15   3  13  15  12   7  10  15  15  15   3  16  15   3   5  16  15   1   6
12   9  15   2   9   9   6  15   4   2  13   7   2   2   2   4  13   9   3   8
 8  16   6   5   5  11  13   8   1   1   3   8   4  14   5  16   8   4  16  10
```

```
 4  15  11   7  15   4   2  14  14  14  10   8   7  11  16   7   9  16   9  13
 7   8  10   4   4  11   4  11   3  13  11   9   2  12   8  12   3   5   7   7
 2  16   9   6  12  15  15   5   2  11   9  13   1  14  14   2  12  13  13  10
10   2   7  15   6   6   9   1   6   3   7   6   4   4   3   8  16  10   4  16
 5   3   5  11   9  10   3   7   4   9  16   2  14   7   1  10   1  12  11  11
 1  12   2   5  14  12   7   4  11   2   6  10  16   6   2   4  11   2   4   1
 6   9   4   8  11   7  10   6   8   1   5   4   3   2   4  11   2   4   5  14
12   5  14  16   5   9  14   3   1   4  12  14   8  16  10   1   6  15   8   5
16  11  12  13  16   8  11   9   5  10   8   7  12   1  15   9  11  11   1   3
 8   1  13   9   2   1   1   2   9   6   4  15   5  15  12   6  13   3  12   9
15  10   1  14   1   5   8  16  12   5   1  15  13  10   7  14   5   6   3   4
 9  13  15   2  13  14  12  12   7  12  14   1   6   3   5   5  15   9  14   8
14   7   8   3   3   2   6  13  15   8  13  12  10  13   9  16   8   7  16  15
13   6   6  10   8  16  16  10  16  15   3   5   9   8   6  15  14   2   2   2
 3  14  16   1  10   3   5  15  10  16   2   3  15   5  11  13  10   8  15   6
11   4   3  12   7  13  13   8  13   7  15  11  11   9  13   3   7  14  10  12
```

INDEX